Left and Right in Global Politics

Few notions are as universal as the idea of a left–right divide in politics. Despite its death being frequently foretold, the left–right metaphor remains the most common lens through which to interpret political life locally, nationally, and globally. *Left and Right in Global Politics* argues that the left–right divide connects these different levels in a world political debate. Interpreting the left–right dichotomy as an enduring debate about equality, Noël and Thérien analyze opinion polls and social discourses to demonstrate how this debate shapes both individual and collective views of public affairs. Setting their findings in a historical perspective, they then show that for more than two centuries the conflict between progressives and conservatives has structured both domestic and international politics. They conclude by discussing the implications of their argument for the analysis of world politics, and contend that the left–right opposition is here to stay.

ALAIN NOËL is Professor in the Department of Political Science of the Université de Montréal.

JEAN-PHILIPPE THÉRIEN is Professor in the Department of Political Science of the Université de Montréal.

Left and Right in Global Politics

ALAIN NOËL and JEAN-PHILIPPE THÉRIEN
Université de Montréal

CAMBRIDGE
UNIVERSITY PRESS

CAMBRIDGE UNIVERSITY PRESS
Cambridge, New York, Melbourne, Madrid, Cape Town, Singapore, São Paulo, Delhi

Cambridge University Press
The Edinburgh Building, Cambridge CB2 8RU, UK

Published in the United States of America by Cambridge University Press, New York

www.cambridge.org
Information on this title: www.cambridge.org/9780521705837

First published 2008

Printed in the United Kingdom at the University Press, Cambridge

A *catalogue record for this publication is available from the British Library*

Library of Congress Cataloguing in Publication data
Noël, Alain.
    Left and right in global politics / Alain Noël, Jean-Philippe Thérien.
      p.   cm.
    Includes bibliographical references and index.
    ISBN 978-0-521-88001-5 (hardback : alk. paper) – ISBN 978-0-521-70583-7
    (pbk. : alk. paper)
    1. Right and left (Political science)–History.   2. Conservatism–History.
    3. Liberalism–History.   4. World politics–History.   I. Thérien, Jean-Philippe.
    II. Title.
    JA83.N64 2008
    327.1–dc22
    2008006274

ISBN 978-0-521-88001-5 hardback
ISBN 978-0-521-70583-7 paperback

Contents

List of tables	*page* vi
List of figures	vii
Acknowledgements	viii
Introduction	1
1 A clash over equality	6
2 A worldwide value divide	32
3 Two tales of globalization	56
4 The rise of the modern state system (1776–1945)	83
5 The age of universality (1945–1980)	107
6 The triumph of market democracy (1980–2007)	137
7 Twenty-first-century rapprochement	166
8 The core currency of political exchange	198
Conclusion	231
Index	236

Tables

2.1 Country means, mean deviations, and percentages of
don't know/no answer, left–right self-placement,
1999–2001   *page* 36

2.2 Relationships between left–right self-placement
and attitudes about social justice and government
intervention, on a world scale, 1999–2001   43

2.3 Relationships between left–right self-placement
and qualities respondents find important to encourage
in children, on a world scale, 1999–2001   45

2.4 Relationships between left–right self-placement
and attitudes toward life, on a world scale, 1999–2001   45

2.5 Relationships between socio-economic attributes
and left–right self-placement, on a world scale, 1999–2001   46

2.6 Scores for relationships between left–right
self-placement and attitudes about social justice,
competition, and government intervention, in seventy-six
countries, 1999–2001   49

Figures

1.1 The left, the right, authority, and liberty   *page* 25

2.1 Left–right self-placement in the world, 1999–2001   34

2.2 Left–right self-placement in the United Kingdom,
the Netherlands, and Israel, 1999–2001   41

3.1 Share of people living on less than $1 a day
(% of population), 1981–2001   61

3.2 Number of electoral democracies, 1987–2005   68

3.3 GDP per capita in the poorest and the richest
countries, 1960–1962 and 2000–2002   70

3.4 Aid as a percentage of developed countries'
GNP, 1955–2006   75

Acknowledgements

Everyone has an idea about the left and the right. This is why these notions are so engaging and so fascinating. Their universal relevance, however, also makes the two terms difficult to grasp in a systematic manner. As with every concept that seems meaningful and clear to all, "the left" and "the right" encompass a wide range of values and perceptions. In trying to make sense of these different standpoints, we were helped by a number of people, who discussed the issues at stake, made suggestions, and were always willing to share their views, usually firmly held, about the significance of left and right in global politics.

First thoughts and early drafts were presented at conferences or meetings in Canada, Egypt, France, Germany, Italy, Mexico, Québec, Switzerland, and the United States. The book benefited very much from this exposure to views from different parts and cultures of the world. We are grateful to the organizers and participants of these different gatherings for the occasion they gave us to exchange ideas with them and for their comments.

In the academic year 2004–05, both of us were visiting scholars in France, the country where the contemporary notions of left and right were born, a fitting environment to give a first impulse to this project. Alain was a guest of the Politiques publiques, Action politique, Territoires research centre (PACTE), at the Institut d'études politiques de Grenoble, a superb location for research and writing. Philippe Warin and Bruno Jobert, in particular, provided support and opportunities. Jean-Philippe spent the first half of the year at the Centre d'études et de recherches internationales (CERI) in Paris. Later that year, he was invited by the Centro de estudios internacionales (CEI) of the Colegio de México, which offered a nicely complementary setting in a country of the global South. He is grateful to Christophe Jaffrelot and Marie-Claude Smouts in Paris, and to Jean-François Prud'homme and Maria del Carmen Pardo in Mexico City for their hospitality and encouragement.

At the Université de Montréal and elsewhere, a number of people provided support or advice. Jean-Philippe wishes to thank, in particular, André-J. Bélanger, Steven Bernstein, David Black, André Blais, Charles Blattberg, Andrew Cooper, François Crépeau, Graciela Ducatenzeiler, Evelyne Dufault, Luc Duhamel, Michel Fortmann, Anna Maria Gentili, Chloé Germain-Thérien, John Groom, Richard Jolly, Stéphane Lutard, Gordon Mace, Frédéric Mérand, Karen Mundy, Richard Nadeau, Lou Pauly, Vincent Pouliot, Ignacy Sachs, Denis Saint-Martin, Samir Saul, Brigitte Schroeder, Tim Shaw, Larry Swatuk, François Thérien, Guillaume Thérien, Urs Thomas, Thomas Weiss, and Marie-Joëlle Zahar. Alain is particularly grateful to Keith Banting, Yannick Barthe, Bernard Cantin, Sarah Fortin, Alain-G. Gagnon, Jane Jenson, Guy Laforest, Jean Laponce, Lutz Leisering, Jacques de Maillard, Marie-France Raynault, and Philip Resnick.

Producing a book is a collective undertaking. At different stages in the process we benefited from the help of talented and devoted research assistants, namely Sébastien Dallaire, who did much of the World Values Survey work, Frédéric Sirois, Sylvie Thibault, and Antonino Geraci. Financial support for the project was provided by the Social Sciences and Humanities Research Council of Canada (SSHRC) and the Fonds québécois de la recherche sur la société et la culture (FQRSC), and is gratefully acknowledged. As one may expect, the final steps were most satisfying. We had the chance to see our manuscript kindly and professionally handled by John Haslam and Carrie Cheek at Cambridge University Press, and by Jamie Hood and Christopher Feeney at Out of House Publishing. It was a pleasure to work with each of them. Finally, we thank our first readers, who provided insightful comments and feedback. These are the anonymous reviewers at Cambridge University Press, as well as Jim Caporaso, Andrew Gamble, Bahgat Korany, and Craig Murphy.

This book claims that global politics is shaped and constructed through enduring and consistent ideological debates. If we are correct, not all readers will agree with us. We hope, however, that each will find this journey on the left and on the right engaging and...worth debating.

Introduction

Ravi Kanbur is one of the world's top specialists in development economics. Born in India and trained in England, at Cambridge and Oxford, he has taught at a number of universities in the United Kingdom and the United States, and has held various high-ranking positions with the World Bank. In 1998, he was asked to lead the team that would prepare the 2000/2001 issue of the *World Development Report*, the Bank's flagship annual publication, which would focus on "Attacking Poverty." In June 2000, before the release of the report, Kanbur resigned over disagreements on the final version. At the time, some said that the divergences were minor. The head of the World Bank, James Wolfensohn, even argued that it was merely a dispute over the order of the chapters! Others suggested that much more was at stake and that the United States Treasury Secretary, Lawrence H. Summers, was himself involved in re-writing parts of the report.

Whatever the case, the matter certainly appeared important to Kanbur. At a conference he addressed later the same year, he raised the question indirectly through a discussion of the fundamental disagreements that underlie global debates on poverty and development.[1] Inside as well as outside international organizations, Kanbur explained, there are two broad, contending views on how best to attack poverty. The first view rallies most of the economists working in finance ministries, in international financial institutions, and in universities, and the second is primarily defended by those, not usually economists, who are associated with social ministries, aid agencies, and non-governmental organizations. Most social and political actors position themselves in line with one of these two standpoints, which Ravi Kanbur identifies as "Group A" and "Group B." According to Kanbur, "Group A"

---

[1] Ravi Kanbur, "Economic Policy, Distribution and Poverty: The Nature of Disagreements," *World Development*, vol. 29, no. 6, June 2001, 1083–94.

believes poverty will best be reduced through structural adjustments that promote trade, foreign investment, and rapid economic growth. "Group B" contends instead that in a world where resources and power are unevenly distributed one cannot count simply on market rules and economic growth to alleviate poverty, and must address directly issues of distribution and redistribution.

Of course, Kanbur is aware of the political dimensions of these "disagreements." He identifies all the key actors and understands the depth of their oppositions. His very resignation from the World Bank was a consequence of this conflict between two worldviews. Still, Kanbur cannot find better names for the contenders than "Group A" and "Group B," or "Finance Ministry" and "Civil Society" tendencies.

Why not call "Group A" the right and "Group B" the left? After all, the first "group" privileges market rules and economic growth to counter poverty, and the second one has less confidence in the unfettered working of the market and places distributional outcomes ahead of growth as a priority. Most observers would recognize these opposing diagnostics as typical expressions of the left–right division. More to the point, these "groups" are not real groups. They constitute broad but loosely connected communities of values and ideas. What Kanbur sees is not a set of opposing "groups," but rather the expression of intellectual and political traditions that go far back in our common history and still matter very much in our collective lives.

Like many others, Ravi Kanbur may be reluctant to speak of the left and of the right, because he wants to give a relatively neutral, scientific character to the controversy he presents. Hence, he locates the core disagreements not in political ideas and values, but in differences over levels of aggregation, time horizons, and market structures. More, however, may be at stake in these analytical choices. Indeed, as widespread and as universally understood as they may be, the notions of left and right are not well thought of in the social sciences and in intellectual discourse. They seem somehow too simplistic and too binary. They also seem too political, bringing all arguments down to a face-to-face between two sides, and leaving almost no space for more dispassionate, balanced inquiries and debates. Moreover, international affairs have usually been understood as a distinct realm, shaped by the balance of power between states rather than by an ideological conflict that, many suggest, is restricted to domestic politics. And even there, in national politics, have not the notions of left and right lost most of their meaning and relevance, in an era defined by widely accepted neo-liberal policies or encompassing alternative programs such as the "Third Way"?

This book argues, to the contrary, that global politics is first and foremost a debate between the left and the right. This is so because the left–right cleavage expresses enduring and profound differences about equality, and equality is one of the most fundamental issues of con-troversy in any political community. The debate between the left and the right changes through time and space, and it does not incorporate every possible conflict and event. This conflict nevertheless structures most of our "disagreements," as Ravi Kanbur would say, and it does so in a significant and coherent way. To a large extent, it is this universal debate that makes contemporary politics intelligible within, but also beyond, the boundaries of nation-states.

The book starts with three claims. First, we believe that the world is constructed primarily through debates. This is not to deny the importance of material forces, technology, interests, or power relations, but simply to say that all these factors become socially and politically meaningful through the interpretations that we make of them. Before a country, a group, or a person can promote specific interests, one must first determine what these interests are, and make them understandable to others through discourse.

Second, we think of politics as global. Debates about the state of the world are conducted concurrently within, across, and above national borders, in processes that remain distinct but that are also intercon-nected and coherent. In other words, the old opposition between international and domestic politics is no longer tenable, if it ever was. Curiously, although this view of global politics is increasingly accepted, not much has been said about the nature and structure of global political deliberations.

Third, the ubiquity and the global character of debates do not mean that we live in a cacophonic world, a linguistic free-for-all where everybody would speak but no one would listen. On the contrary, there is a structure to our disagreements, a vocabulary and a grammar that make the process intelligible to all. In this grammar, the left–right dichotomy occupies a special place, as the most enduring, universal, and encompassing of all political cleavages.

Global politics is thus constructed through an ongoing debate between the left and the right. Indeed, the politics of the world, no matter on what scale, is most often a politics of left versus right. Whether they take place in global forums, in international organizations, in national legislatures, or in local associations, all our political debates are connected to the old, universal conflict over the meaning of equality, which divides progressives and conservatives. This is not to deny that there are civilizations, national identities, and other cleavages that shape global politics. But none of these differences governs our debates as thoroughly as the debate between the left and the right. Understanding the nature of our disagreements gives us a key to apprehend the world, and no key opens as many doors as the left–right key.

The first chapter explains what the left–right distinction means, and how it shapes politics. This distinction is critical, we argue, because it concerns not only interests but also deeply held values and principles. Chapters 2 and 3 demonstrate how profound and significant is the left–right opposition. Chapter 2 considers public opinion trends, and shows how, all over the world, ordinary citizens position themselves along the left–right spectrum, and organize their ideas and attitudes accordingly. Whatever social scientists may think of this dichotomy, it undoubtedly makes sense to the citizens of the world. Chapter 3 focuses on the discourse of elites, and presents two radically different portraits of global politics. The first is drawn by the right and appears relatively optimistic, the second comes from the left and offers a much darker picture of the world's past, present, and future.

The following chapters turn to history to explain how the global debate between the left and the right has evolved over time, from the end of the eighteenth to the beginning of the twenty-first century. Chapter 4 retraces the evolution of this opposition over the long period between the American Revolution and the end of the Second World War, which saw the emergence of the modern state system. Chapter 5 covers the period from 1945 to 1980, marked by the appeal of universal rights and by new world tensions. It examines the rise of the mixed economy, the expansion of the welfare state, the East–West divide, and the North–South conflict. In each case, we find, the left–right alignment defined the opponents and framed their disagreements.

Chapters 6 and 7 focus on more recent trends. Taking stock of the failure of communism and of the ascendancy of liberal democracy, Chapter 6 explains that the last two decades have been dominated by a turn to the right, both domestically and internationally. In economic and social policy as well as in global development, market rules, economic objectives, and efficiency have prevailed over state intervention, social preoccupations, and redistribution. Chapter 7 examines how at the turn of this century the left has been gradually forced to redefine its priorities and strategies, just as the right has become more sensitive to social concerns. In these years, the left–right debate slowly entered into a phase of more open dialogue and convergence. Yet, as we will see, this long-standing opposition is unlikely to vanish any time soon.

Finally, Chapter 8 extends the implications of our argument for the study of global politics. It considers, in particular, the relevance of left and right for the interpretation of emerging issues like the politics of identity, the war on terrorism, and environmental protection. This chapter also explains how the left–right debate sheds light on the main theoretical discussions that confront the community of political scientists today.

1 | *A clash over equality*

On August 24, 2006, the General Assembly of the International Astronomical Union (IAU) took a vote in Prague on the proper definition of the term "planet." Following years of intense debate, the IAU's decision was far from insignificant. As a result of the vote, Pluto lost its status as the solar system's ninth planet, and was reclassified in the diplomatically named category of "dwarf planets." The dispute over Pluto's nature, which had been raging for years, had become a major source of embarrassment for astronomers in 2005, when Michael Brown, a scientist working at the California Institute of Technology, discovered Xena, a celestial body larger than Pluto. Although it was passed with a clear majority, the IAU's vote did not stop the controversy between opponents and fans of Pluto. While the discoverer of Xena himself maintained that the IAU decision was "the right scientific choice," astronomer Alan Stern of the Southwest Research Institute in Colorado – who had sold the US Congress on the idea of funding a space mission to the "last planet" – declared for his part: "This is a sloppy, bad example of how science should be done."[1] Given that Stern's dissatisfaction was shared by several of his colleagues, the IAU is likely to reconsider its definition of "planet" at its next triennial meeting, in 2009. The "Pluto war" is not over yet.

To some, the Pluto controversy may seem odd or atypical. Debates about definitions, however, are far from unique. There is no scientific agreement either on a question as fundamental as "when does human life begin?" In *Roe* v. *Wade*, the 1973 Supreme Court decision that established the right to abortion in the United States, Justice Harry Blackmun, who wrote the majority opinion, explained that "when

---

[1] Govert Schilling, "Pluto: Underworld Character Kicked Out of Planetary Family," *Science*, vol. 313, September 1, 2006, 1214–15; Tom McNichol, "Beyond Cool: NASA Cost-Cutters Want to Kill a Pioneering Probe to the Ice-Cold Edge of the Solar System. First They Have to Reckon with the Pluto Underground," *Wired*, vol. 9, no. 4, April 2001, 116–28.

those trained in the respective disciplines of medicine, philosophy, and theology are unable to arrive at any consensus, the judiciary, at this point in the development of man's knowledge, is not in a position to speculate as to the answer." The Court ruled on different grounds, arguing that the mother's interest should be the first consideration in the first trimester of pregnancy, while the state's interests in protecting the unborn would prevail in the third.[2] It is doubtful that the progress of human knowledge will ever lead to a definitive, universally accepted answer to this difficult question. If anything, progress raises even more uncertainties of this type – concerning at what point clinical death should be declared, for instance. Reaching consensus on definitions does not become easier as we move from natural to social objects. What is a democracy? What is a just war? What is pornography? Who should be counted as poor? Where does Europe end? Is Québec a nation? All of these questions are matters for deliberation and debate.

Controversies about definitions are ubiquitous, in all fields of human knowledge, for two reasons. First, reality is not made of categories. We make up categories and apply them as best as we can to a world that is basically continuous, a seamless web of facts and events.[3] Second, naming something is also taking a stand. "Every name," writes Deborah Stone, "is a symbol, not the thing itself, and in the choice of names lies judgment, comparison, evaluation, and above all the potential for disagreement."[4] This does not mean that our discourses are pure inventions, totally disconnected from the "real world." What we say may be more or less accurate, or more or less supported by arguments and evidence. It means, rather, that in a social context, it matters whether Pluto is considered a planet, and whether life is said to begin in the first trimester of pregnancy.

People always debate about the proper categories and about their definitions. We care deeply about such debates because they provide

---

[2] United States Supreme Court, *Roe* v. *Wade*, 410 U.S. 113 (1973).

[3] "Disputes about the truth of classification," writes Ian Hacking, "precede anything we now call science ... There is nothing in the world but individual entities. Classes, groups, genera, are a fiction." Ian Hacking, "Inaugural Lecture: Chair of Philosophy and History of Scientific Concepts," *Economy and Society*, vol. 31, no. 1, February 2002, 1–14, p. 5; see also Deborah Stone, *Policy Paradox: The Art of Political Decision Making*, revised edition, New York, W. W. Norton, 2002, pp. 378–79.

[4] Stone, *Policy Paradox*, p. 310.

the narratives through which we see the world, our communities, and ourselves. We care as well because debates contribute to change the world. As we name and rename our environment, we shape our cultures and our social relations. In recent years, these discursive processes have been key preoccupations for constructivists, a group of scholars who call attention to the importance of ideas and language in politics. To further advance the constructivist project, however, analysts must better take into account the content and structure of social debates, as well as the dialectical nature of political interactions. This implies keeping in mind that disagreements are part of the human condition. In political life, no disagreement is as profound as the left–right opposition. It is to this quintessential political debate that we can now turn.

Left and right in global politics

The right begins for us much further left than you think. (Édouard Vaillant, socialist member of the National Assembly, Paris, 1907).[5]

From the beginning of the modern era, the public sphere in which social and political debates take place has had supranational dimensions. The ideas of the Enlightenment, for instance, circulated across borders, in both Europe and America. Yet, as the philosopher Charles Taylor explains, it is only recently that the public sphere "has been imaginatively expanded to include all the (properly behaved) members of the global community."[6] In this sense, political debates are increasingly global. Of course, the world public sphere does not encompass all possible debates, many issues being mostly of concern for politics on a smaller scale. Its existence, however, provides every debate with a global connection. More specifically, the world public sphere creates a shared background and vocabulary, which helps to bridge local, national, continental, and global deliberations.

   Current analyses of world politics note this public sphere, but they are rarely attentive to the structure of global deliberations. If anything,

---

[5] Marcel Gauchet, "La droite et la gauche," quoted in Pierre Nora (ed.), *Les lieux de mémoire. III. Les France: 1. Conflits et partages*, Paris, Gallimard, 1992, p. 417 (our translation).

[6] Charles Taylor, *Modern Social Imaginaries*, Durham, Duke University Press, 2004, p. 179.

they tend to assume that current debates lack coherence, compared to those that prevailed in the past. Globalization, write David Held and Anthony McGrew, disrupts "established paradigms and political orthodoxies," and leaves us without "coherent readings" or clear political "responses."[7] This diagnostic is not new. At the beginning of the 1990s, Anthony Giddens was already arguing that globalization had emptied the terms "right" and "left" of much of their meaning, each political perspective being "in its own way exhausted."[8] In a similar fashion, Zaki Laïdi concluded that the end of the Cold War had engendered a "world without meaning," devoid of clear collective projects to debate. In the past, proposed the French scholar, sharp cleavages between the left and the right, between the East and the West, and between the North and the South gave rise to well-defined claims and identities, and they generated coherent understandings of the world. With the disappearance of these cleavages, social actors would now lack common references, and fight instead over identity, religion, and culture, engaging in conflicts condemned to be endless and unsolvable.[9]

We argue, on the contrary, that today's global debates can best be understood as an expression of the old conflict between the left and the right. After all, what is it that divides partisans and adversaries of globalization if it is not a left–right conflict over markets, public intervention, and social justice? Interestingly, after they announced the end of traditional politics as a consequence of globalization, Held, Giddens, and Laïdi all attempted to define new objectives for the contemporary left. Held, for instance, seeks to define a global social democratic alternative, to establish a cosmopolitan common ground.[10] Likewise, Anthony Giddens, who was the foremost proponent of a "Third Way" beyond the left and the right, now wants to move "beyond where third way thinking has got so far," and to define a new

---

[7] David Held and Anthony McGrew, *Globalization/Anti-Globalization*, Cambridge, Polity Press, 2002, p. 2.

[8] Anthony Giddens, *Beyond Left and Right: The Future of Radical Politics*, Cambridge, Polity Press, 1994, pp. 78 and 251.

[9] Zaki Laïdi, *A World without Meaning: The Crisis of Meaning in International Politics*, London, Routledge, 1998.

[10] David Held, *Global Covenant: The Social Democratic Alternative to the Washington Consensus*, Cambridge, Polity Press, 2004, pp. 163–67; Held and McGrew, *Globalization/Anti-Globalization*, pp. 130–31.

progressive agenda for the world.[11] Zaki Laïdi also has his own
proposals for a renewed left, better able to address globalization and
modernity.[12] Fascinated by the social and political transformations of
their era, these authors first announced the end of old cleavages and
ideas, then identified a new division around globalization, which they
found insufficiently rigorous, and ended up trying to reinvent the distinction between the left and the right. The left–right divide, however,
may have been there all along.

Few notions, indeed, are as ubiquitous as the idea of a division
between the left and the right in politics. In public opinion surveys all
over the world, self-placement on a left–right scale stands out as
something of a "superissue," which "tends to assimilate all important
issues" and consistently proves to be one of the best predictors of a
person's political attitudes and behavior.[13] In most countries, political
life is defined by this dichotomy. The left and the right have distinct
views on globalization and they have reacted differently to the war in
Iraq. The two sides also take different positions on nuclear energy, on
the future of the European Union, and on same-sex marriage. The
right now dominates in American and French politics, while the left
has come back to power in Latin America and India. Everywhere,
newspapers analyze the respective stands, strengths, and divisions of
the two camps, to evaluate where a country, or the world, seems to be
heading.

Ronald Inglehart suggests quite appropriately that the core meaning
of the distinction "is whether one supports or opposes social change
in an egalitarian direction."[14] The question, however, may be more
complex than it seems. Indeed, if there are emotional disagreements
about what constitutes a planet, one can easily imagine that there is no
consensus on what exactly are the left and the right in politics.

Many political scientists actually think that the two terms are better
left undefined, as vague notions that play useful roles in political life

[11] Anthony Giddens, "Introduction. Neoprogressivism. A New Agenda for Social
Democracy," in Anthony Giddens (ed.), *The Progressive Manifesto*,
Cambridge, Polity Press, 2003, pp. 1–6.

[12] Zaki Laïdi, *La gauche à venir: politique et mondialisation*, Paris, Editions de
l'Aube, 2001.

[13] Ronald Inglehart, *Culture Shift in Advanced Industrial Society*, Princeton
University Press, 1989, pp. 292–93.

[14] *Ibid.*, p. 293.

but have no scientific or even descriptive relevance. They see two major problems with the use of the notions of left and right as analytical concepts. First, they note that these notions cover a broad range of political positions, which change across space and time, and argue that any definition simplifies reality and leaves out important movements and parties. Is it possible, for instance, to find a meaningful definition that would draw together Adolf Hitler, Winston Churchill, Augusto Pinochet, and George W. Bush, against Lenin, Franklin Delano Roosevelt, Nelson Mandela, and Tony Blair? Second, it is often pointed out that, even in a given place and time, the notions of left and right remain relative. It is always a question of being on the left or right of someone. As the quotation from Édouard Vaillant given above indicates, political positions are very much a matter of . . . debate! The best we can do, conclude some experts, is to build modest, time- and space-specific typologies of various ideological preferences. Doing otherwise would smack of essentialism, a perspective that assumes phenomena have inherent, distinctive features, which give them their true and universal meaning.[15]

This reluctance to define the left and the right is misplaced on two counts. First, as even the most prudent authors recognize, the left–right division is a genuine social fact that can hardly be ignored. Second, the conventional fear of essentialism is misguided.

Consider, first, the undeniable reality of the left–right dichotomy. Social scientists, argues René Rémond, have not invented this notion; they have found it in the real practices of political actors, all over the world and for more than a century. Observers have repeatedly predicted the demise of the division, but repeatedly as well they have seen it persist, as the most powerful of all political cleavages.[16] This distinction can be challenged as a working concept, but it cannot be abolished as a phenomenon.[17] This is the case because the left–right

---

[15] Among the many authors adopting this position, see: René Rémond, *Les droites en France*, Paris, Aubier-Montaigne, 1982, pp. 18–37; Roger Eatwell, "The Nature of the Right, 1: Is There an 'Essentialist' Philosophical Core?," in Roger Eatwell and Noël O'Sullivan (eds.), *The Nature of the Right: European and American Politics and Political Thought since 1789*, London, Pinter, 1989, pp. 47–60; Jean-Marie Denquin, *Science politique*, fourth edition, Paris, PUF, 1992, pp. 337–41; Agnès Alexandre-Collier and Xavier Jardin, *Anatomie des droites européennes*, Paris, Armand Colin, 2004, pp. 10–20.

[16] Rémond, *Les droites en France*, p. 29.

[17] Denquin, *Science politique*, p. 341.

opposition is an important social fact, one of those "things like money, sovereignty, and rights, which have no material reality but exist only because people collectively believe they exist and act accordingly."[18] Social facts can be broadly defined as sets of shared memories and narratives that shape individual and collective behavior. Abstract and constructed socially though they may be, social facts are nonetheless real and influential, and they should not be discarded lightly, as vague or hopeless notions.

Understood as a social fact, the left–right distinction can make sense, even though its specific contours change over time and across space. Such variations are indeed the hallmark of long-lasting and widespread collective representations, which endure precisely because they are flexible. The power of the left–right division, explains Marcel Gauchet, lies in its indefinite capacity to be enriched and renewed. This cleavage functions as a memory tool because it is open. It creates continuity in histories that are discontinuous and unites political families through time and space, in society-wide conflicts that can appear perennial and meaningful.[19] This analytical perspective implies that we need not worry too much about essentialism, the second point raised above. Whether a cultural representation exists is a question that can best be assessed with empirical evidence. It cannot be affirmed uncritically, but neither should it be ruled out a priori, by an epistemological skepticism that would "be just as dogmatic as appeals to occult essences."[20] History provides the best safeguard against loose essentialist arguments. Indeed, the left–right distinction has a well-established genealogy, anchored in the travails of the French Revolution and in the development of democracy and socialism in Europe.

Before turning to this genealogy, some clarification about antecedents needs to be offered. First, social dichotomies featuring the left and the right are much older than the modern, democratic distinction. "Wherever one looks," writes psychologist Chris McManus, "on any continent, in any historical period or in any culture, right and left have

---

[18] Martha Finnemore and Kathryn Sikkink, "Taking Stock: The Constructivist Research Program in International Relations and Comparative Politics," *Annual Review of Political Science*, vol. 4, 2001, 391–416, p. 393.

[19] Gauchet, "La droite et la gauche," p. 416.

[20] Alexander Wendt, *Social Theory of International Politics*, Cambridge University Press, 1999, pp. 63–64.

their symbolic associations and always it is right that is good and left that is bad."[21] Early Indo-Europeans and tribal societies all over the world have tended to equate the right–left division with the male–female distinction, and to associate the right with positive symbols such as life, gods, cleanliness, and superiority, and the left with their opposites: death, mortals, dirtiness, and inferiority. In classical Greece, the same dichotomies held, the right being associated with symbols for male, straight, light, and good, and the left with representations for female, crooked, darkness, and evil. In the Christian, Jewish, and Islamic traditions, the elect are on the right of God and the damned on His left. Buddhists see the path to paradise as bifurcated, the right branch leading to Nirvana.[22] Everywhere, noted sociologist Robert Hertz in 1909, "the right hand is the symbol and model of all aristocracy, the left hand of all common people."[23] The languages of the world convey the same message, the words for right generally being associated with qualities and the words for left with defaults. In Latin, for instance, the terms are *dexter* and *sinister*.[24] It is useful to keep in mind these ancient roots. The idea of some sort of symbolic continuity appears intriguing and plausible, although one should not lose sight of the distinctive character of modern usage.

Political debates about social justice are also ancient, going much further back in history than the contemporary debates between the left and the right. "Right from the time of the ancient Greeks," argues D. D. Raphael, "there have been two, apparently inconsistent, ideas of distributive justice," one stressing merit and deservingness, the other equal worth and needs.[25] This divergence, as Raphael points out, is very close to the one defining the contemporary left–right cleavage.

The genealogy of the left–right debate as a social fact, then, is the story of the gradual and eventually universal association between an old, familiar spatial metaphor and a modern debate about justice. This association was not necessary. Other metaphors, or a multitude of

[21] Chris McManus, *Right Hand, Left Hand: The Origins of Asymmetry in Brains, Bodies, Atoms and Cultures*, Cambridge, MA, Harvard University Press, 2002, p. 35.

[22] *Ibid.*, pp. 21–33.   [23] Robert Hertz, quoted in *ibid.*, p. 20.

[24] J. A. Laponce, *Left and Right: The Topography of Political Perceptions*, University of Toronto Press, 1981, pp. 38–41; McManus, *Right Hand, Left Hand*, pp. 60–65.

[25] D. D. Raphael, *Concepts of Justice*, Oxford University Press, 2001, p. 5.

metaphors, could have expressed the cleavages driving contemporary political life.[26] Colors, for instance, have often played such a role, and they have many of the qualities of the left–right representation, allowing a range of positions from the various shades of blue to those of red, along with the outlying tints of green, orange, or yellow. Many popular revolutions have been draped in colors, from the red of the French and Russian Revolutions to the orange of the recent Ukrainian democratic movement. In the end, it was the left and the right, however, which prevailed as the universal political metaphor. These two poor classificatory words, remarks Gauchet with wonder, condensed like no others the passions, the emotions, the ideas, and the memories of entire generations, all over the world.[27]

The standard narrative starts with the French Revolution. In France as elsewhere, prior to the Revolution, the main political metaphor was not horizontal but vertical. It distinguished three estates, ranked in a descending order, from the clergy to the nobility to the commoners.[28] In June 1789, the Third Estate proclaimed itself a National Assembly and successfully invited the other two estates to join in constitutional discussions. This illegal act created an unprecedented situation, and placed the different orders on an equal plane. At the outset, however, the delegates did not constitute parties. They aspired on the contrary to unity, and hoped a consensus could emerge out of their free deliberations.[29] In practice, the Assembly proved unruly and chaotic, with few rules of procedure, much noise and interruption, and voting by standing or sitting. By the end of August, a pattern had emerged out of this disorder, with partisans of the king and of gradual change moving to the right of the president, and more ardent promoters of liberty and equality to the left.[30] Some tried to be independent and move around but, as explained in his memoirs by a member of the National Assembly from the nobility, in the end one had to "abandon absolutely the left side," where he "was condemned to always vote

---

[26] McManus, *Right Hand, Left Hand*, pp. 260–61; Gauchet, "La droite et la gauche," p. 446; Laponce, *Left and Right*, p. 27.

[27] Gauchet, "La droite et la gauche," p. 442.

[28] Laponce, *Left and Right*, p. 47.

[29] Michel Vovelle, "La gauche sous la Révolution: naissance d'une notion," in Jean-Jacques Becker and Gilles Candar (eds.), *Histoire des gauches en France. Volume 1: L'héritage du XIXe siècle*, Paris, La Découverte, 2004, pp. 53–54.

[30] *Ibid.*, p. 50; Laponce, *Left and Right*, pp. 48–49.

alone and consequently condemned to the boos of the tribunes."[31] Participants and observers increasingly acknowledged the spatial division of the National Assembly, and this arrangement solidified as an important political convention.

For most of the nineteenth century, however, the distinction between the left and the right remained confined to one institution, in one country. It pertained solely to the life of France's National Assembly, and belonged to the technical vocabulary of parliamentary affairs. When universal male suffrage was adopted in 1848, French politicians and electors spoke instead of a sharp opposition between the republicans and the conservatives, or the reds and the whites, the two camps historically in favor of or opposed to the Revolution.[32] The cleavage was more or less the same as the one between the left and the right in the Assembly, but the spatial metaphor had not become commonplace, let alone universal. The left–right division was not, yet, a ubiquitous social fact.

The turning point came in the 1890s, with the rise of socialism. Until then, the parliamentary left was defined primarily by its support for the republic, for democracy, and for laicism, against a right still attached to the monarchy, to limited enfranchisement, and to state support for religious institutions. With the end of the nineteenth century, however, a new left emerged, which was not only republican but also socialist. Representative of an increasingly organized and mobilized working class and tied to an international movement, the socialists challenged the republicans, who clung to a *laissez-faire* attitude in matters of social and economic development. After 1893, socialist parties made electoral gains and gradually took over the left of the National Assembly, pushing the republicans to the right.[33] On both sides, then, there were elected representatives who believed in the republic and claimed to be on the left. The old republicans had become "men from the centre that hard times forced to sit on the right."[34] Politicians were struggling to redefine parliamentary labels, in a way that could highlight differences between opponents as well as similarities

---

[31] Baron de Gauville, quoted in Gauchet, "La droite et la gauche," p. 398 (our translation).

[32] Gauchet, "La droite et la gauche," pp. 399, 409, and 412–13.

[33] Gilles Candar, "La gauche en République (1871–1899)," in Becker and Candar (eds.), *Histoire des gauches en France. Volume 1*, pp. 117–22.

[34] Joseph Barthélemy, quoted in *ibid.*, p. 117.

and possible alliances between like-minded parties. In the process, the left–right metaphor took on its contemporary meaning, as a permanent cleavage about equality, which is sufficiently open to be redefined with time and allow shifting alliances, without losing its relevance as a collective representation of the enduring conflict that divides democracies. More importantly, the left–right metaphor reached beyond the French parliamentary arena, to define two perennial camps, two enduring political cultures within French society.[35] Through the socialist movement, this metaphor then spread more or less rapidly throughout Europe and across the world.[36]

The contemporary left–right division, then, is less a child of the French Revolution than an offspring of democratic socialism. This suggests that the defining issue is not democracy itself, or revolution and change versus authority and order, but rather what was called in the nineteenth century the "social question," namely the issue of equality. Norberto Bobbio, who considers the different definitions that have been proposed for the left–right distinction, concludes likewise that the contemporary opposition is a product of the late nineteenth century and concerns equality. The left, argues Bobbio, is "more egalitarian," and the right "more inegalitarian."[37] Bobbio's definition has been faulted for being essentialist but, as we have seen above, this is a baseless criticism. A collective representation as powerful as this one must have an intelligible, enduring meaning. More problematic, in our view, is the negative definition Bobbio gives for the right, which he understands simply as less in favor of equality than the left.

Consider once again the French republicans, who were gradually pushed to the right by the socialists. As champions of the republic, of universal suffrage, and of public schools, they certainly were not against equality. They were pessimistic, however, about the possibilities of changing society through public intervention, and more confident in the potential of individuals in a society that would reward effort and merit. "Undoubtedly," recognized Jules Ferry, a republican politician who headed the French government in the 1880s, "the fight for

[35] Gauchet, "La droite et la gauche," pp. 416.
[36] *Ibid.*, pp. 446–47; Laponce, *Left and Right*, pp. 52–56.
[37] Norberto Bobbio, *Left and Right: The Significance of a Political Distinction*, University of Chicago Press, 1996, pp. 56 and 65.

life is harsh, and it is certainly legitimate to dream of a society better organized than this society of struggle and competition that is ours, a more fraternal society; but none of us and none of those who will succeed us will ever see even the threshold of this promised land."[38] Ferry's equality was the equality of citizens in rights and in opportunities, not in intrinsic worth and needs.

The split between the republicans and the socialists reproduces the debate over social justice that D. D. Raphael traces as far back as classical Greece. In a democratic society, however, this debate is not only for philosophers. It is constitutive of the public sphere, and structures politics through and through. This is the case because the opposition between the left and the right raises the central contradiction of a new society, a liberal one, premised on the equality of all citizens in rights but still marked by profound inequalities.

Liberal democracies were built in opposition to older, hierarchical orders, in the name of equality and individual rights.[39] The shift in perspective was huge and difficult, because up to then inequality had been understood as the natural order of things. The family, the Church, social classes, even the animal kingdom were seen as hierarchies designed by God. Ranks and places defined a natural order that was normal and right, and could only be challenged at one's peril, as many tales and myths demonstrated.[40] Breaking with such a social imaginary was neither easy nor rapid. To stay with the case of France, it was not until the second half of the nineteenth century that universal male suffrage and democratic rights were firmly established. Elsewhere in Europe, the main advances in male suffrage took place only between 1880 and 1920. For women the vote came even later, between 1918 and 1918.[41] In many countries of the world, and for nearly 40 percent of the world's population, such basic democratic rights remain unachieved to this day.[42]

The first liberal debates, then, pitted defenders of the old order against democrats. With the gradual entrenchment of individual rights, however, democrats themselves split over the meaning of equality. This

---

[38] Jules Ferry, quoted in Candar, "La gauche en République (1871–1899)," p. 117 (our translation).

[39] Taylor, *Modern Social Imaginaries*, p. 22.   [40] *Ibid.*, pp. 9–19.

[41] Stefano Bartolini, *The Political Mobilization of the European Left, 1860–1980: The Class Cleavage*, Cambridge University Press, 2000, pp. 209–15.

[42] See www.freedomhouse.org.

division was confirmed and institutionalized with the rise of socialism, which gave the left–right metaphor its contemporary meaning and contributed to its broad diffusion. On the right stood liberals and democrats who believed it was not only sufficient but also best to let individuals work their way forward, in a context guaranteeing them equal rights and fair opportunities. On the left were those who contended that equality remained an illusion without collective institutions assuring truly equal opportunities and minimally equal conditions for all.

Although there was some continuity and various alliances, the modern right was not simply a new incarnation for old conservatives clinging to a bygone hierarchical order. It was first and foremost a liberal right, which also claimed to be on the side of equality, the equality of right-bearing citizens free to pursue happiness and economic success and to accumulate wealth for themselves and for their children, without undue interference from the state. Less concerned by unachieved potential, unmet needs, and social solidarity than the left, this liberal right nevertheless defined a moral position, which was not simply backward looking or self-interested. The modern right was not, Bobbio notwithstanding, "inegalitarian." It was, shall we say, differently egalitarian.

Consider, for instance, the American debate on affirmative action. This controversy, which is an instance of the broader left–right debate, does not pit the promotion of equality against the defense of self-interest or, worse, of inequality. It opposes two contending conceptions of equality, both solidly anchored in the liberal tradition. Affirmative action's detractors argue that in hiring and admission decisions, only decisions based on merit offer a fair and equal treatment to all. Taking race into consideration appears to them as hazardous, given the difficulty of defining race, and can even be seen as an insidious form of racism. It is thus in the name of equality that these opponents reject affirmative action. On the other side, affirmative action supporters agree that equal treatment and merit are important, but they consider that American history has left a legacy of discrimination that weighs heavily against minority candidates. They also point to a number of exceptions to the neutral rules advocated by opponents of affirmative action, exceptions that do not seem to clash with these opponents' "color-blind" conception of fairness. The children of alumni, major donors, or well-known people, for instance, are often given preference in college admissions.[43] Supporters of affirmative action appeal to a more demanding conception of equality, one that considers not only the rules governing a presumably level playing-field, but also the conditions under which the players may reach this field, or not. The two sides claim the high moral ground of equality, but in different ways.

Contrasting worldviews

The contemporary opposition between the left and the right is thus a conflict over the meaning of equality in a modern, predominantly liberal society. This is not a conflict about modernity as such, opposing reaction and progress, but rather a conflict within modernity, on the manner in which shared principles should be implemented, not only in a country but also in the world.

This is the distinction that one of the founders of modern neoliberal thought, Friedrich A. von Hayek, had in mind when he wrote emphatically that he was not a conservative but a liberal, because he advocated principled social transformations. The conservative attitude, complained Hayek, is backward looking and dominated by "a fear of change, a timid distrust of the new as such, while the liberal position is based on courage and confidence, on a preparedness to let change run its course even if we cannot predict where it will lead." In the fight against collectivism, he explained, liberals "cannot be content with simply helping to apply the brake." They must propose principles, a direction, and avenues for change.[44]

Aren't conservatives nevertheless on the right of the political spectrum? Yes, because, in practice, they share the skepticism expressed by a liberal like Jules Ferry, and the distrust of public intervention of someone like Hayek. The point is simply that conservatism, or a preference for the status quo, is not what distinguishes most clearly the right from the left.[45] Margaret Thatcher, for instance, one of the most important right-wing politicians of our era, meant to transform Britain in a radical way, not to preserve its established institutions and practices.

[43] Stone, *Policy Paradox*, pp. 393–95.
[44] Friedrich A. von Hayek, "Why I Am Not a Conservative," in *The Constitution of Liberty*, University of Chicago Press, 1960, pp. 397–411.
[45] Bobbio, *Left and Right*, p. 56.

Further distinctions could be outlined for a number of other terms and ideas associated in one way or another with the left and the right. George Lakoff, for instance, a specialist in linguistics and cognitive science, suggests that parents on the right and on the left do not have the same views about raising children. Parents on the right would be guided by a "strict father" model, which would privilege rules, authority, self-discipline, and self-reliance. Parents on the left would follow instead a "nurturant parent" model, stressing empathy, respect, communication, personal fulfillment, and the exploration of a range of ideas and experiences.[46] These models correspond to distinct views about society. In the "strict father" perspective, life is difficult and competitive, and children must build character, so as to sink or swim by themselves. The struggle for survival is tough, but it is also moral, because it rewards the most deserving. Victims of external disasters caused by nature or accidents should thus be helped, but persons who are in trouble by their own fault must accept the consequences of their irresponsibility, otherwise they will never learn to discipline themselves. The "nurturant parent" worldview stresses instead empathy, open-mindedness, and cooperation. Personal fulfillment comes in this case with the development of social ties, in a spirit of respect, fairness, and interdependence. Helping others does not hurt them and does not distort critical social mechanisms. On the contrary, mutual support reinforces social trust and happiness for all.[47]

Lakoff's focus on family metaphors highlights important foundations of the left–right debate, with examples that are typical of contemporary American debates. To some extent country-specific, his analysis is nevertheless extremely useful in pointing to the moral character of the universal debate between the left and the right. The "strict father" model is indeed very close to the values generally associated with nineteenth-century social Darwinism. On the opposite side, and closer to us, consider how left-of-centre Bill Clinton explains how he was raised, by his uncle, aunts, and grand-parents, to believe "that no one is perfect but most people are good; that people can't be judged only by their worst or weakest moments...Perhaps most important, I learned that everyone has a story – of dreams and

---

[46] George Lakoff, *Moral Politics: What Conservatives Know That Liberals Don't*, University of Chicago Press, 1996, pp. 32–36.
[47] *Ibid.*, pp. 65–140.

nightmares, hope and heartache, love and loss, courage and fear, sacrifice and selfishness."[48] Empathy, respect, and communication prevailed here over the struggle for survival.

People on the left and on the right promote different standards of equality precisely because they have different views about human nature and society, different expectations about life in a community. These contrasting views are constitutive of the modern political debate, and were articulated from the very beginning by philosophers like Thomas Hobbes and John Locke on one side, and Jean-Jacques Rousseau, Karl Marx, and Friedrich Engels on the other.

Thomas Hobbes, who wrote his *Leviathan* (1651) during the English Civil Wars, was pessimistic about human nature, which he saw as governed by competition, envy, and fear. Without a strong authoritarian government, humans were condemned to live in a permanent state of war, "where every man is enemy to every man." In such a violent state of nature, men would be unable to produce, invest, invent, or create, and their life would remain "solitary, poor, nasty, brutish, and short."[49] More moderate, John Locke nevertheless converged with Hobbes in favoring a state strong enough to protect individual property, in his view the cornerstone of individual autonomy, which would be threatened without laws and legal institutions.[50] Jean-Jacques Rousseau, on the contrary, saw human nature as intrinsically good and compassionate, and property as usurpation and theft, the source of all that is corrupt in society: "you are undone," he affirmed in his 1754 discourse on the origin of inequality among men, "if you once forget that the fruits of the earth belong to us all, and the earth itself to nobody."[51] Karl Marx and Friedrich Engels likewise associated inequality and alienation with the division of labor and with the rise of private property, even though they were less sanguine about a primitive stage that remained limited by scarcity and "surrounded by superstition." The distribution of labor and its products in

---

[48] Bill Clinton, *My Life*, New York, Alfred A. Knopf, 2004, p. 15.

[49] Thomas Hobbes, *Leviathan* (1651), Chapter 13, www.constitution.org/th/leviatha.htm.

[50] Robert Castel, *L'insécurité sociale: qu'est-ce qu'être protégé?*, Paris, Seuil, 2003, pp. 12–17.

[51] Jean-Jacques Rousseau, "A Discourse on a Subject Proposed by the Academy of Dijon: What Is the Origin of Inequality Among Men, and Is It Authorised by Natural Law," Part II (1754), trans. G. D. H. Cole, www.constitution.org/jjr/ineq.htm.

the family, they wrote in *The German Ideology*, very early established a form of "latent slavery." Only communism on a world-scale, in a modern context of abundance, could do away with the alienation associated with "the consolidation of what we ourselves produce into an objective power above us, growing out of our control, thwarting our expectations, bringing to naught our calculations."[52]

Like Hobbes and Locke, those on the right tend to be pessimistic about human nature, about the fight for life, and about the possibilities of progress through collective action or public intervention. At best, they think, such interventions will be ineffective. At worst, they will create perverse incentives or be captured by special interests seeking privileges. The ideal for them is to let individuals use their talents and their drive to succeed, so as to assure economic growth and social progress, which in the end will benefit all of society. The state's primary role, in this context, is to protect individuals and their property, in a society that remains potentially dangerous, greed and envy being indelible features of human nature.

For the left, human nature is, on the contrary, a source of optimism, each person being seen as fundamentally good and compassionate. Problems start with the organization of society, which creates inequality and may corrupt character. This implies that only collective and public solutions can provide adequate responses to social ills. Insecurity, here, is associated less with threats to individuals and their property than with the always uncertain fate of vulnerable persons, in a society driven by competition. The state must of course prevent violence and theft, prevention being preferable to punishment, but it should also create equal opportunities, offer protection against social risks, and redistribute income, to counter the perils associated with a market economy.[53]

In a tongue-in-cheek comment, Canadian philosopher Joseph Heath contrasts these opposite views of human nature by proposing that each side endures its peculiar kind of unthinking militants. The left, he

---

[52] Karl Marx and Friedrich Engels, *The German Ideology* (1845–46; first published in 1932), Sections entitled "Private Property and Communism" and "[5. Development of the Productive Forces as a Material Premise of Communism]," www.marxists.org.

[53] The contrast between these two notions of insecurity, which underpins the right's focus on crime and the left's preoccupation with social security, is well presented in Castel, *L'insécurité sociale*, pp. 19–32.

writes, attracts "bleeding hearts," persons "who have never met a claim to victimhood that does not cry out for redress and compensation," and seem "temperamentally incapable of saying no to the underdog." The right, on the other hand, must deal with "jerks," who want to cut taxes and social programs "simply because they don't care about anybody but themselves," are unabashedly self-interested, and "may even have a mean streak."[54]

More broadly, one could identify a vast array of cultural attitudes and predispositions associated with being on the left or on the right. "Le ski," cries a woman played by Emmanuelle Béart in a 2004 French movie, "c'est de droite!" Skiing is right-wing.[55] Béart's character refers to downhill skiing, an expensive sport that requires fancy equipment and is practiced in highly organized and commercial settings. She does not say so, but Nordic and backcountry skiing may have more of a leftist touch. For Margaret Thatcher, buses were apparently collectivist, left-wing contraptions. "A man," she said, "who, beyond the age of 26, finds himself on a bus can count himself as a failure."[56] Jean Jaélic, a little-known French conservative who wrote a book on the right in the early 1960s, proposed an entire classification of characteristics of the left and of the right. In his view, for instance, soup, mountain hiking, and the morning were disciplined, rigorous right-wing preferences, whereas aperitifs, beach holidays, and the afternoon were lax, frivolous left-wing inclinations.[57] More recently, a French survey found that people who identify with the right tend to buy Peugeot cars whereas those on the left are more likely to choose Renault, a formerly state-owned enterprise.[58] Much could be said about the political relevance of such categorizations but, as we will show in Chapter 2, public opinion surveys do indicate significant relationships between political orientations and cultural attitudes. One should keep in mind, however, that Italians have not

---

[54] Joseph Heath, "The Last Word: Thoughts on a United Right," *Policy Options*, vol. 25, no. 1, December 2003–January 2004, 116 (www.irpp.org).

[55] The movie is *À boire*, by Marion Vernoux (France, 2004).

[56] Margaret Thatcher (1986), quoted in the *Wikipedia Free Encyclopedia* (http://en.wikiquote.org/wiki/Margaret_Thatcher).

[57] Jean Jaélic, *La droite, cette inconnue*, Paris, Les sept couleurs, 1963, p. 129.

[58] Ludovic Hitzmann, "Élection présidentielle française: La gauche aime Renault, la droite Peugeot," *La Presse* (Montréal), May 7, 2007. The most right-wing French prefer Ford cars!

been able yet to solve the heated controversy over the right- or left-wing character of Nutella![59]

On one side, then, we have the right, which is pessimistic about human nature, sees life as a tough competition among individuals, seeks security against the ever-present possibility of violence, and defines equality in terms of personal rights. On the other side is the left, which is more optimistic about humanity, considers that communities can successfully cooperate, wants the state to protect people against social risks, and hopes to achieve what it sees as real equality.

Expectations differ accordingly. Given its pessimistic outlook on human motivations and collective potential, the right tends to be satisfied with the state of the world. Considering where we started and where we could be, possibly back in a Hobbesian state of nature, life is not so bad after all. In any case, trying collectively to do too much is likely to fail and to create, in the process, all kinds of "perverse effects."[60] At the end of the 1980s, American economist John Kenneth Galbraith described his country, governed for a decade by the right, as driven by a "culture of contentment."[61] The left, on the contrary, is ever unsatisfied, even when it is in power. Confident in the potential of all human beings and in our societies' capacity to transform themselves for the better, leftists tend to find progress too timid and too slow. This is why the adjective "critical" is often understood as just another word for left.

What about authority? Many authors argue that, being more concerned by violence and insecurity and more positive about hierarchies based on merit, the right is also more likely to be authoritarian than the left.[62] Favorable to discipline and law and order, the right would be more tolerant of strong leaders. This may be true, but one should recognize that authoritarian, even violent, tendencies also exist on the left, as the history of communism makes perfectly clear. The cleavage over authority is simply not the decisive one.

---

[59] Éric Jozsef, "De gauche ou de droite, le Nutella?," *Le Devoir* (Montréal), February 4, 2005, p. A1.

[60] Albert O. Hirschman, *The Rhetoric of Reaction: Perversity, Futility, Jeopardy*, Cambridge, MA, Harvard University Press, 1991.

[61] John Kenneth Galbraith, *The Culture of Contentment*, Boston, Houghton Mifflin, 1992.

[62] See Roger Eatwell, "The Rise of 'Left–right' Terminology: The Confusions of Social Science," in Eatwell and O'Sullivan (eds.), *The Nature of the Right*, pp. 51–52.

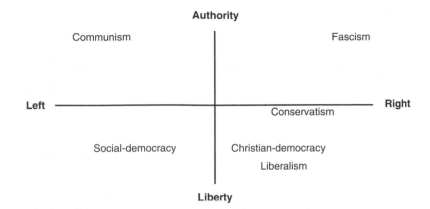

Figure 1.1 The left, the right, authority, and liberty
Source: adapted from Hans Eysenck.[63]

One way to integrate the fact that both sides of the political spectrum may harbor authoritarian elements is to treat the authority–liberty opposition as a secondary axis of differentiation, cutting vertically across the left–right horizontal axis. Such a representation, which creates four possible positions, was proposed by psychologist Hans Eysenck in the early 1950s. In this perspective, presented in Figure 1.1, the left can be authoritarian or liberal (going from communists to social-democrats), and so can the right (with fascists at one end, and conservatives, liberals, and Christian-democrats at the other).[64] Eysenck's distinction is useful in underlining the fact that no side has the monopoly of authoritarian tendencies. His spatial model also allows one to see that a variety of positions are possible, from moderate centrist stances, to more extreme ones.

Interestingly, in European history, both communist and fascist extremists entered the political arena by claiming that they were neither from the left nor from the right. They constituted radical alternatives, in rupture with the established debates about the meaning and promises of liberalism.[65] The choice between the parliamentary right and the parliamentary left, said French communist leader Maurice Thorez in 1934, was merely a choice between "cholera and

---

[63] Hans Eysenck, *The Psychology of Politics*, London, Routledge, 1954, p. 110.
[64] Eatwell, "The Rise of 'Left–right' Terminology," pp. 42–3.
[65] Gauchet, "La droite et la gauche," pp. 427–28 and 431.

the plague."[66] In the end, one should recognize that both sides may engender authoritarian forces. Left-wing authoritarianism is usually legitimated in the name of equality and of people's democracy; right-wing authoritarianism in the name of security, order, and tradition.

The left–right cleavage, then, is a powerful social fact, an ideological division that has coherence and that holds because people collectively believe in its significance and act accordingly. This conflict, which gradually became universal around the beginning of the twentieth century, opposes two views of human nature and two conceptions of equality, and it shapes many cultural traits as well as most of the world's political debates. In constant evolution, the left–right duality is constructed by a variety of agents, be they individuals, groups, movements, parties, or states. It also constitutes these agents, contributing to define their identities and to situate them more or less in opposition or in alliance with other social actors. The left–right metaphor structures the primary cleavage through which, together, we debate the world.

Isn't global politics more complex?

Many readers may object that a single ideological cleavage cannot a world make, and they would be right. A number of issues unrelated or weakly related to the left–right division fuel political debates. Our point is simply that no other question tells us as much as this one about the conflicts governing our societies. Let us consider, briefly, a number of plausible counter-arguments.

First, some would reject the very idea of reducing world debates to two master narratives, arguing that this analytic choice is simplistic, reductive, and possibly inimical to democratic debates, best premised on diversity. Against this objection, we can only bring back the classical response of René Rémond, who agreed that the left–right duality simplified reality, but noted that this was how social actors understood politics.[67] In general, humans tend to represent the world with binary classifications and polar opposites, and it is hardly surprising that politics is also understood in dichotomous terms, with one

---

[66] A few months later, Thorez joined in a "Popular Front" with other parties of the left. Thorez is quoted in Gauchet, "La droite et la gauche," p. 428 (our translation).

[67] Rémond, *Les droites en France*, p. 29.

dichotomy prevailing over all others.[68] From a scientific point of view, such classifications may appear insufficient but, in the social world, they constitute powerful representations. As such, they are important social facts.

Second, as mentioned above, attempts to define the left–right opposition are often seen as essentialist, because both terms actually change in meaning across time and space. These notions would be, so to speak, empty vessels ready to convey different material depending on the context. Again, this is largely true. Left and right are relative notions that take on different meanings according to the circumstances. These terms, however, also have a history, anchored in the development of liberal democracy, and as such they have an enduring significance, which most people across the world perceive easily. However difficult to pin down and define, the left–right cleavage looks like common sense to most citizens. Nobody hesitates, polls regularly demonstrate, when it comes to placing a party or a well-known public figure on the left or on the right. There is this little something, this "je ne sais quoi" that says it all.[69] The left–right opposition may pertain to the type of understanding that philosopher Michael Polanyi calls tacit knowledge, "the things people know but cannot put into words, much less formulate as rules."[70] The distinction is no less operative as a source of political mobilization.

Third, it has been repeatedly argued over the years that the left–right cleavage was a fading division, gradually superseded by other oppositions, more relevant for our era. Over time, various authors have talked about the end of ideology or of history, the new cleavages of post-industrial society, the rise of post-materialism, the emergence of the women's movement or of green politics, the fragmentation of politics into issue-oriented conflicts, or the predominance of personality and electoral marketing over traditional partisan divisions, all these hypotheses converging to predict the demise of the old battle lines, born in the nineteenth century. For one thing, the left–right cleavage

---

[68] Laponce, *Left and Right*, pp. 14–23; McManus, *Right Hand, Left Hand*, p. 36; Bobbio, *Left and Right*, pp. 1–2.

[69] Maxime Dury, *La droite et la gauche: les lois de la représentation politique*, Paris, Éditions Eska, 2001, pp. 16–17.

[70] Stone, *Policy Paradox*, p. 290–91. To illustrate the notion, Deborah Stone gives the example of Supreme Court Justice Potter Stewart who said about obscenity: "I can't define it but I know it when I see it."

has never been the sole dimension of political life. In Europe, for instance, cleavages between Catholics and Protestants, and between urban and rural areas have played a distinctive role alongside the dominant class cleavages that fueled the debate between socialist and conservative parties.[71] The existence of other cleavages, however, did not imply that the left–right division was not operative. It simply made its translation into discourse and institutions more complex, giving rise to hybrid species such as Christian-democratic or agrarian parties. The same is true today. The issues and cleavages of the day tend to be incorporated into the core left–right dichotomy, by voters who read them through familiar lenses, and by candidates and parties who have good strategic reasons to integrate rising preoccupations into their programs.[72] Even scholars who speak of emerging political cleavages around new values acknowledge that these "new" cleavages remain deeply anchored in the left–right division, and sometimes slip into calling the "new" social forces at work the "new left" and the "new right."[73]

Fourth, many internationalists would counter that world politics is a distinct realm, a system where power rules and in which ideological debates about equality play little role. For realism, the dominant school of thought in international relations, domestic politics and ideologies have less importance than systemic factors, and the prevailing balance of power best explains the behavior of states. Countries go to war because of security interests, not because they are motivated by ideas from the left or from the right. Classical in the study of international relations, this standpoint has been a subject of debate for years, and these debates cannot be addressed, let alone settled, here. Two arguments can nevertheless be advanced. The first is that even

---

[71] Seymour Martin Lipset and Stein Rokkan, "Cleavage Structures, Party Systems, and Voter Alignments: An Introduction," in Seymour Martin Lipset and Stein Rokkan (eds.), *Party Systems and Voter Alignments*, New York, Free Press, 1967, pp. 1–64.

[72] Jacques Thomassen and Hermann Schmitt, "Policy Representation," *European Journal of Political Research*, vol. 32, no. 2, October 1997, 165–84; Herbert Kitschelt, *The Transformation of European Social Democracy*, Cambridge University Press, 1994.

[73] Ronald Inglehart, *Culture Shift in Advanced Industrial Society*, pp. 292–300; Russell J. Dalton, *Democratic Challenges, Democratic Choices: The Erosion of Political Support in Advanced Industrial Democracies*, Oxford University Press, 2004, p. 144.

realists recognize that ideas and internal politics matter. Their claim is simply that they are not the main explanatory factor at work.[74] On our part, we do not argue that the left–right debate, or any debate, explains everything. We simply contend that debates matter and that, on a global scale, no debate matters as much as this one. The second argument is that there are many international developments that realism explains poorly, in particular with respect to international cooperation, the capacity of advanced democracies to compete in a peaceful way, and the ongoing progress of international institutions.[75] To account for such phenomena, approaches more sensitive to the role of domestic forces are likely to be helpful. In this perspective, several studies have established that, in democratic countries at least, foreign policy is largely driven by partisan preferences. As Brian Rathbun observed, "the values that parties represent in domestic politics ... are often the values underlying their foreign policy as well."[76] Quite predictably, the left–right cleavage that is so central at home has ramifications abroad. It has been noted, for instance, that leftist governments tend to be more favorable to antimilitarism, humanitarianism, and multilateralism.[77] One should thus accept that, even in the international arena, shared norms and ideas contribute to shape the behavior of states.[78]

A fifth counter-argument would emphasize the importance of civilizations and portray the left–right division as a Western imposition, which in many countries remains at best an artificial importation, without deep cultural or social roots. The best advocate of such a position is Samuel Huntington, who argues that the defining conflicts

---

[74] For a classic statement, see Kenneth N. Waltz, *Man, the State, and War: A Theoretical Analysis*, revised edition, New York, Columbia University Press, 2001.

[75] G. John Ikenberry, *After Victory: Institutions, Strategic Restraint, and the Rebuilding of Order after Major Wars*, Princeton University Press, 2001, p. 13.

[76] Brian C. Rathbun, *Partisan Interventions: European Party Politics and Peace Enforcement in the Balkans*, Ithaca, Cornell University Press, 2004, p. 2.

[77] *Ibid.*, pp. 21–22; Brian C. Rathbun, "Hierarchy and Community at Home and Abroad: Evidence of a Common Structure of Domestic and Foreign Policy Beliefs in American Elites," *Journal of Conflict Resolution*, vol. 51, no. 3, June 2007, 379–407.

[78] Thomas Risse, "'Let's Argue!': Communicative Action in World Politics," *International Organization*, vol. 54, no. 1, Winter 2000, 1–39; Harald Müller, "Arguing, Bargaining and All That: Communicative Action, Rationalist Theory and the Logic of Appropriateness in International Relations," *European Journal of International Relations*, vol. 10, no. 3, 2004, 395–435.

of the years to come will not be over ideology or economic interests, but rather over cultural differences, between the West and Islamic countries in particular.[79] This idea of clashing civilizations is appealing because it is a huge and simple representation, which allows one to paint a big picture with only a few strokes. Intellectuals on the right, notably, have acclaimed a view stressing distinct traditions more than universal traits, and force and insecurity more than cooperation and distribution. On the left, on the contrary, this pessimistic worldview has been broadly denounced. Whatever the case, Huntington's perspective neglects the critical differences that remain within countries sharing cultural characteristics. It overlooks the fact that, all over the world, no matter in what "civilization," social and political actors disagree about the course their country should take. These divisions, we believe, are most often organized along the left–right dimension. In the end, however, this is primarily an empirical question. As we will show in the coming chapters, there are good reasons to suggest that the politics of left and right is truly global, which easily cuts across cultures and civilizations.

Finally, one could contend that the idea of a global political clash over equality is not so much wrong as trivial. Everyone knows, this argument would go, that the left and the right are perennial political categories, and there is not much to conclude from a statement of the obvious. The previous paragraphs suggest on the contrary that the left–right argument is far from uncontroversial. While it is true that most people have a good grasp of the opposition between the left and the right, this is not always the case for social scientists, except perhaps when they think as citizens. In political science, for example, the idea of a basic conflict between two competing worldviews has often been neglected as too vague and too normative. The politics of left and right may appear transparent to citizens and militants, but it has not yet entered the world of the professional analyst of global politics.

Conclusion

Globalization has often been presented as an epochal transformation propelled by technological, economic, and cultural forces, at the

---

[79] Samuel P. Huntington, *The Clash of Civilizations and the Remaking of World Order*, New York, Simon and Schuster, 1998.

expense of established political institutions and practices. The process, however, is also deeply political. For one thing, globalization is determined by the decisions and actions of states and international organizations, which build infrastructures, change regulations, and cooperate with each other. At the same time, globalization is a political transformation in itself, giving rise to new and more interconnected ideas, identities, forums, and conflicts. The world, rightly note Richard Higgott and Morten Ougaard, is becoming more and more like a polity, an increasingly interdependent system, with dense networks of relationships, and a growing sense of community.[80]

The general idea of a world community has been put forward and promoted for a number of years, with various images and representations stressing the unity of humanity. We have *Only One Earth*, stated a widely read and pioneering book, published in 1972 by economist Barbara Ward and biologist René Dubos. We must thus begin, added in 1987 the World Commission on Environment and Development headed by former Norwegian Prime Minister Gro Harlem Brundtland, to envision *Our Common Future*. Doing so and working in partnership for development, emphasized in 2005 the Commission for Africa launched a year earlier by Tony Blair, is in *Our Common Interest*.[81]

The least we can say is that, as a community, humanity remains far from such a unity of purpose. Metaphors of unity may thus not provide the most appropriate representations for the global polity. The world is not and may not become a democratic, global order. But for a long time it has been a public sphere where public debates about common purposes have been taking place. And these debates, we argue, have a structure. They are primarily a conflict between the left and the right over the meaning of equality, within and among nations.

---

[80] Richard Higgott and Morten Ougaard, "Introduction: Beyond System and Society – Towards a Global Polity?," in Morten Ougaard and Richard Higgott (eds.), *Towards a Global Polity*, London, Routledge, 2002, pp. 2–3.

[81] Barbara Ward and René Dubos, *Only One Earth: The Care and Maintenance of a Small Planet*, New York, W. W. Norton, 1972; World Commission on Environment and Development, *Our Common Future*, Oxford University Press, 1987; Commission for Africa, *Our Common Interest: Report*, London, Commission for Africa, March 2005 (www.commissionforafrica.org).

2 | A *worldwide value divide*

How widespread really is the language of left and right? One could recognize the clash about equality just described, but consider it largely a concern for experts and politicians, at a distance from the preoccupations and views of most people around the world. Outside the Western world, in particular, the left–right dichotomy may seem less relevant as a heuristic tool. This chapter uses global public opinion trends to demonstrate, on the contrary, that practically everywhere citizens understand this representation and position themselves along an axis going from left to right. The left–right cleavage is neither Western, nor *passé*. It is ubiquitous and very much contemporary.

This chapter presents worldwide survey results that establish the near-universal relevance of the left–right division and its coherence for most people, who associate the two sides with the expected attitudes about equality, redistribution, and the role of the state. Country-specific data also confirms that these findings hold across very different regions and cultures of the world. The left–right debate is truly global. Indeed, in both national and comparative studies of public opinion, no cognitive instrument, no scale measuring personal values is more powerful than the way respondents locate themselves on the left–right continuum. Even scholars who claim that the left–right cleavage is in decline or in transformation cannot but conclude that it still incorporates most of the other attitude differences they seek to explain. This opposition is the most central value divide that political parties built as they struggled for, and about, democracy. Encompassing and enduring, this ideological division survived both its origins in class politics and the contemporary transition to post-industrial societies. Simple and stable, but also multi-faceted, the left–right dichotomy helps citizens all over the world organize their views according to their most important values, and as they do so, achieve consistency in the face of complexity.

A universal divide

The left–right value divide is rarely, in itself, an object of inquiry. At the same time, it is so central to the construction of public opinion that most studies of political attitudes take it into consideration. Consequently, there is good data available to assess the significance of the left and the right across the world. One source, in particular, stands out. Since 1981, a worldwide network of social scientists coordinated by Ronald Inglehart, the World Values Survey (WVS), has conducted compatible public opinion surveys on every continent, to assess socio-cultural and political change in a systematic and global fashion.[1] The data used here, which covers seventy-eight societies, was collected between 1999 and 2001. This data was made public in 2004.

In each society included in the World Values Survey, a representative sample of at least 1,000 people is built and the same questions are asked, so as to develop a worldwide database permitting comparison of cultural and political trends across time and space. Because the data is widely available, a large number of studies have relied on the World Values Survey, and they provide a strong intellectual background for cross-cultural analysis. These studies can also be replicated, which facilitates the testing of rival hypotheses and the pursuit of debates around divergent interpretations.

The 1999–2001 wave of the World Values Survey included societies with various cultures, traditions, and political institutions. In all these countries, respondents were asked to locate themselves on a 1 to 10 scale going from the left (1) to the right (10).[2] Figure 2.1 shows the worldwide distribution of respondents on this scale (19.7 percent of respondents said they did not know; 2.7 percent did not answer the question).

Following Ronald Inglehart, we could interpret this distribution as indicating that 55 percent of the world's population is on the left (between 1 and 5) and 45 percent on the right (between 6 and 10).[3] The fact that the distribution is basically normal and centered around 5,

---

[1] See www.worldvaluessurvey.org.

[2] The exact question (V139) is: "In political matters, people talk of 'the left' and 'the right.' How would you place yours views on this scale, generally speaking?"

[3] This is how he reads similar results in Ronald Inglehart, *Modernization and Postmodernization: Cultural, Economic, and Political Change in 43 Societies*, Princeton University Press, 1997, p. 319.

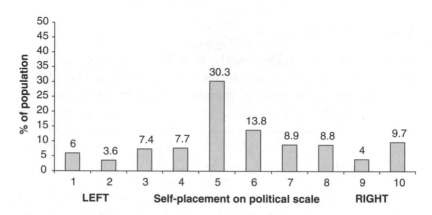

Figure 2.1 Left–right self-placement in the world, 1999–2001
Source: World Values Survey.

however, suggests a different reading. Even though the scale goes from 1 to 10 and has a middle point at 5.5, it is most likely that respondents who want to locate themselves at the centre see 5 as the middle and choose it accordingly. In this perspective, we would rather say that 24.7 percent of the world's respondents place themselves on the left, 30.3 percent at the centre, and 45.2 percent on the right. Our interpretation is indeed confirmed when World Values Survey data is compared with other survey results.[4]

Results from the World Values Survey suggest that all over the world respondents understand the notions of left and right and are able to apply them to interpret their own position. World respondents also form a basically normal distribution, the most important categories being clustered around the centre. The World Values Survey mean for the world is 5.66, and only Vietnam sticks out, with an average that is more than 2 points away from this global mean.

[4] We compared the World Values Survey data with data from another international team, the Comparative Study of Electoral Systems (CSES). The CSES used a 0 to 10 scale, instead of 1 to 10, to evaluate the left–right self-placement of respondents in 32 countries of Asia, Eastern and Western Europe, South and North America, and Oceania, between 1996 and 2001. In the CSES survey, 33.5 percent of the respondents located themselves at 5 (compared to 30.3 percent in the World Values Survey). When we combined the 0 and 1 positions of the CSES scale to have the same number of categories on each side of the median, the correlation coefficient between the two distributions equaled 0.96. See www.cses.org.

In Vietnam, a country where the 2001 World Values Survey was one of the first scientific public opinion surveys ever conducted, and where many responses seemed to reflect a prudent and almost unanimous expression of satisfaction with the existing communist regime, 65 percent of respondents located themselves on the extreme right (at 10), and 86 percent at 8, 9, or 10. In this one case, responses may be unreliable, or unrelated to the conventional understanding of left and right in politics.[5]

Another striking feature of Figure 2.1 is the relative weakness, in people's self-placement, of the left compared to the centre and the right. Psychologist Chris McManus found similar asymmetries in older European data, with "a moderate but consistent excess of right over left, there being almost three people on the right for every two on the left." In his view, this bias can be attributed to the fact that in all cultures right is a positive word, associated with "the norm, the dominant, and the good."[6] In more political terms, one may hypothesize that the left attracts people who question the established order and seek change, an attitude that may be less prevalent than a bias in favor of the status quo, especially in more traditional cultures.[7]

Global patterns obviously mask important variations. The left–right cleavage is first and foremost a political construction and, as such, it is likely to be quite different from one country to another. Table 2.1 presents the mean, the mean deviation and the percentage of non-response for the different countries included in the 1999–2001 World Values Survey, in increasing order of mean.

Consider, first, the percentage of respondents who said they did not know or would not answer the left–right self-placement question.

[5] The Vietnam survey is presented in Russell J. Dalton and Nhu-Ngoc T. Ong, "The Vietnamese Public in Transition: The 2001 World Values Survey," Center for the Study of Democracy, University of California, Irvine, 2001 (www.democ.uci.edu). Doubts on the quality of responses given in a context where people may be afraid of speaking against the authorities are raised in: Minh Nhut Duong, "Grassroots Democracy in Vietnamese Communes," Centre for Democratic Institutions, Australian National University, 2004, p. 29 (www.cdi.anu.edu.au). For an even more critical point of view raising doubts about the entire study, see the transcript of a 2001 interview with Vietnamese dissident Duong Thu Huong (www.vietquoc.com/news2001/na122901.htm).
[6] Chris McManus, *Right Hand, Left Hand: The Origins of Asymmetry in Brains, Bodies, Atoms and Cultures*, Cambridge, MA, Harvard University Press, 2002, pp. 261–64.
[7] Inglehart, *Modernization and Postmodernization*, pp. 70–71, 76–77, and 320.

Table 2.1. *Country means, mean deviations, and percentages of don't know/no answer, left–right self-placement, 1999–2001*

Country	Mean	Mean deviation	Don't Know/ No answer (%)
Zimbabwe	3.66	2.07	18.5
Montenegro	4.72	1.91	33.1
Spain	4.74	1.47	21.8
Iran	4.82	1.87	40.8
France	4.86	1.64	17.4
Russian Federation	4.92	1.48	36.0
Slovenia	4.99	1.12	28.0
United Kingdom	5.08	1.11	18.9
Bosnia and Herzegovina	5.09	1.29	12.6
Israel	5.09	2.29	7.2
Netherlands	5.09	1.38	4.1
Hungary	5.11	1.07	22.8
Greece	5.13	1.59	11.6
Slovakia	5.14	1.48	15.9
Republic of Macedonia	5.21	1.75	22.7
Chile	5.24	1.60	16.3
Belgium	5.26	1.33	18.2
Croatia	5.27	1.23	24.2
Portugal	5.27	1.76	23.0
Switzerland	5.31	1.41	19.6
Albania	5.34	2.33	5.2
Australia	5.34	1.32	12.5
Germany	5.34	1.39	16.6
Sweden	5.34	1.72	4.2
Poland	5.35	1.73	22.1
Republic of Korea	5.35	1.76	0.0
Italy	5.36	1.75	21.5
Luxembourg	5.37	1.38	25.6
Armenia	5.39	1.73	21.1
Lithuania	5.41	1.69	37.8
Austria	5.43	1.21	19.1
Ukraine	5.49	1.88	37.4
Denmark	5.51	1.62	9.6
Nigeria	5.51	2.21	2.8
Serbia	5.53	1.77	30.9
Uganda	5.55	2.71	15.3

Table 2.1. (*cont.*)

Country	Mean	Mean deviation	Don't Know/ No answer (%)
Azerbaijan	5.54	1.84	32.8
Canada	5.55	1.39	13.8
Norway	5.57	1.41	2.7
Republic of Moldova	5.58	2.29	33.1
Ireland	5.62	1.23	17.8
Northern Ireland	5.65	1.43	21.1
World	5.65	1.86	22.4
India	5.66	2.30	46.4
Uruguay	5.66	1.97	8.7
Belarus	5.68	1.50	48.5
South Africa	5.68	1.95	10.1
Peru	5.69	1.80	13.3
Japan	5.70	1.42	24.6
Finland	5.77	1.69	12.2
Iceland	5.78	3.21	9.5
Malta	5.80	1.25	2.9
New Zealand	5.80	1.47	27.1
United States of America	5.80	1.51	5.4
Latvia	5.83	1.51	33.1
Romania	5.83	1.72	44.6
Turkey	5.84	2.07	3.7
Bulgaria	5.85	1.95	32.7
Morocco	5.88	2.55	73.1
Brazil	5.90	2.41	12.5
Jordan	5.90	2.07	64.1
Estonia	5.93	1.32	31.5
Georgia	5.93	1.95	19.9
Pakistan	5.94	1.21	87.7
Czech Republic	5.96	1.83	7.9
Argentina	5.99	1.63	32.0
Algeria	6.22	2.08	54.0
El Salvador	6.30	2.35	19.9
Venezuela	6.32	2.14	18.4
Philippines	6.45	1.85	4.3
Taiwan	6.57	1.40	3.1
Indonesia	6.62	1.70	18.2
Puerto Rico	6.62	2.22	12.4
Colombia	6.63	1.96	8.5

Table 2.1. (*cont.*)

Country	Mean	Mean deviation	Don't Know/ No answer (%)
Dominican Republic	6.65	2.34	4.1
Mexico	6.65	2.47	33.4
Tanzania	6.75	3.11	30.8
Bangladesh	7.56	2.17	23.1
Vietnam	9.07	1.21	4.4

Source: World Values Survey.

There is significant variation in these percentages and, in some cases, relatively high levels of non-response. One should keep in mind, however, that on any question, a number of citizens simply will not answer. The world proportion of non-responses on left–right self-placement is at 22.4 percent and the percentages are almost as high in old democracies, where left–right semantics has long been central in public discourse, such as France, where the terms were invented (17.4 percent), or the United Kingdom (18.9 percent).

Above the world rate of non-responses, we find thirty cases out of seventy-eight. Seventeen of these can be considered true outliers, 10 points above the world rate: ten outliers are in the former Soviet sphere of influence, five in the Islamic world, and one in Asia (India), and one in Latin America (Mexico). Many factors may explain the importance of non-response in the former Soviet sphere of influence. First, the left–right labels were distorted and trivialized by the communist regimes, which made their subsequent use by democratic parties more problematic. Second, apart from being associated with the idea of substantive equality, the term "left" usually connotes a greater openness toward social and political change. In post-communist democracies, however, change was first associated with market-oriented reforms, which often implied less, not more, equality. Finally, many of those who benefited materially from market-oriented reforms were part of the old communist establishment and often legitimized their position and privileges with reference to symbols and arguments from the left. "In light of these opportunities for semantic confusion about the meaning of left and right in the aftermath of communism," noted a group of experts, "it would demonstrate the formidable power of

such formal concepts for the intellectual clarification of party competition if opinion surveys revealed even a modest tendency on the
part of respondents to employ left–right placements of self and others
(parties) with specific policy positions in mind."[8] As we show below,
this is exactly what happens with citizens and elites of the region.
Insofar as they appropriate the left–right distinction, and around
70 percent do, respondents from the former Soviet sphere of influence
do so in conformity with our expectations.

Among Islamic countries, the high level of non-response probably
has more to do with the lack of democracy than with cultural or
religious orientations. Bangladesh, Indonesia, and Turkey have non-
response rates below or near the world proportion. The populations
of these nations are overwhelmingly Muslim (from 83 percent for
Bangladesh to 99.8 percent for Turkey), but benefit from political
regimes that are open and democratic compared to other Muslim
countries.[9] Algeria, Iran, Jordan, Morocco, and Pakistan, by contrast,
all countries whose populations are more than 90 percent Muslim,
have more authoritarian regimes and very high rates of non-response.[10]
Likewise, the rate of non-response for Mexico could be explained
by the non-consolidated nature of democracy until 2000. India, an old
and well-established democracy, appears more puzzling and would
require further inquiry. All in all, however, these proportions of non-
responses confirm the importance of democratic debates in constructing meaningful left–right oppositions, across various cultural
and geographical areas.

If we turn to the left–right means, the country with the most leftist
average is Zimbabwe (3,66), and the one furthest on the right, if we
leave Vietnam aside, is Bangladesh (7.56). Zimbabwe, Vietnam,
Bangladesh, and Tanzania are the only cases with means more than
1 point away from the world mean, which implies that all countries
share broadly similar distributions. There are nevertheless important
remaining differences. At one end, Zimbabwe, Montenegro, Spain,

---

[8] Herbert Kitschelt, Zdenka Mansfeldova, Radoslaw Markowski, and Gábor
Tóka, *Post-Communist Party Systems: Competition, Representation, and Inter-
Party Cooperation*, Cambridge University Press, 1999, p. 283.

[9] Freedom House rates Bangladesh, Indonesia, and Turkey as partially free, with
combined scores, respectively, of 8, 7, and 7 (www.freedomhouse.org).

[10] Freedom House classifies these countries as non-free or partially free, with
combined scores at or above 10 (www.freedomhouse.org).

Iran, France, the Russian Federation, and Slovenia have means below 5, and at the other, Algeria, El Salvador, Venezuela, the Philippines, Taiwan, Indonesia, Puerto Rico, Colombia, the Dominican Republic, Mexico, Tanzania, Bangladesh, and Vietnam are above 6. In Spain, for instance, 40 percent of respondents locate themselves between 1 and 4, and only 26 percent pick scores between 6 and 10. In Taiwan, by contrast, merely 4 percent of citizens chose 1, 2, 3, or 4, and 70 percent opted for a score of 6 or above.

Overall, there are more left-leaning countries in Eastern and Western Europe and more right-leaning ones in Latin America and Asia. This result seems in line with Inglehart's characterization of Latin America and Asia as poorer, more traditional societies.[11] The presence of many outliers, however, warns us against sweeping cultural accounts. Chile and the Republic of Korea, for instance, have left-leaning scores, whereas Finland and the Czech Republic have rightward ones. As political categories, it needs to be emphasized, the left and the right are always constructed through a country's history.

Using a different dataset, Pippa Norris finds a strong correlation between left–right self-placement and voting behavior.[12] Given her theoretical preoccupations, Norris tends to assume that personal ideology determines voting, which is not wrong, of course, at the individual level. In a broader social perspective, however, left–right self-placement can also be understood as reflective of the varying success parties have had in defining the relevant political alternatives for a country's electorate. Norris also lends support to this complementary hypothesis, with her findings on the impact of electoral rules. Compared to majoritarian or combined electoral systems, proportional representation systems give parties less incentive to adopt catch-all, centrist platforms, and they tend to make political cleavages more pronounced, accentuating the difference between the left and the right.[13] Figure 2.2 illustrates this conclusion, with the contrasting distributions of left–right self-placement in first-past-the-post Britain and in proportional representation Netherlands. Also included

---

[11] Inglehart, *Modernization and Postmodernization*, p. 335.
[12] Pippa Norris, *Electoral Engineering: Voting Rules and Political Behavior*, Cambridge University Press, 2004, pp. 104–19. Norris used the data provided by the Comparative Study of Electoral Systems team (see footnote 4, this chapter).
[13] *Ibid.*, pp. 119–23.

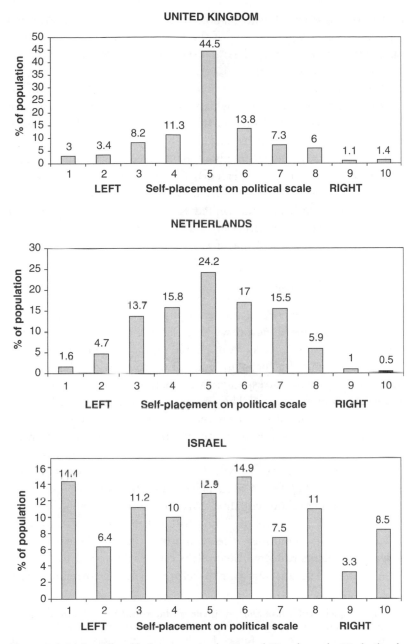

Figure 2.2 Left–right self-placement in the United Kingdom, the Netherlands, and Israel, 1999–2001
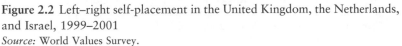
Source: World Values Survey.

is the striking case of Israel, another country with a proportional representation system and one of the highest mean deviations in our sample (note that, for the sake of presentation, the vertical scale varies from one case to another).

One should note, as well, that averages mask important variations in the strength of the center, which ranges from very low scores in Vietnam (3 percent), Israel (13 percent), Nigeria (14 percent), Tanzania (15 percent), Albania (16 percent), Uganda (17 percent), and Algeria (18 percent), to about half the electorate in Hungary (52 percent), Slovenia (51 percent), Croatia (51 percent), Pakistan (50 percent), Bosnia and Herzegovina (49 percent), India (47 percent), Latvia (45 percent), and the United Kingdom (45 percent). Present and relevant everywhere, the left and the right clearly tell different stories about the political life of each society.

Divided over equality

The universal prevalence of the left–right labels does not prove that they mean the same thing everywhere, let alone that they reflect the coherent values one expects from people on the left and on the right. The literature on public behavior and voting does suggest that left and right self-placement corresponds to predictable patterns of attitudes and electoral preferences.[14] This literature, however, is usually based on a smaller group of countries than that presented here, and it is often guided by questions only tangentially related to the left–right cleavage.

This section considers the world as a whole to test whether, in a global perspective, left–right self-placement truly corresponds to the expected attitudes about equality, government intervention, or social justice. Table 2.2 presents the relationships between a person's ideological stance and a number of relevant questions. All these questions asked respondents to locate themselves on a scale from 1 to 10, 1 to 5, or 1 to 4. The answers can therefore easily be correlated with

---

[14] Ronald Inglehart, *Culture Shift in Advanced Industrial Society*, Princeton University Press, 1989, pp. 292–93; Inglehart, *Modernization and Postmodernization*, p. 320; Russell J. Dalton, *Citizen Politics: Public Opinion and Political Parties in Advanced Industrial Democracies*, third edition, Chatham, NJ, Chatham House, 2002, pp. 201–03; Norris, *Electoral Engineering*, p. 118.

Table 2.2. *Relationships between left–right self-placement and attitudes about social justice and government intervention, on a world scale, 1999–2001*

Should incomes be made more equal (1), or do we need larger income differences as incentives for individual effort (10)?	0.110***
Should your country aim to be an egalitarian society where the gap between rich and poor is small, regardless of achievement (1), or a competitive society where wealth is distributed according to one's achievement (5)?	0.059***
Should your country aim to be a society with extensive social welfare but high taxes (1), or one where taxes are low and individuals take responsibility for themselves (5)?	0.100***
Do you think that competition is good and stimulates people to work hard and develop new ideas (1), or that competition is harmful and brings out the worst in people (10)?	−0.065***
Do you think the government should take more responsibility to ensure that everyone is provided for (1), or that people should take more responsibility to provide for themselves (10)?	0.078***
Should the government let anyone come in the country who wants to (1), or prohibit people coming here from other countries (4)?	0.039***
Homosexuality is never justifiable (1), or always justifiable (10)?	−0.108***
Abortion is never justifiable (1), or always justifiable (10)?	−0.125***

Note: All these correlations are significant at 0.001 level (***).[15]
Source: World Values Survey.

left–right self-placement. A positive sign indicates that the two scales increase together, a negative sign that they progress in opposite directions.

The results of Table 2.2 are all statistically significant and in the expected direction. The more a person is on the right, the more she is likely to think that we need larger income differences as incentives for individual effort, that her country should aim to be a competitive society where wealth is distributed according to one's achievement,

[15] As recommended by the World Values Survey team, the results were adjusted with weights correcting for national characteristics.

and also one where taxes are low and individuals take responsibility for themselves. A person on the right is also less inclined to consider that competition is harmful and that government should take more responsibility to ensure that everyone is provided for. On the left, on the contrary, respondents prefer an egalitarian society with extensive social protection provided by the government, and they tend to believe that competition is harmful and brings out the worst in people.

These findings are very much in line with our understanding of the left and the right as anchored in distinct conceptions of equality in a democratic society, the first focused on unmet needs and solidarity, the other on opportunity and individual achievement. Each conception privileges specific social mechanisms: redistribution and state intervention for the left, competition and markets for the right. The worldwide scope of the World Values Survey suggests that these conceptions run across different social and political cultures, and constitute a widespread tacit knowledge about politics, a vocabulary people may not be able to define precisely but understand very well. The specific contours of the left and the right undoubtedly vary across space and time, but these notions are not empty vessels that can be filled with any possible meaning. This conclusion is reinforced when we consider responses unrelated to equality as such, but associated with the broader sets of values linked to the left and the right. In Table 2.2, for instance, one can see that those on the right are more likely to have reservations about immigration to their country, about homosexuality, and about abortion. Table 2.3 is consistent with this pattern, with results describing the relationship between left–right self-placement and the qualities respondents find the most important to encourage in children.

As George Lakoff would have predicted, the child qualities that are most strongly associated with the left are imagination and independence, and the qualities that correlate most powerfully with being on the right are religious faith and obedience. All in all, people on the right favor faith, obedience, hard work, and thrift while people on the left grant more importance to imagination, independence, tolerance and respect for other people, determination and perseverance, a feeling of responsibility, and unselfishness.

Persons on the left and the right are also likely to have distinct attitudes toward life, the former being more optimistic about human nature but also more critical about their country and the world, and

Table 2.3. *Relationships between left–right self-placement and qualities respondents find important to encourage in children, on a world scale, 1999–2001*

Independence	−0.035***
Hard work	0.027***
Feeling of responsibility	−0.024***
Imagination	−0.043***
Tolerance and respect for other people	−0.029***
Thrift, saving money and things	0.026***
Determination, perseverance	−0.024***
Religious faith	0.093***
Unselfishness	−0.016***
Obedience	0.035***

Note: All these correlations are significant at 0.001 level (***).
Source: World Values Survey.

Table 2.4. *Relationships between left–right self-placement and attitudes toward life, on a world scale, 1999–2001*

Generally speaking, would you say that most people can be trusted (1), or that you need to be very careful in dealing with people (2)?	0.026***
All things considered, how satisfied are you with your life as a whole these days? Choose a score between 1 (dissatisfied) and 10 (satisfied).	0.085***
Taking all things together, would you say you are very happy (1), quite happy (2), not very happy (3), or not at all happy (4)?	−0.072***

Note: All these correlations are significant at 0.001 level (***).
Source: World Values Survey.

the latter more pessimistic about humanity but more satisfied with the status quo. Table 2.4 presents results in line with these predictions.

On a world scale, people on the right tend to be less trustful and to believe that one needs to be very careful in dealing with people. They are, however, more satisfied with their life and happier. There are, of course, numerous determinants of happiness, including a person's economic and social situation and religious faith, and it is not our aim

Table 2.5. *Relationships between socio-economic attributes and left–right self-placement, on a world scale, 1999–2001*

Sex (Male: 1; Female: 2)	−0.008*
Age	0.012***
Highest educational level attained, from no formal education (1) to university-level with degree (9)	−0.043***
Income	0.010**

Note: Significant at 0.05 level (*), at 0.01 level (**), or at 0.001 level (***).
Source: World Values Survey.

to probe this matter in detail. Everything else being equal, however, attitudes toward life correspond very well to the expectations we have about leftist and rightist views of society.

Can we say something more, globally, about these persons who place themselves on the left and on the right and who, collectively, harbor coherent views about equality, politics, education, and life? Table 2.5 presents some socio-economic correlates of left–right self-placement.

Our results show that women have a slight tendency to be less on the right than men. This relationship must be interpreted prudently, not only because it is weak, but also because the global pattern masks a number of countervailing trends. In the past, women were more on the right than men, probably because they were also more religious. In recent generations, the pattern has been reversed, to create a gender gap between more progressive women and more conservative men. In new democracies, on the other hand, older women may be more to the left than men and than younger women. Politically, these different trends are significant and make gender an important dimension of electoral strategies. Added up, as they are in our limited test, current trends more or less cancel each other out.[16] Still, generational patterns suggest that in the long run a gender gap will persist, with women more to the left than men.[17]

Age is significantly associated with left–right self-placement. In advanced democracies, in particular, the younger generations tend to be more to the left than the older cohorts. In post-communist countries,

[16] Norris, *Electoral Engineering*, pp. 116–18.
[17] Ronald Inglehart and Pippa Norris, *Rising Tide: Gender Equality and Cultural Change around the World*, Cambridge University Press, 2003, pp. 98–100.

the reverse may be true, younger generations being disaffected with a culture and values associated with the fallen communist regimes, and more attracted by the promises of a competitive, market-oriented society.[18] Still, overall the pattern holds, and younger respondents are in general more to the left.

Educational level is negatively associated with left–right self-placement. Everything else being equal, the more formal education a person has, the more likely she is to be on the left. This finding may appear intriguing, because more educated persons also tend to be wealthier, but education has often been associated with the development of leftist views.[19] Income level, the variable that best captures a respondent's social position is, as expected, positively associated with left–right self-placement. Respondents who are better placed in the social hierarchy and wealthier appear more likely to be convinced that merit lies behind the individual's social condition.

Civilization divides?

One could accept the evidence, so far, that left and right perceptions are universal, coherent, and broadly associated with distinctive views about social justice and, yet, still have doubts about the relevance of such conclusions for societies that have non-Western traditions and cultures. In these societies, other cleavages could be more meaningful or give the left–right labels other meanings. To shed some light on this admittedly complex question, we took a closer look at national cases, from different continents and cultural areas.

For each country in our set, we tested the correlation between respondents' left–right orientations and their answers to the questions presented in Table 2.2 on equality ("Should incomes be made more equal or do we need incentives for individual effort?"), on competition ("Do you think that competition is good and stimulates people to work hard and develop new ideas, or that competition is harmful and brings out the worst in people?"), and on the role of government ("Should government take more responsibility or should people take more responsibility?"). Countries where the three correlations yielded significant results in the expected direction were given a score of 1 (3/3), those with one or two significant correlations got a 0.33 (1/3) or a

---

[18] Norris, *Electoral Engineering*, pp. 114–15.   [19] *Ibid.*, pp. 112–13.

0.66 (2/3), and those where all answers yielded results that were either non-significant or in the wrong direction received a 0 (0/3). When we had results for only two questions, the same logic was applied, with scores of 1 (2/2), 0.5 (1/2), or 0 (0/2). Table 2.6 presents these scores for different geographical or cultural areas of the world.

More than half of the countries (forty-three out of seventy-six) have a score of 1 or of 0.66, which means that their citizens' self-placement on a left–right axis predicts fairly well what they think about equality, competition, and the role of government. At the same time, almost one out of four cases has a 0 (eighteen out of seventy-six), indicating a lack of correspondence between ideological labels and attitudes about politics. The rest have a score of 0.33 or 0.5, having significant results for one out of three or out of two questions.

In Western Europe (including Turkey) and among Anglo-Saxon democracies, most countries have a score of 1. The main exceptions, with 0, are Ireland and Portugal. In the former Soviet sphere of influence, results are almost as strong, with only two scores of 0 out of twenty-three cases (Hungary and Slovenia). Results are more contrasted in the Asia-Pacific region, with two scores of 1, four of 0.66 or 0.5, and three of 0. In Latin America, and in the Middle East and Africa, scores of 0 predominate (six out of eleven in Latin America; five out of ten in the Middle East and Africa), followed by scores of 0.33 (three in each region). In line with the cultural or civilization argument, one could present these results as a proof that the left–right division is a Western concept, more meaningful in the West and in the North than in the East and the South. Many exceptions, however, militate against such a cultural interpretation. In Asia, Bangladesh, India, Indonesia, Japan, the Philippines, and Vietnam have scores above 0.5; and so do Algeria, Bangladesh, Indonesia, Kazakstan, and Turkey in the Muslim world.

As with non-response rates, the most plausible explanation to account for the differences observed in Table 2.6 relates to variations in the democratic context. Among countries with scores of 1, a majority are old democracies (fifteen out of twenty-seven), with at least twenty years of regular multi-party elections. The rest are mostly new democracies, or countries at the crossroads, which could be classified as semi-democratic.[20] At the other end, among countries

---

[20] On democracy, we follow the distinctions proposed in Inglehart and Norris, *Rising Tide*, pp. 165–71.

Table 2.6. Scores for relationships between left–right self-placement and attitudes about social justice, competition, and government intervention, in seventy-six countries, 1999–2001

Western Europe		Anglo-Saxon Democracies		Former Soviet Sphere of Influence		Latin America		Asia-Pacific		Middle East and Africa	
Austria	0.66	Australia	1	Albania	1	Argentina	0	Bangladesh	1	Algeria	1
Belgium	0.66	Canada	0.66	Armenia	0.66	Brazil	0	India	0.66	Iran	0
Denmark	1	Ireland	0	Azerbaijan	0.33	Chile	0.33	Indonesia	0.5	Israel	0
Finland	1	New Zealand	1	Belarus	0.66	Colombia	0.5	Japan	0.66	Jordan	0
France	1	United Kingdom	1	Bosnia-H.	0.33	Dominican R.	0.33	Korea	0	Morocco	0
Germany	1	United States	1	Bulgaria	1	El Salvador	0	Pakistan	0	Nigeria	0.5
Greece	0.5			Croatia	0.33	Mexico	0	Philippines	0.66	S. Africa	0.33
Iceland	1			Czech R.	1	Peru	0.33	Taiwan	0	Tanzania	0.33
Italy	1			Estonia	0.66	Puerto Rico	0	Vietnam	1	Uganda	0
Luxembourg	1			Georgia	0.33	Uruguay	1			Zimbabwe	0.33
Malta	0.66			Hungary	0	Venezuela	0				
Netherlands	1			Kazakstan	1						
Norway	1			Latvia	1						
Portugal	0			Lithuania	0.66						
Sweden	1			Macedonia	0.66						
Switzerland	1			Moldova	0.66						

Table 2.6. (*cont.*)

Western Europe	Anglo-Saxon Democracies	Former Soviet Sphere of Influence	Latin America	Asia-Pacific	Middle East and Africa
Turkey 1		Poland 0.33			
		Romania 0.66			
		Russian F. 1			
		Serbia-M. 0.66			
		Slovakia 1			
		Slovenia 0			
		Ukraine 0.66			

Note: Scores represent the proportion of relationships that are significant and in the right direction (out of three or in some cases out of two questions).
Source: World Values Survey.

with scores of 0, there are almost no old democracies (three out of eighteen).

The left–right cleavage is a social construction, and it makes sense that a long experience with democratic rule is more likely to produce a public with a coherent understanding of what it means. In the Middle East and Africa, for instance, where all of our cases except Israel are either non-democratic or semi-democratic, one is not surprised to find limited evidence of a conventionally ideological public. This broad-brush institutional explanation, however, is not sufficient to explain all variations of significance. It fails to make sense, in particular, of the remarkable difference between Latin America and the former Soviet sphere of influence.

Both regions experienced democratization in the period that Samuel Huntington famously called the "third wave of democratization," between 1974 and the late 1990s.[21] Latin America was first, with most transitions from military to democratic rule taking place in the late 1970s and early 1980s,[22] and the Soviet sphere of influence came later, at the turn of the 1990s. Relatively older and presumably more established, Latin American democracies nevertheless seem to have electorates that are less structured along the left–right dimension than East European publics. Among our eleven Latin American cases, six have a 0 score and only one has a score of 1 (Uruguay). No country has a score of 0.66. In comparison, in the former Soviet bloc, there are only two 0s out of twenty-three cases, and sixteen scores of 0.66 or above. How can we account for these differences?

Consider, first, the case of Latin America. Until the recent process of democratization, many Latin American countries simply did not have

---

[21] Samuel P. Huntington, *The Third Wave: Democratization in the Late Twentieth Century*, Norman, University of Oklahoma Press, 1991. Adam Przeworski and his co-authors fail to discern distinct "waves" and question Huntington's periodization and "oceanic metaphor." Whatever the case, this period was certainly critical for democracy in Latin America and Eastern Europe. Adam Przeworski, Michael E. Alvarez, José Antonio Cheibub, and Fernando Limongi, *Democracy and Development: Political Institutions and Well-Being in the World, 1950–1990*, Cambridge University Press, 2000, pp. 40–45.

[22] Scott Mainwaring and Frances Hagopian, "Introduction: The Third Wave of Democratization in Latin America," in Frances Hagopian and Scott P. Mainwaring (eds.), *The Third Wave of Democratization in Latin America: Advances and Setbacks*, Cambridge University Press, 2005, pp. 1–3.

institutionalized party systems helping to draw a clear line between the left and the right.[23] Populism, personalism, and clientelism obscured partisan and ideological divisions. The effects of this historical legacy were compounded by the conditions that prevailed in the late 1970s and 1980s, when democracy was re-established. Indeed, the new democracies were less triumphant than "ushered in...by the effects of economic crisis on incumbent authoritarian regimes."[24] For more than a decade, democratization was "associated with increased poverty, economic inequality, and great declines in both relative and absolute standards of living."[25] In this harsh context, trade unions, social movements, and even individual participation in politics declined.[26] Political parties were plagued by their difficulty in meeting the high expectations raised by democracy and by their frequent turn toward the neoliberal policies they had denounced to get elected.[27] To many citizens of Latin America, democracy appeared more a personal contest among like-minded politicians than an opportunity to debate contending views about justice.[28]

With the major exception of Uruguay, a country which inherited from its past an institutionalized party system, the political orientations of the Latin American public thus seemed to be shaped in an unconventional fashion. To put this conclusion in perspective, however,

[23] Dietrich Rueschemeyer, Evelyne Huber Stephens, and John D. Stephens, *Capitalist Development and Democracy*, University of Chicago Press, 1992, p. 293.

[24] *Ibid.*, p. 216; Ruth Berins Collier, *Paths toward Democracy: The Working Class and Elites in Western Europe and South America*, Cambridge University Press, 1999, pp. 13, 187, and 197.

[25] Marcus J. Kurtz, "The Dilemmas of Democracy in the Open Economy: Lessons from Latin America," *World Politics*, vol. 56, no. 2, January 2004, 262–302, p. 280.

[26] *Ibid.*, p. 264; Kurt Weyland, "Neoliberalism and Democracy in Latin America: A Mixed Record," *Latin American Politics and Society*, vol. 46, no. 1, Spring 2004, 135–57.

[27] *Ibid.*, p. 148; Susan Stokes, *Mandates and Democracy: Neoliberalism by Surprise in Latin America*, Cambridge University Press, 2001.

[28] Frances Hagopian, "Democracy and Political Representation in Latin America: Pause, Reorganization, or Decline?," in Felipe Agüero and Jeffrey Stark (eds.), *Fault Lines of Democracy in Post-Transition Latin America*, Miami, North-South Center Press at the University of Miami, 1998, pp. 112–13; Jorge I. Domínguez, "Constructing Democratic Governance in Latin America: Taking Stock of the 1990s," in Jorge I. Domínguez and Michael Shifter (eds.), *Constructing Democratic Governance in Latin America*, second edition, Baltimore, Johns Hopkins University Press, 2003, pp. 358–66.

it should be noted that on social issues such as abortion and homo-sexuality, Latin Americans are very much divided along left–right lines. In addition, the leftist wave that swept across Latin America at the beginning of the twenty-first century suggests that the left–right divide may gradually be taking root in the region. Only time will tell whether the recent turn to the left will make a difference and meet the expectations of the Latin American population. What is already clear, however, is that the left–right semantics has been re-established in the Latin American public sphere.

Also intriguing are the Eastern European cases, where the transition to democracy gave rise to populist rhetoric in defense of neoliberalism, without emptying the left–right cleavage of its meaning, as can be seen in Table 2.6.[29] In contrast to Latin America, where party systems and ideological structures remained inchoate, the transition from communism created a strong polarization between "social protectionists and market liberalizers."[30] Generally, this polarization opposed ex-communists and anti-communists. In some cases, it also involved new parties of the left that rejected the legacy of communism but sought to define a European-type social-democratic path to the market economy.[31] In spite of the complexity associated with such labels in countries with a communist past, the left–right dichotomy was thus defined basically as it is in advanced democracies, and it helped citizens make sense of politics.[32] Hungary, here, may be an exception. In this case, the ruling Communist Party was an early advocate of market capitalism, and this political stance generated a large consensus, which led politicians and voters to "associate the meaning of the left–right semantics less with economic policy than with socio-cultural issues."[33]

Our examination of public views across the world suggests that the left–right divide is an ideological cleavage that political parties build

---

[29] Kurt Weyland, "Neoliberal Populism in Latin America and Eastern Europe," *Comparative Politics*, vol. 31, no. 4, July 1999, 379–401.

[30] Kitschelt, Mansfeldova, Markowski, and Tóka, *Post-Communist Party Systems*, p. 389.

[31] Timothy Frye, "The Perils of Polarization: Economic Performance in the Postcommunist World," *World Politics*, vol. 54, no. 3, April 2002, 308–37, pp. 312–13.

[32] Kitschelt, Mansfeldova, Markowski, and Tóka, *Post-Communist Party Systems*, p. 402.

[33] *Ibid.*, p. 386.

over time, to reach voters and present meaningful competitive stances in the public sphere. To a large extent, the left–right terminology is thus a product of democratic governance. Yet, even in less competitive, authoritarian systems, notions of left and right have a place in public debates. In Iran, for instance, the ruling elites divide into a reformist and a conservative camp, and fight over the possibilities of democratization, cultural opening, and economic liberalization. To be sure, many of the reformists are not "Jeffersonian democrats," and they still believe in the unity of mosque and state.[34] Likewise, the country's conservatives do not have the commitment to freedom that one usually finds among right-wing politicians in liberal democracies. Still, this protracted conflict highlights a clear and familiar ideological cleavage, which the Iranian daily press readily interprets as one where right is opposed to left.[35] Our data on Iran indicates that this conflict does not structure public opinion as powerfully as it would in old, well-established democracies, where political debates are open and well publicized. Just a few years of electoral democracy, however, could make a difference, as can be seen in the former Soviet sphere of influence, where the left–right semantics rapidly demonstrated its "formidable power."[36]

Conclusion

Studies of the cultural divides that shape the world tend to draw lines between countries and civilizations. Divergences between the West and the Islamic world, in particular, are seen as profound and significant. These divergences, argue Ronald Inglehart and Pippa Norris, are not located so much in distinctive levels of support for democracy, as in markedly different views about gender equality, divorce, abortion, and homosexuality.[37] It is not our intention to deny such differences. In this book, however, we wish to emphasize, as do

---

[34] Jahangir Amuzegar, "Iran's Crumbling Revolution," *Foreign Affairs*, vol. 82, no. 1, January/February 2003, 44–58.

[35] Afshin Matin-asgari, "From Social Democracy to Social Democracy: The Twentieth-Century Odyssey of the Iranian Left," in Stephanie Cronin (ed.), *Reformers and Revolutionaries in Modern Iran: New Perspectives on the Iranian Left*, London, Routledge, 2004, p. 50.

[36] *Ibid.*, p. 283.

[37] Ronald Inglehart and Pippa Norris, "The True Clash of Civilizations," *Foreign Policy*, no. 135, March/April 2003, 67–74.

Inglehart and Norris in their own argument, the common ground that also connects peoples, across these cultural divides. More precisely, we seek to bring to light the common divisions that, around the world, political parties and social movements establish to debate the content of liberal democracy. These common divergences, and the social dynamic they embody, make it possible to speak of a global public sphere, intelligible for ordinary citizens as well as for the elites.

Since it first appeared more than 200 years ago, the left–right value divide has survived the transformation of class structures and the rise of new post-materialist values in advanced democracies. This divide helps citizens integrate into coherent patterns their attitudes and ideas about politics. The left and the right separate, in particular, citizens who favor equality, social protection, and government intervention, from those who consider we should maintain incentives for individual effort, accept competition, and keep taxes as low as possible. In turn, these core values organize the way most people think about a host of social choices, whether they concern democracy, homosexuality, or abortion. Even values that people think should be encouraged in children diverge according to whether their proponents are on the left or on the right. People on the right also tend to be less confident in their fellow citizens but more satisfied and happy with their life, possibly because they are higher in the social hierarchy and wealthier.

In new democracies, the left–right schema is evoked in the public sphere, but it is not always anchored as solidly in public opinion, and does not shape values and attitudes as powerfully as in older democracies. This situation, however, is evolving rapidly. For one thing, electoral democracy is spreading throughout the world. In 1987, 40 percent of the world's countries were electoral democracies. In 2005, this proportion had climbed to 64 percent, for a total of 122 electoral democracies.[38] It does not usually take long before electoral competition begins to structure public views about social justice. Even in Latin America, where the process proved more difficult, politics is increasingly polarized along familiar lines. Everywhere, in time, the democratic process tends to give rise to the conventional left–right cleavage about equality.

---

[38] Freedom House, "Freedom in the World 2006: Selected Data from Freedom House's Annual Global Survey of Political Rights and Civil Liberties," New York, Freedom House, 2006 (www.freedomhouse.org).

3 | *Two tales of globalization*

It was the best of times, it was the worst of times, it was the age of wisdom, it was the age of foolishness, it was the epoch of belief, it was the epoch of incredulity, it was the season of Light, it was the season of Darkness, it was the spring of hope, it was the winter of despair, we had everything before us, we had nothing before us, we were all going direct to Heaven, we were all going direct the other way (Charles Dickens, *A Tale of Two Cities*, 1859)

To say that the world is more and more complex is today considered conventional wisdom. Three overarching factors justify this almost universal perception. First, the communications technology revolution has fostered a formidable compression of space and time. Second, globalization has brought about an unprecedented increase in economic, political, social, and cultural interaction among populations of all regions and countries. Finally, the international scene, which was traditionally dominated by sovereign states, now has to adapt to the rise of new actors, both collective (including international institutions, sub-state governments, transnational corporations, and non-governmental organizations) and individual (including migrants, refugees, tourists, and terrorists). The fundamental changes underway in global politics have quite naturally engendered a vast diversity of reactions among experts. Far from being altogether cacophonic, however, these multiple viewpoints can well be understood as the expression of a coherent dialogue.

Whereas the previous chapter concerned the attitudes of citizens, this chapter focuses on the discourse of opinion leaders, and shows that their debates on world affairs can be summarized in two narratives, proposed by the right and the left. As explained earlier, the right generally believes that the global order is working well, even though there is obviously room for improvement. Given their insistence on the egoistic tendencies of individuals, conservatives are forever mindful of human folly. Since they have low expectations regarding domestic as well as international politics, they are more easily contented with the circumstances in which they find themselves. For the left, on the contrary, the levels of global inequality and injustice make it simply impossible to draw a favorable portrait of the world situation. Progressives, who lay stress on the altruistic aspect of human nature, have higher ambitions, and they are repeatedly disappointed by the slowness of social change. In short, the worldview of the "satisfied" is systematically different from that of the "critics." As E. H. Carr suggested in his classic study of international relations, radicals tend to be "utopian" and conservatives like to appear "realist."[1]

Reducing the political dynamic to a binary opposition cannot, of course, fully account for all aspects of global debates. Anyone observing the political scene, even at a distance, is well aware that neither the right nor the left is monolithic. The alignment of views becomes increasingly blurred the closer one gets to the center of the left–right spectrum. Yet, notwithstanding the many nuances that may be factored in and the many counter-examples that one could cite, there is no doubt that conservative elites have developed a more positive vision of the world than their progressive counterparts. Although the narratives examined in this chapter do not exist in a pure form, they do in point of fact represent what Max Weber called ideal types: intellectual constructions that make it possible to identify "the primary lines of argument and . . . the fundamental points of disagreement" in a discussion.[2] And, as we shall see, while the right and the left do not share the same outlook on global politics, experts from both camps are able to marshal an arsenal of facts and figures to support their point of view.

The world of the satisfied

Built upon considerations that are at once technological, economic, political, social, and cultural, the right's interpretation strives to demonstrate that "globalization works,"[3] that development is heading

---

[1] E. H. Carr, *The Twenty Years' Crisis, 1919–1939: An Introduction to the Study of International Relations*, New York, Palgrave, 2001 (first edition 1939), p. 18.

[2] David Held and Anthony McGrew, *Globalization/Anti-Globalization*, Cambridge, Polity Press, 2002, p. 3.

[3] Martin Wolf, *Why Globalization Works*, New Haven, Yale University Press, 2004.

in the right direction, that history constantly begets progress, and that, in the final analysis, the world could be much worse off than it is. Consider, first, the expansion of new technologies. Anyone can see that life today is far easier than it was in the past. Martin Wolf, chief economic commentator of the *Financial Times*, remarks that contrary to the nightmare described by George Orwell in his novel *1984*, "modern computer and telecommunications technology liberates rather than imprisons."[4] The transfer of data from one corner of the planet to another is not only less and less costly, but has also become practically instantaneous. By increasing the mobility of goods, services, and capital – as well as that of ideas and fashions – the communications revolution has helped to bring peoples closer together, and give concrete meaning to the trope of the "global village" coined by Marshall McLuhan in the 1960s.

The technical changes of the past twenty years have spawned a host of new opportunities. Above all, they have promoted economic growth across the globe as recent innovations have made it possible to draw greater benefit from the comparative advantages that each country derives from its factors of production.[5] In other words, the tremendous progress achieved in the fields of electronics, computers, and transportation has helped to strengthen the competitiveness of states and firms, and to enhance the efficiency of the international division of labor. Consumers are unquestionably the major benefi-ciaries of the resulting transformation of the global system of pro-duction, for they now have access to goods and services of a higher quality and at a lower price than ever before.

The technological progress witnessed over the past generation has contributed immensely to the maintenance of a healthy international economy. Between 1970 and 2002, world production grew at an average yearly rate of 3–4 percent, and this trend is on the upswing.[6] During the same period, the international exchange of goods and services expanded at even higher rates, with a 6 percent annual average increase.[7] Most experts agree that this sustained growth in

---

[4] *Ibid.*, p. 120.
[5] World Commission on the Social Dimension of Globalization, *A Fair Globalization: Creating Opportunities for All*, Geneva, International Labour Office, 2004, p. 27, paragraph 140.
[6] IMF, *Annual Report 2003*, Washington, DC, IMF, 2003, p. 8, Figure 1.1.
[7] *Ibid.*

trade is one of the mainstays of the recent phase of globalization. And nowhere is the positive impact of globalization more evident than in the way it has led to an improvement in the economic and social conditions prevailing in poor countries.

In this connection, it must be acknowledged that developing countries have been taking a more and more active part in the ongoing technological revolution, a phenomenon due largely to their greater integration within global production networks. India, China, and Brazil, notably, have become leaders in the telecommunications and computer industries. A particularly striking trend is the gradual shrinking of the digital gap between North and South. Whereas in 1994 internet users in the developed countries outnumbered those in the developing countries by a ratio of 73:1, in 2004 the ratio was down to a mere 8:1.[8] Undeniably, the South continues to lag behind the North in the areas of technology and research and development. This said, the technological revolution is doubly advantageous for poor countries. It allows these nations to speed up the course of history and skip certain stages that today's developed countries had to go through in the past; and at the same time makes it possible for them to be connected in real time to the international networks through which data and knowledge are disseminated.

The growth in world trade has accelerated the economic take-off of the developing countries and strengthened their position in global markets. Between 1960 and 2002, the South saw its share of world exports of goods increase from less than one-fourth to one-third.[9] Parallel to this growth in volume, the trade of the developing countries also underwent significant qualitative changes. Poor states are no longer simply commodity exporters, as they had been in colonial times. While in 1980 the great bulk (75 percent) of exports from Third World countries still comprised raw materials, today 70 percent of their foreign sales are made up of manufactured goods.[10] Between

---

[8] International Telecommunication Union, Figure: "Internet users per 100 inhabitants" (www.itu.int/wsis/tunis/newsroom/stats/charts/ChartA3_72dpi. jpg).

[9] UNCTAD, *Development and Globalization: Facts and Figures*, New York and Geneva, United Nations, 2004, p. 50.

[10] UNCTAD, *Economic Development in Africa: Trade Performance and Commodity Dependence*, New York and Geneva, United Nations, 2003, p. 2.

1980 and 1998, the South's share of the global trade in high technology products rose from 20 to 30 percent.[11]

In the financial sphere, there has been a definite improvement in the situation of developing countries. The debt problem, the cause of so much suffering during the 1980s, is now in the process of being resolved. Globally, the debt/gross national income ratio is on the decline.[12] In addition, a number of severely indebted poor countries have been able to take advantage of the favorable terms of reimbursement proposed by the IMF as part of the HIPC (Highly Indebted Poor Countries) Initiative that was set up in 1999. By 2005, the debt load of twenty-seven countries had thus been reduced by a total of $32 billion in net present value terms.[13] The G8's proposal to cancel the multilateral debt of the poorest countries represents the latest illustration of the international community's strong willingness to move beyond the debt crisis. What is more, the Third World has been attracting an ever-greater number of international investors in recent years. Between the late 1980s and 2002 the developing countries' share of foreign direct investment rose from 18 to 25 percent of the world total.[14] Finally, development assistance, which had gone down during the 1990s, has once again begun to increase in the wake of the 2002 Monterrey Summit on development financing. In 2005 aid reached the record amount of $106 billion.[15]

The economic vigor of the developing countries has made it possible to realize unprecedented progress with respect to poverty reduction. At the end of the 1990s, one UN agency enthusiastically declared, "income poverty has fallen faster in the past fifty years than in the previous fifty decades."[16] Although such an assertion is not easy to verify, the progress achieved in recent years has indeed been impressive. According to World Bank figures, the number of individuals

---

[11] Richard Kozul-Wright and Paul Rayment, *Globalization Reloaded: An UNCTAD Perspective*, Geneva, UNCTAD Discussion Papers, no. 167, January 2004, p. 9.

[12] UNCTAD, *Development and Globalization*, p. 30.

[13] IMF, *Factsheet: Debt Relief under the Heavily Indebted Poor Countries (HIPC) Initiative*, Washington, DC, IMF, 2005.

[14] UNCTAD, *Development and Globalization*, p. 32.

[15] OECD, "Aid Flows Top USD 100 Billion in 2005" (www.oecd.org/document/40/0,2340,en_2649_33721_36418344_1_1_1_1,00.html).

[16] UNDP, *Human Development Report 1997: Human Development to Eradicate Poverty*, New York, Oxford University Press, 1997, p. 24.

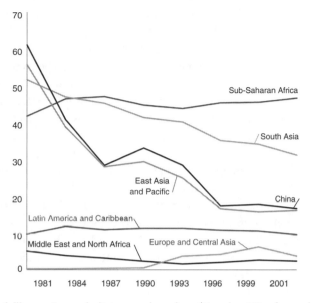

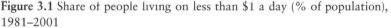

Figure 3.1 Share of people living on less than $1 a day (% of population), 1981–2001
Source: World Bank, *World Bank Development Indicators 2004*, Washington, DC, World Bank, 2004, p.1 (www.worldbank.org/data/wdi2004/worldview.htm).

living in absolute poverty, that is, with an income of $1 per day or less, declined from 1.5 billion in 1981 to 1.1 billion in 2001.[17]

The magnitude of this success is even more striking when translated into relative terms. In barely twenty years, the proportion of people living in extreme poverty in developing countries dropped by almost half, from 40 to 21 percent of the global population (Figure 3.1).[18] In China and South Asia, the effects of economic growth have been quite simply spectacular, if one considers that in these two regions alone more than 500 million people have been able to escape from poverty.[19] The recent reduction in poverty has been accompanied by all manner of positive spin-offs, but two of them are especially noteworthy. First,

---

[17] World Bank, "Global Poverty down by Half since 1981 but Progress Uneven as Economic Growth Eludes Many Countries," Washington, DC, World Bank, 2004 (http://web.worldbank.org/WBSITE/EXTERNAL/NEWS/0,, content MDK:20194973~menuPK: 34463~pagePK:64003015~piPK: 64003012~theSitePK:4607,00.html).
[18] *Ibid.* [19] *Ibid.*

population-weighted international inequality is now diminishing. The Gini coefficient for weighted international inequality indeed dropped by 10 percent between 1965 and 2000.[20] Second, a new "global middle class" is currently emerging. According to the World Bank, by 2030, the number of people in developing countries belonging to this global middle class will go up from 400 million to 1.2 billion.[21]

One of the benefits of globalization is to foster greater mobility among workers. Taking advantage of this new international context, migrant workers have made a growing contribution to economic growth and development. In 2005, the remittances of these workers to Third World countries amounted to more than $160 billion, thereby becoming a source of development financing much more important than foreign aid. Remittances have the added advantage of being more stable than aid flows, as they do not depend on the state of public finances in the migrant workers' host countries.[22] Qualified workers living abroad furthermore play a crucial role in the economic and social transformation of their countries of origin. Expatriate Indian professionals, for example, are the primary wellsprings of knowledge and capital flows toward India. In Taiwan, half the companies located in the country's largest research park were founded by workers who had spent time in the United States.[23]

The recent evolution of the international economy owes much to the consensus that gradually crystallized through the 1980s in favor of market liberalization and globalization. Up to that point, the economic policies of the developing and socialist countries were by and large interventionist, protectionist, and bureaucratic. Unable to satisfy the rising aspirations of their populations and meet the challenges of international competition, that approach was finally shelved and replaced by a new one focused on private enterprise, the opening of borders, and fiscal discipline. The collapse of communism in 1989,

[20] Branko Milanovic, *Worlds Apart: Measuring International and Global Inequality*, Princeton University Press, 2005, p. 85.

[21] World Bank, *Global Economic Prospects 2007: Managing the Next Wave of Globalization*, Washington, DC, World Bank, 2007, p. xvi.

[22] Dilip Ratha, "Remittances: A Lifeline for Development," *Finance and Development*, vol. 42, no. 4, December 2005 (www.imf.org/external/pubs/ft/fandd/2005/12/basics.htm).

[23] Mario Cervantes and Dominique Guellec, "The Brain Drain: Old Myths, New Realities," *OECD Observer*, no. 231–32, May 2002 (www.oecdobserver.org/news/fullstory.php/aid/673/The_brain_drain:_Old_myths,_new_realities.html).

which heralded the triumph of the capitalist economic model over that of the planned economy, was the emblem *par excellence* of this policy shift. After a period of adjustment, undoubtedly painful but perfectly natural given the dilapidation of their infrastructures and the absence of any business culture, the countries of Eastern Europe slowly but surely found their way back toward growth. Thanks to their methodical and efficient adjustment policies, Bulgaria, the Czech Republic, Estonia, Hungary, Latvia, Lithuania, Poland, Romania, Slovenia, and Slovakia even entered the European Union alongside some of the most thriving economies in the world.

While the liberal consensus caused less of a shock in the South than it did in the former socialist countries, the reforms introduced there were nonetheless profound. Having experimented with various forms of inward-looking development, poor countries finally understood that the opening up of trade was a precondition for growth. Third World governments manifested their new free-trade stance most notably by joining *en masse* the WTO, an international organization whose *raison d'être* is precisely the liberalization of trade. It should be recalled that the GATT – the WTO's predecessor – had always been regarded as a club for rich countries. Today, however, the situation has changed entirely, as 80 percent of WTO members are from the South.

Since the early 1990s, developing countries have radically altered their attitudes toward foreign investment and transnational corporations. Breaking with the distrust that colored their policies for so long, they have adopted an array of financial liberalization measures with a view to attracting private capital. This new approach goes a long way to explaining why, as noted earlier, the South has recently received much higher levels of foreign direct investment. It has also allowed some emerging countries, like Brazil, South Korea, and Mexico, to become major players in international capital markets, and has fostered the unparalleled expansion of Third World transnational firms.

The prosperous countries of Asia and Latin America are not the only ones to have felt the effects of the new liberal consensus that has taken shape in the developing world. Since 2001, Africa, too, has embarked on the road toward significant economic renewal through the adoption of a vast development program, the New Partnership for Africa's Development (NEPAD), which draws on the principles of the market economy.[24] Elaborated on the initiative of the heads of state of Algeria, South Africa, Egypt, Nigeria, and Senegal, the NEPAD signals a new stage in African history, for it has gone further than any earlier project in identifying the true problems of Africa in the area of political and economic governance. With the aim of putting a halt to the continent's structural dependence on international loans and handouts, NEPAD emphasizes the role of the private sector as the only possible key to African development. NEPAD was extremely well received by the international community, which has promised to take an active part in the realization of its objectives, so long as African governments make good on their commitment to adopt structural reforms that will improve the business climate in the region.

The recent period has also witnessed incomparable social progress at the global level. This is particularly true when it comes to health. In barely forty years, life expectancy in developing countries has shot up by eighteen years.[25] In China, it has gone up by a spectacular twenty-nine years.[26] During the 1990s, some sixty countries saw their infant mortality rate drop by at least a third. Inoculation campaigns have resulted in the almost total eradication of diseases such as smallpox and polio.[27] Victories have started to be won in the struggle against AIDS, particularly in Brazil, Uganda, and Thailand. Education is another area where major advances have been accomplished. Over the past thirty years, illiteracy throughout the Third World has been reduced by half.[28] Today, more than 80 percent of children attend primary school. Whereas there were three times as many post-secondary students in the North as in the South in 1950, the greatest

[24] See www.nepad.org/2005/files/home.php

[25] UNDP, *Human Development Report 2004: Cultural Liberty in Today's Diverse World*, New York, Oxford University Press, 2004, p. 142; see also UNDP, *Human Development Report 1992: Global Dimensions of Human Development*, New York, Oxford University Press, 1992, p. 14.

[26] Richard Jolly, Louis Emmerij, Dharam Ghai, and Frédéric Lapeyre, *UN Contributions to Development Thinking and Practice*, Bloomington, Indiana University Press, 2004, p. 252.

[27] Richard Jolly, *Global Goals: The UN Experience*, New York, UNDP, Human Development Report Office, 2003 (http://hdr.undp.org/publications/papers.cfm).

[28] World Bank, "World Bank/IMF Report Calls for Urgent Action on Poverty Reduction by All Countries" (http://web.worldbank.org/WBSITE/EXTERNAL/NEWS/0,,contentMDK:20194751~ menuPK:34463~pagePK: 64003015~piPK:64003012~ theSitePK: 4607,00.html).

number of students at this level is now in the South.[29] And while it is true that access to schooling remains more difficult for women in the developing countries, there has been progress toward gender equality at all levels of education.[30]

In addition to education, the economy has also provided leverage for the promotion of greater equality between men and women. Indeed, the accelerated industrialization of the Third World has given a large number of women the opportunity to escape the pressures stemming from a patriarchal family system or informal economic networks. The growth of export sectors and the spread of tax-free zones, especially in Asia and Latin America, have strongly contributed to the emancipation of women and to the consolidation of their rights. By allowing women to improve both their social status and their financial situation, globalization has directly enhanced the well-being of families, for one can easily understand that children whose mother earns a higher income tend to be better nourished and better educated.[31]

There is further cause for celebration when one considers the awareness of environmental issues that has blossomed worldwide in the last twenty years or so. The new environmental concerns have resulted in greater energy efficiency in both the developed and developing countries, such that everywhere more riches are being produced with less energy.[32] In one decade, carbon dioxide emissions have dropped from 4.1 to 3.8 metric tons per capita.[33] Since the adoption of the Montreal Protocol on ozone-depleting substances, the consumption of chlorofluorocarbons (CFC) has diminished substantially.[34] And all around the world, nature conservancy areas are on the increase.[35] Yet in the long term, the two most positive changes

[29] Jolly, Emmerij, Ghai, and Lapeyre, *UN Contributions to Development Thinking and Practice*, p. 254.

[30] UNESCO, *Global Monitoring Report 2003–04: Gender and Education for All: The Leap to Equality*, Paris, UNESCO, 2003.

[31] World Commission on the Social Dimension of Globalization, *A Fair Globalization*, p. 48, paragraph 217.

[32] UN, *Follow-up to the Outcome of the Millennium Summit: Implementation of the United Nations Millennium Declaration: Report of the Secretary-General*, New York, UN General Assembly, 58th session, A/58/323, September 2, 2003, p. 29 (www.un.org/ga/58/documentation/list3.html).

[33] World Bank, *World Bank Development Indicators 2004*, Washington, DC, World Bank, 2004, p. 10.

[34] UN, *Follow-up to the Outcome of the Millennium Summit*, p. 11.

[35] *Ibid.*, p. 28.

are probably that the leaders of the G8 countries agreed to cut greenhouse gas emissions in half by 2050, and that the leadership role of the private sector in addressing environmental problems is increasingly recognized.

Lastly, in the political sphere, the world today is more peaceful and more democratic than ever before. This two-fold evolution actually comes as no surprise to anyone aware of the well-established fact that democracies do not wage war against each other. From a historical perspective, what is most striking is that, despite a number of significant crises, no conflict opposing major powers has erupted into war in more than half a century. Also, contrary to a widespread opinion, the number of wars has declined significantly since the fall of the Berlin Wall. According to the most credible data available, there were twenty-one major armed conflicts taking place in 2002 compared to thirty-three in 1990.[36] Of course, there are still too many civil wars going on, but on the whole the international system is safer and less anarchic than in the past.

The prolonged stability of the international order can to a great extent be attributed to the leadership of the United States. Given the fact that no nation in modern history has wielded a military, economic, technological, and cultural domination comparable to that of the American superpower, especially since the end of the Cold War, the United States is naturally subject to constant protestation and criticism. Nevertheless, this country remains the only political player able to answer the collective needs of the international community in regard to security, trade, development, and the environment.[37] Neither Europe, nor China, nor Russia, nor the United Nations has the resources necessary to fulfil this role. Those who contest US hegemony do not realize that without this leadership the international system would be faced with a dangerous power vacuum.[38] The resultant "apolar" world would inevitably become more volatile and dangerous than any of the international system's historical configurations.

[36] SIPRI, *SIPRI Yearbook 2004: Armaments, Disarmaments and International Security*, Oxford University Press, 2004, p. 110, Table 2A.1.

[37] Fareed Zakaria, "Hating America," *Foreign Policy*, no. 144, September–October 2004, 47–49.

[38] Niall Ferguson, "A World without Power," *Foreign Policy*, no. 143, July–August 2004, 32–39; see also by the same author *Colossus: The Price of America's Empire*, New York, Penguin Press, 2004.

The last hundred years must, furthermore, be seen as the century of democracy. The full meaning of this observation appears clearly at the global level. Indeed, international power is far less oligarchic than at any other moment in history. The League of Nations, created in 1919 to maintain peace, never comprised more than sixty member-states and was always dominated by the Western countries. In 1945, a mere fifty-one states took part in the foundation of the United Nations, yet in 2007 that international body had 192 members, with the vast majority from developing countries. The movement toward democratization appears all the more impressive when one looks at the extensive transformations that have occurred within the domestic structures of governance. In 1900, more than half of the world population lived under a colonial regime and universal suffrage did not exist in any country. A hundred years later multi-party democracy is on the verge of establishing itself as a universal political regime.

The data provided by Freedom House helps to measure the recent flourishing of democracy. At the end of the 1980s, only 66 countries out of 167 (40 percent) could qualify as electoral democracies. By 2005 the number of electoral democracies had jumped to 122, representing 64 percent of all UN member states (Figure 3.2).[39] In addition, between 1972 and 2005 the number of countries regarded as "free" – that is, those where civil liberties are protected, the media are independent, and real political competition exists – rose from forty-three to eighty-nine (i.e. from 35 to 46 percent of the world population). Conversely, during the same period, the number of countries regarded as "unfree" – that is, where civil liberties are systematically violated – fell from sixty-nine to forty-five (i.e. from 47 to 36 percent of the world population).[40] The number of "unfree" countries of course remains too high, but one can assume that it will decline as market liberalization progresses. In fact, the states with the worst human rights records, such as Burma, North Korea, Cuba, Sudan, and Syria, are among those least integrated in the networks of globalization.

In spite of the positive picture that can be drawn of global politics, it must of course be recognized that the world remains confronted with

---

[39] Adrian Karatnycky, "Freedom in the World," Freedom House, 2005 (www. freedomhouse.org/template.cfm?page=130 & year=2005).

[40] *Ibid.* Freedom House also refers to a group of "partly free countries" that are not taken into consideration here.

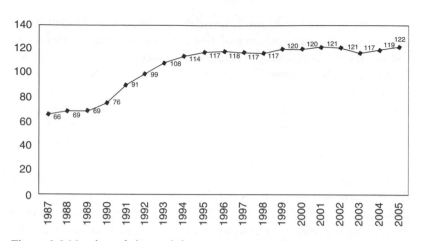

Figure 3.2 Number of electoral democracies, 1987–2005
Source: Freedom House, "Freedom in the World 2006: Selected Data from Freedom House's Annual Global Survey of Political Rights and Civil Liberties, 2006" (www.freedomhouse.org/uploads/pdf/Charts2006.pdf).

a range of difficulties. At the beginning of the twenty-first century the most serious problems are without a doubt those related to the threat that terrorism poses for the defence of freedom. It is heartening that thanks to the strengthening of national and international security measures, the threat has been reduced.[41] On the other hand, the terrorist scourge has become contagious. Whereas in the past it was restricted to unstable regimes, particularly in the Middle East and Latin America, there is today no region or country that is safe. Moreover, in the wake of the September 11, 2001 attacks against the United States, the human cost of terrorism has been going up, and considering that terrorists have grown ever-bolder, no one today can dismiss the hypothesis of a "big one" – a kamikaze attack using biological, chemical, or nuclear weapons.[42] Even though it sometimes requires difficult compromises in the area of human rights, the fight against terrorism must therefore remain a central concern of all societies that value democracy. To be victorious, that struggle demands, first and foremost,

[41] US Department of State, *Country Reports on Terrorism 2006*, Washington, DC, US Department of State Publication 11409, 2007, p. 14.
[42] World Economic Forum, *Global Governance Initiative: Annual Report 2004*, London, Communications Development, 2004, p. 8.

the marshalling of all available military, police, financial, and diplomatic resources, at both the national and international level. But it also requires the realization that security depends on the vigilance of every citizen.

The world of the critics

Experts on the left share a reading of the situation that is quite different from the one presented above. Though divided on issues such as the effects of globalization or the role of the state, progressives are united in their dissatisfaction with the prevailing world order. Grounded in a critical approach that applies to both the national and international arena, the view from the left is one of inadequately distributed wealth, over-concentrated political power, and the repeated flouting of the rule of law. The main arguments underpinning the left's critical outlook can be summarized as follows.

What characterizes global politics is, above all, the growing inequality of economic power. Over recent decades, the gulf between the richest and the poorest has become grotesque. Whereas in 1960–62, the average income of the twenty wealthiest countries was fifty-three times greater than that of the twenty poorest countries, forty years later, the ratio was 121:1 (Figure 3.3). A battery of additional statistics demonstrates the egregious level of the concentration of wealth. For example, the countries of the North, with 15 percent of the world's population, control 80 percent of global wealth, while nearly three billion people live on less than two dollars a day.[43] The richest 1 percent of the world's population has an income equal to that of the poorest 57 percent.[44] *Forbes* magazine has furthermore estimated that in 2004 there were 587 billionaires in the world, a super-elite whose combined assets of some $1.9 trillion was comparable to the collective GDP of the 170 poorest states.[45]

---

[43] World Bank, "Poverty Reduction: The Future of Global Development and Peace," keynote address delivered by the President of the World Bank, James D. Wolfensohn, at the University of Pennsylvania, Philadelphia, March 27, 2003, pp. 1–2.

[44] UNDP, *Human Development Report 2002: Deepening Democracy in a Fragmented World*, New York, Oxford University Press, 2002, p. 19.

[45] Jamie Chapman, "Forbes Report: Billionaires' Wealth Grew by 36 percent in Last Year," International Committee of the Fourth International (ICFI), March 9, 2004 (www.wsws.org/articles/2004/mar2004/forb-m09.shtml).

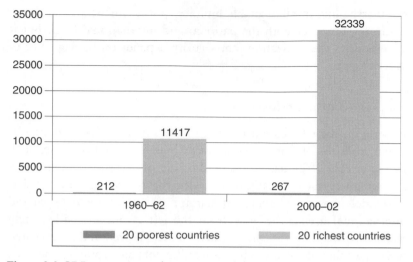

Figure 3.3 GDP per capita in the poorest and the richest countries, 1960–1962 and 2000–2002

Source: World Commission on the Social Dimension of Globalization, *A Fair Globalization: Creating Opportunities for All*, Geneva, ILO, 2004, p. 37, Figure 11 (www.ilo.org/public/english/wcsdg/index.htm).

Although economic inequality is the result of numerous factors, it is nourished to a large extent by the difference in access to technology. At the dawn of the twenty-first century, developed countries held 97 percent of patents, while the United States alone contained more computers than the rest of the world.[46] At the same time, half the population in the South had never placed a telephone call.[47] Clearly, the promises of greater and more equitably shared prosperity often associated with globalization have remained a long way from being fulfilled. In fact, since the acceleration of globalization in the early 1990s, the world GDP per capita growth rate has slowed relative to the previous three decades.[48] The 1990s were particularly dramatic

---

[46] See Oxfam-America, "Essential Facts about International Trade," 2004 (www.oxfamamerica.org/advocacy/art6417.html) and Kofi A. Annan, *"We the Peoples:" The Role of the United Nations in the 21st Century*, New York, United Nations, 2000, p. 32.

[47] *Ibid.*, p. 15.

[48] World Commission on the Social Dimension of Globalization, *A Fair Globalization*, p. 35, paragraph 174.

for a group of fifty-four developing countries that suffered a decline in their income during that period.[49] Within this economic environment, low-income countries, representing 40 percent of the world population, stand among the most excluded, receiving barely 3 cents of every dollar of wealth created worldwide.[50]

The little headway that has been achieved in the fight against poverty remains disappointing. Entire regions – Sub-Saharan Africa, Latin America, Central Asia, and Eastern Europe – are home to a greater number of citizens living on less than $1 a day than in 1980.[51] The situation in Sub-Saharan Africa has deteriorated to such a degree that its per capita GDP fell by $200 between 1974 and 2000.[52] The standard of living in Central Asia is now comparable to that of the least advanced countries. On the other hand, in places where extreme poverty has actually diminished, the benefits of growth have been shared in extremely unequal ways. In China, for instance, the recent economic boom has considerably broadened the gap between the country's coastal and rural regions. Ultimately, economic success seems to depend far less on individual talents and skills than on geographic or ethnic origins, and gender. Gender stands out as a particularly decisive ground for discrimination, given that women constitute the vast majority among vulnerable groups such as refugees, unregistered workers, the poor, and the hungry.

The problem of poverty in wealthy nations is, of course, less severe than in the developing countries. The North is nevertheless characterized by very acute economic disparities. In countries as different as the United States, Italy, and Sweden, income gaps expanded between 1980 and 1990.[53] In the United States, the richest 1 percent of the population has seen its share of national income increase steadily over the last decades. In 2000 that share was 17 percent, a level that had

[49] UNDP, *Human Development Report 2003: Millennium Development Goals: A Compact among Nations to End Human Poverty*, New York, Oxford University Press, 2003, p. 34.

[50] UNCTAD, "UNCTAD XI Press Room: Trade and Poverty," Geneva, 2003 (www.unctadxi.org/templates/Page____508.aspx).

[51] World Bank, *World Bank Development Indicators 2004*, p. 3.

[52] United Nations Foundation, "Many African Economies Worse off Than after Decolonization," New York, UN Wire, May 27, 2004 (www.unwire.org/UNWire/20040602/449_24458.asp).

[53] World Commission on the Social Dimension of Globalization, *A Fair Globalization*, p. 43, Figure 16.

not been experienced since the 1920s.[54] Even though the case of the USA may be an extreme one, income disparities are growing pretty much throughout the developed world and relative poverty is on the rise. It is currently estimated that over 10 percent of the OECD population – that is, more than 100 million individuals – has a disposable income that is less than half of the national median.[55]

While the prevailing neoliberal discourse declares trade to be the best way to speed up economic growth, the benefits of the recent market expansion are still very badly distributed. First, international trade flows continue to be largely dominated by the developed countries, whose share of merchandise exports in 2002 was 63.5 percent, almost unchanged in relation to 1960 (64.7 percent).[56] Second, the growth of trade in the Third World is highly concentrated: twelve countries – essentially from Asia and Latin America – account for 75 percent of the manufactured goods exported from the South.[57] Africa, on the other hand, has been pushed further and further to the margins, outside the trade circuits of globalization. Forever dependent on the export of primary products, African countries saw their share of world exports shrink from 6 to 2 percent between 1998 and 2002.[58]

Despite the considerable efforts made by poor countries to liberalize their economies over the past twenty years, the rules of international trade continue to be strongly biased in favour of the rich countries. The annual cost of the protectionism practiced by the developed countries *vis-à-vis* the developing countries is estimated to be roughly $150 billion.[59] A number of obstacles – high tariffs, quotas, subsidies, environmental, and health standards – continually restrict exports from the South to the North. It is well known, for example, that the

---

[54] *Ibid.*, p. 42, paragraph 198.
[55] Michael Förster and Marco Mira d'Ercole, "Tackling Poverty," *OECD Observer*, no. 248, March 2005, p. 21 (www.oecdobserver.org/news/fullstory.php/aid/1586/tackling_poverty.html). See also UNDP, *Human Development Report 1997*, p. 24.
[56] UNCTAD, *Development and Globalization*, p. 49.
[57] World Commission on the Social Dimension of Globalization, *A Fair Globalization*, p. 26, Figure 3.
[58] UNCTAD, *Economic Development in Africa: Trade Performance and Commodity Dependence*, New York and Geneva, United Nations, UNCTAD, 2003, p. 1.
[59] Supachai Panitchpakdi, "The Doha Development Agenda: Challenges and Opportunities for the Arab World," address by the Director-General of the WTO, Geneva, September 9, 2002, p. 1.

tariffs imposed by the developed countries on developing countries are higher than those they impose on other developed countries. This said, the issue of subsidies is certainly the one that has given rise to the sharpest debates in North–South trade relations recently. In the agricultural sector alone, the subsidies granted by the governments of OECD countries amount to around $330 billion annually.[60] Some have cynically remarked that a European cow received a daily subsidy of $2 – more, that is, than the average income of an African citizen. This abundance of public funds seems all the more unjustifiable in light of its very doubtful social usefulness: 70 percent of agricultural subsidies in the developed countries are granted to farmers whose incomes are above the national average.

Transnational corporations, overwhelmingly based in the developed countries, are responsible to a large degree for the concentration of wealth and the exacerbation of international trade imbalances. The economic power of these firms is due, first, to the fact that they account for two-thirds of international trade.[61] Many industries, especially those involved in the production of commodities, are under the sway of a very small number of corporations. Three companies control 65 percent of the banana market; in the aluminum and copper industries ten corporations control, respectively, 60 percent and 58.5 percent of world production.[62] What is more, transnational corporations possess resources that dwarf those of many states: fifty-one transnationals are among the hundred top economic units in the world. In 2001, Wal-Mart's annual sales exceeded the GDP of Indonesia, and those of Royal Dutch Shell were greater than the GDP of Venezuela.[63] Against this backdrop it is easy to understand why power relations between transnational corporations and Third World governments often favour the former to the detriment of the latter.

The operation of the international financial system is another factor facilitating the globalization of inequalities. Whereas it would be logical for capital to be flowing from the rich countries toward the

---

[60] World Bank, "Global Poverty Down by Half Since 1981."
[61] World Commission on the Social Dimension of Globalization, *A Fair Globalization*, p. 32, paragraph 150.
[62] United Nations, *Commodity Atlas*, New York and Geneva, UNCTAD and Common Fund for Commodities, 2004, p. 3, 5, and 13.
[63] CorpWatch, "Corporate Globalization Fact Sheet," San Francisco, CorpWatch, 2001 (www.corpwatch.org/article.php?id=914).

poor countries so as to compensate for the lack of domestic savings, it is actually the opposite that has been taking place for many years. In 2004, the net transfer of financial resources from the South to the North has approached the record sum of $350 billion.[64] Furthermore, in spite of the heightened attention of the international community, the debt problem remains a serious brake on development efforts. The debt volume of the developing countries and the former socialist countries taken together has expanded significantly during the past decade. In 2001, debt reimbursements were estimated at close to $300 billion, while interest payments alone reached almost $100 billion.[65] However well intentioned, the debt relief measures that have been introduced over the years have remained plainly insufficient. On one hand, their implementation has been subject to an exceedingly slow process. On the other, their impact continues to be limited because they neglect certain key aspects, such as private debts and volatility in commodity prices.

The financial crisis faced by the Third World is aggravated by the relative decline of development assistance. From 1960 to 2005, foreign aid dropped from 0.5 to 0.33 percent of the rich countries' Gross National Income[66] (Figure 3.4). The objective to which the developed countries committed themselves in the 1970s – to devote 0.7 percent of their Gross National Product to foreign aid – has until now been attained only by a group of five small countries (Denmark, Luxembourg, the Netherlands, Norway, and Sweden). It is particularly distressing to note that international aid adds up to a mere 10 percent of global military spending. Furthermore, assistance remains strongly oriented toward countries representing strategic or commercial interests (China, former Yugoslavia, Iraq, Pakistan) rather than the poorest nations. Although welcome, the recent rise in net official development assistance cannot erase the fact that the peace dividends that were to derive from the end of the Cold War have never materialized.

The developed countries' lack of generosity jeopardizes the achievement of the Millennium Development Goals (MDGs) adopted by

---

[64] United Nations, *World Economic and Social Survey 2005*, New York, United Nations, 2005, p. x.

[65] UNCTAD, *Development and Globalization*, pp. 28–29.

[66] OECD, *Development Co-operation Report*, Paris, OECD, various years. The term Gross National Income has replaced the term Gross National Product in the OECD's new System of National Accounts.

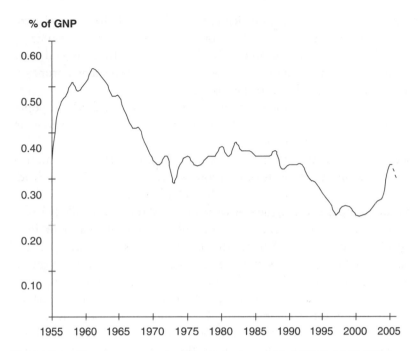

% of GNP

Figure 3.4 Aid as a percentage of developed countries' GNP, 1955–2006
Note: Preliminary estimate for 2006. Since 2000, Gross National Product (GNP) has been modified and renamed Gross National Income by the OECD.
Source: OECD, *Development Co-operation Report*, Paris, OECD, various years.

147 heads of state in 2000, which propose a 50 percent reduction in extreme poverty by 2015. Since reaching these objectives would require international aid to be increased significantly, all indications are that they will end up on the long list of disappointments that have regularly marked the history of North–South relations. In accordance with this pessimistic forecast, the UN has estimated that if the current trend is maintained, Africa would attain the MDGs not in 2015 but in 2147.[67] Yet a number of statistics on consumption patterns show that the international community's indifference toward development can hardly be justified by the scarcity of resources. At the end of the 1990s Americans were spending more on cosmetics – $8 billion – than the $6 billion needed to ensure basic education for all. Europeans were

[67] United Nations, "More Cash and Effort Needed to Help Africa Reach Anti-poverty Goals – UN Official," UN News Centre, September 16, 2004 (www.un.org/apps/news/story.asp? NewsID=11892 & Cr=millennium&Cr1=).

buying $11 billion worth of ice cream while $9 billion would have sufficed to provide water and sanitation for all. And it was estimated that the cost of basic health and education worldwide would have been $13 billion, in comparison with the $17 billion that Europeans and Americans paid out for pet food.[68]

Because of this hostile economic environment, Third World populations continue to live in conditions of hardship that most people in the developed countries would find intolerable. In a time when global wealth has reached unheard of levels and agricultural production is enough to meet the needs of everyone on earth, 800 million individuals go hungry.[69] Each year 10 million children die of curable diseases as commonplace as diarrhea. A woman is 100 times more likely to die during pregnancy or childbirth in Sub-Saharan Africa than in a developed country.[70] Among the infectious diseases ravaging the South, AIDS is no doubt the one that has attracted the most media attention because it also affects the North. It is often forgotten that 95 percent of HIV cases – that is, more than 40 million individuals – are located in the developing world. The most dramatic consequence of the AIDS epidemic is to have reduced life expectancy in some thirty countries; in certain states, such as Botswana, Lesotho, Swaziland, and Zimbabwe, life expectancy has been reduced by over twenty years.[71] Thus, the division between rich and poor is literally a matter of life and death, and this situation will most likely persist so long as a mere 10 percent of medical research resources are devoted to problems affecting 90 percent of the world's population.[72]

International inequalities are also legion in the sphere of labor. For one thing, capital mobility and the high rates of unemployment prevalent in the Third World restrict the bargaining power of employees of companies that are integrated in the global production system.[73] Yet most workers in the South do not even enjoy the privilege of negotiating their labor conditions, since they are employed within the

---

[68] UNDP, *Human Development Report 1998: Consumption for Human Development*, New York, Oxford University Press, 1998, p. 37.

[69] UNDP, "Millennium Development Goals: A Status Report," New York, UNDP, 2003 (http://hdr.undp.org/reports/global/2003/).

[70] UNDP, *Human Development Report 2003*, p. 97.

[71] *Ibid.*, p. 43.   [72] *Ibid.*, p. 158.

[73] World Commission on the Social Dimension of Globalization, *A Fair Globalization*, p. 46, paragraph 210.

informal economy: lacking resources and trapped in the demands of daily survival, they often have no social protection other than that provided by their family. The situation of the 218 million child laborers is another issue of great concern. More than half of them (126 million) work in conditions considered dangerous and often verging on slavery; more than one-third (73 million) are under 10 years of age.[74] Finally, the international differences in opportunity and income engender a brain drain that hampers the development of many countries. The exodus of African professionals has taken on particularly dramatic proportions: 300,000 of them work in Europe and North America.[75] According to one assessment, approximately one-third of all Third World professionals in the research and development field live in the developed countries.[76] The brain drain constitutes a prime example of the ways in which the South subsidizes growth in the North.

The production and consumption model that underpins globalization, furthermore, raises serious environmental issues. The standard of living in developed countries cannot be sustained in the long term because it cannot be generalized over the whole planet. These countries are currently responsible for 56 percent of global consumption, while the poorest 40 percent of the world's population account for only 11 percent. It has been estimated that for the living standard of everyone in the world to be equal to that of the rich countries, 2.6 additional planet Earths would be needed.[77] The global warming caused by unchecked industrial development is admittedly one of the greatest menaces facing the environment. The United Nations Environment Programme predicts that over the next century the Earth's temperature will rise to levels unheard of in the history of humanity, with widespread droughts and floods as the inevitable results.[78] In the

[74] UNICEF, "Child Labour" (www.unicef.org/protection/index_ childlabour. html) and ILO, "Facts on Child Labour" (www.ilo.org/public/english/bureau/ inf/fact/index.htm).
[75] Cervantes and Guellec, "The Brain Drain." [76] *Ibid.*
[77] United Nations Commission on Sustainable Development, "Factsheet about Consumption and Production Patterns," document prepared for the World Summit on Sustainable Development, Johannesburg, August 26–September 4, 2002 (www.johannesburgsummit.org/html/media_info/pressreleases_ factsheets/wssd9_consumption.pdf).
[78] UNEP, "How Will Global Warming Affect My World? A Simplified Guide to the IPCC's 'Climate Change 2001: Impacts, Adaptation and Vulnerability,' "

countries of the South, the environmental issue is inextricably linked to poverty, given that the worst problem remains access to water. More than one billion people have no access to drinking water, and more than a third of the world's population (2.4 billion people) do not have adequate sanitation facilities.[79] Contaminated water and unhealthy sewage systems are the cause of 5 million deaths per year and the source of 80 percent of the infectious diseases that afflict developing countries.[80] The environmental problems in the rich countries are no doubt different from those in the poor countries, but the solution in all cases depends on the awareness that to be viable economic growth must be subordinated to social priorities.

From a political point of view, the international system faces chronic insecurity and a significant democratic deficit. Even though inter-state conflicts have in recent years been less numerous than intra-state conflicts (Chechnya, Democratic Republic of the Congo, Liberia, Rwanda, Sudan, former Yugoslavia, etc.), the world continues to find itself in the throes of war and organized violence. However shocking this situation may be, it is not entirely surprising in light of the fact that the yearly global arms trade amounts to $1 trillion, while the UN's regular budget hovers around $3.2 billion.[81] In most instances, poverty and economic disparities are the engines that drive armed conflicts. The rise of international terrorism, moreover, can only be fully understood as another consequence of the failure of economic development. Since the end of the Cold War, the international community has constantly run into the same problem in trying to manage crisis upon crisis: it has proven to be completely incapable of establishing the primacy of law and morality over national interests. As a result of its illegitimacy and illegality, the war launched by the United States against Iraq in 2003 offers the perfect illustration of this syndrome, aptly demonstrating that what does or does not constitute a threat to international security is determined by the rule of "might makes right."

Geneva, 2003 (www.unep.org/themes/climatechange/PDF/ipcc_wgii_guide-E.pdf).

[79] UNDP, *Human Development Report 2003*, p. 103.

[80] See Annan, "*We the Peoples*," p. 60.

[81] See SIPRI, "Recent Trends in Military Expenditure" (www.sipri.org/contents/milap/milex/mex_trends.html) and Angela Drakulich (ed.), *A Global Agenda: Issues before the 60th General Assembly of the United Nations*, New York, United Nations Association of the USA, 2005, pp. 293–95.

While all states have proclaimed their support for democracy, the international system continues to be profoundly anti-democratic. In the political and strategic spheres, all important decisions are subject to the veto of the five powers that, at the end of the Second World War, granted themselves permanent seats on the UN Security Council (United States, Russia, United Kingdom, France, and China). The dedication of these countries to the cause of peace is, moreover, dubious, given that taken together they are responsible for 77 percent of global arms exports.[82] The primary international economic institutions – the IMF, the World Bank, and the WTO – are completely dominated by the Western countries. The United States has, *de jure* or *de facto*, the power to block any major reform of these institutions that does not meet with its approval. In fact, the ascendancy of the US government and corporations over the world economy has, since the disintegration of the USSR, become so great that more and more observers characterize the contemporary global order as "imperial."

On the domestic level, the democratic malaise stems, first, from the fact that rather than being available to all equally, political power remains everywhere in the hands of an exclusive elite. According to the largest poll ever conducted – a survey commissioned by the UN in preparation for the Millennium Summit and covering sixty countries – two-thirds of the 57,000 respondents felt their government did not reflect "the will of the people."[83] In many states, basic human rights are violated with the full knowledge of the authorities. Faced with this situation, the response of international institutions has been generally passive; when they do take action, they often apply a double standard based on economic and political considerations. Far from affecting the Third World alone, this disregard for human rights also concerns developed countries, where governments increasingly tend to "sacrifice the global values of human rights in a blind pursuit of security."[84]

---

[82] SIPRI (by Björn Hagelin, Mark Bromley, and Siemon T. Wezeman), "Appendix 12A. The Volume of Transfers of Major Conventional Weapons: By Recipients and Suppliers, 1999–2003," Stockholm, 2004, p. 5 (http://web.sipri.org/contents/armstrad/app12A2004.pdf).

[83] Annan, "*We the Peoples,*" p. 16.

[84] Amnesty International, "Report 2004: War on Global Values – Attacks by Armed Groups and Governments Fuel Mistrust, Fear and Division," press release, London, May 26, 2004 (http://web.amnesty.org/library/index/engPOL100162004?open&of= eng-200).

Even the idea that the advancement of democracy has been slow but nevertheless steady has become groundless. In this connection, Amnesty International noted that in 2003 human rights and international humanitarian law suffered the most important setback in half a century.[85]

Fortunately, in the bleak landscape depicted above there is a ray of hope emanating from the mobilization of civil society, often described as the "other superpower."[86] Global civil society comprises a vast network of 25,000 international non-governmental organizations (NGOs) and an even greater number of groups working on the national and local level.[87] Thanks to the systematic use of information technologies, this network is more and more tightly knit. And, as it expands, global civil society is becoming increasingly representative. While it was admittedly dominated for a long time by organizations from the North, the situation has gradually begun to change. Since the early 1990s, NGOs have definitely developed at a faster rate in poor countries than in rich ones.[88]

The various organizations of civil society are concerned with a broad spectrum of issues (human rights, development, international economy, environment, and gender), but they all pursue a common goal: to promote a globalization that gives priority to solidarity rather than competition. Contrary to a view often expressed in the media, civil society's contribution to the political debate is not restricted to street demonstrations during major diplomatic meetings. For more than a decade, its representatives have participated as legitimate partners in a wide range of international negotiations. The creation of the World Social Forum in 2001 is further proof of how civil society groups are striving to define an alternative social project through a constructive approach. All in all, the rise of civil society offers the hope that one day the management of global affairs may move toward the realization of a more democratic, more humane world.

---

[85] *Ibid.*

[86] Jonathan Schell, "The World's Other Superpower," *The Nation*, April 14, 2003.

[87] Commission on Human Security, *Human Security Now: Protecting and Empowering People*, New York, Commission on Human Security, 2003, p. 88.

[88] Centre for the Study of Global Governance, *Global Civil Society 2003*, Oxford University Press, 2003, Figures 1.2 and 1.3 (www.lse.ac.uk/Depts/global/Yearbook/outline2003.htm).

Conclusion

The two visions set forth in this chapter propose very different diagnoses of global politics and the attitudes that should determine the actions of the international community. The acute differences separating these visions clearly make dialogue difficult. However much one may deplore the situation, it is important to understand that these two interpretations derive from the basic dynamics of the "global public domain."[89] Within that common space, opinion formers who emphasize the economy, freedom, and individual responsibility find themselves constantly opposed to those who stress social issues, equality, and collective responsibility. These differing values have long been associated with the right and the left respectively. Needless to say, statistics on the reduction of absolute poverty or on the increase of the Third World's debt cannot intrinsically be classified as right or left. Nevertheless, political life is such that those who take part in it *choose* to highlight certain facts and figures rather than others. And that *choice* is always linked to a system of values or an ideology. It is, therefore, unlikely that the current debate will one day be resolved on empirical grounds.

It should be reiterated, in closing this chapter, that whether they take place on the domestic or the international level, political discussions can never be reduced to a sparring match between two impermeable camps. Ordinary citizens and experts alike defend ideas that often straddle the discourses of the satisfied and of the critics. For example, the left-leaning American economist Jeffrey Sachs, head of the UN Millennium Project, denounces the international community's meagre efforts in the fight against poverty, while at the same time hailing the benefits of the opening up of markets.[90] On the other hand, Martin Wolf, generally associated with the right, insists on the beneficial role of transnational corporations, yet condemns the hypocrisy of the rich countries' agricultural policies.[91] Clearly, the global political debate is traversed by an infinite number of nuances. Without

---

[89] John Gerard Ruggie, "Reconstituting the Global Public Domain: Issues, Actors, and Practices," *European Journal of International Relations*, vol. 10, no. 4, 2004, 499–531.

[90] Jeffrey Sachs, *The End of Poverty: Economic Possibilities for Our Time*, New York, Penguin Press, 2005, p. 357.

[91] Wolf, *Why Globalization Works*, p. 215.

denying the relevance of analyzing all those nuances, it was not our intention to summarize them here, since such a summary would have necessarily remained incomplete. Our purpose, rather, has been to illuminate the basic positions that both dominate and structure the public sphere. To that end, the ideal-type narratives of the right and the left provide an unmatched conceptual roadmap.

4 | The rise of the modern state system (1776–1945)

The opposition between the left and the right did not emerge spontaneously. The debate as we know it took shape gradually, out of the protracted conflict over the construction of the modern state system. With the rise of liberalism, a world of overlapping hierarchies was gradually challenged by a new one defined by the intrinsic equality of all able-bodied adult men. Disagreements about the exact meaning of this newly affirmed common citizenship were unavoidable, however, and they became inherent in most, if not all, public deliberations.

This chapter retraces the evolution of the opposition between the left and the right over the period between the American Revolution in 1776 and the end of the Second World War in 1945. In this long era of transition, the modern state as we know it, a legitimate bureaucratic and political apparatus presiding over a relatively vast territory, came into being. So did the modern state system, conceived as an international arrangement of stable relationships between sovereign units. The period encompassed here is rich in events which obviously cannot be analyzed in any exhaustive manner. Our aim is simply to offer a better understanding of the ubiquity of left–right debates, by showing how they shaped political views over a range of critical questions across the world. Four themes, central to this period when the modern state and state system were built, are considered: democracy, peace and war, capitalism and socialism, and the colonial enterprise.

The first theme concerns democracy. Long despised as an unworkable and dangerous political regime, the rule of the people became a powerful rallying cry in the wake of the American and French Revolutions, at the end of the eighteenth century. How this new political system would be organized remained, however, far from clear. Conflicts, revolutions, and counter-revolutions gradually determined the institutional contours of democracy in the Western world. At the same time, ongoing debates defined two sides: one continued to privilege hierarchy and order; the other put more faith in equality and

83

popular rule. Gradually, these two camps constituted the modern left and right.

A similar antinomy opposed, in the international arena, those who viewed the world as a democracy writ large, a society of sovereign peoples governed by similar principles and able to cooperate in peace, and those who clung to a more traditional, hierarchical vision of international relations, whereby only power, military strength and, when necessary, war could provide security. In the latter perspective, even democratic revolutions, should they happen, could not transform the ways of a world condemned to remain an anarchical society, prone to violence and governed by force.

By the end of the nineteenth century, two new dimensions were added to these conflicts, in response to the worldwide expansion of capitalism. First, the debate about democracy and equality was extended into a debate about the organization of production and distribution, pitting conservatives and liberals, both favorable to capitalism, against socialists of various stripes. This opposition transformed party politics and shaped, too, the world of work and industrial relations. Second, on a world scale, the debate about force and order also became one about imperialism and colonialism, thus including, at least implicitly, the fate of peoples outside Europe and the white-settler colonies.

Democracy, peace and war, capitalism and socialism, and the colonial enterprise: these four themes are rarely presented in an interconnected fashion when they are examined by historians. The four questions, however, involved several common principles, and they were intimately connected, as core issues in the long political conflict out of which the modern left and right were constructed. It took fierce ideological battles to give a definite contour to these two broader visions, but the disagreements that were then defined proved coherent, and they are still with us today.

Democracy

Until 1776, nothing resembling a national democratic regime existed in the world.[1] In some merchant cities of Europe and in a few remote

---

[1] Charles Tilly, *Contention and Democracy in Europe, 1650–2000*, Cambridge University Press, 2004, p. 66.

peasant communities, there were forms of collective rule that prefigured democracy, but these were fairly limited in scope. Demands for popular rule and rights also emerged in rural and urban rebellions, but they remained few and far between, and more or less inarticulate. The main demands voiced on these occasions concerned distribution, not representation, and certainly not representation as it is understood today. None of these movements, observes political philosopher C. B. Macpherson, "however enraged, would think that its aims could be achieved by its getting the vote."[2] Such rebellions normally were defeated by force and severely repressed.

Democracy, then, had a bad name. Understood as a form of direct rule by the people, this type of regime was overwhelmingly seen as "illegitimate in theory" and "disastrous in practice."[3] The independent city-states of thirteenth-century Italy, for instance, had citizen representation, elected magistrates, and the rule of law, but they were viewed as republican, not democratic systems of governance.[4] In the British Isles, the civil wars of the seventeenth century primarily opposed social classes divided by religion and interest, not by disagreements over the political regime as such. These violent conflicts generated a new configuration of political forces and institutions that was justified in terms of legitimacy and rights, not as a form of democracy. Articulating the preoccupations of men of small property and of independent producers, the Levellers did have a democratic program calling for a written constitution, an "Agreement of the People," and regular and fair elections. They too were defeated, however.[5]

The real breakthrough came with the American Revolution. Set in a new society with rather fluid political structures, this revolution gave rise to a new republic and an unprecedented vision of popular liberties and constitutional rights. At first, the republic was not understood as a democracy, the old notion being identified with direct popular rule in small communities, as well as with instability and excess. A republic, explained James Madison in 1787 in the *Federalist Papers*, differs from a democracy in two respects. First, it is of a much larger size,

[2] C. B. Macpherson, *The Life and Times of Liberal Democracy*, Oxford University Press, 1977, p. 13.
[3] John Dunn, *Setting the People Free: The Story of Democracy*, London, Atlantic Books, 2005, p. 15.
[4] *Ibid.*, p. 58.
[5] Macpherson, *The Life and Times of Liberal Democracy*, pp. 14–15.

both in territory and population. Second, it delegates government to a small number of citizens, chosen as representatives of the larger community and held accountable by various mechanisms, regular elections being the most important.[6] A new form of government was being created, representative democracy, which in due course would be simply referred to as democracy, without the negative connotations long associated with the ancient Greek word.

The establishment of this new political regime was the subject of intense debates throughout the American states, regarding the appropriate forms of the institutions, the principles at stake, and the type of society that could be fostered by democratic rule. Subjects of disagreement were multiple, but early on an opposition divided those who saw democratic equality as an equality of opportunity among free individuals in an open process, and those who insisted on results as well, and sought living conditions as equal as possible. The first feared excessive popular demands, threats to property rights, and an alliance with revolutionary France. The second worried about the rise of a new aristocracy backed up by a strong state and a standing army, and the "Anglicization" and corruption of American government.[7]

Initially, this ideological division did not give rise to a partisan cleavage, because there were no formal political parties in the new democracy. It was not long, however, before the two sides organized into coherent parties. In the election of 1796, voters could choose between the Federalists led by George Washington, John Adams, and Alexander Hamilton, and the Republicans of Thomas Jefferson. An aristocrat and slave-owner worried by commerce and industrialization, Jefferson was an ambiguous figure, and some have portrayed him as driven more by the interests of landowners than by an ideal of equality.[8] In the end, however, Jefferson proved to be a pragmatic politician. He built a party, reached out to city voters, and defined a politics that "had a more popular, egalitarian impetus" than that of

---

[6] Dunn, *Setting the People Free*, pp. 77–78.

[7] Richard J. Ellis, *American Political Cultures*, New York, Oxford University Press, 1993, pp. 45 and 63–67; Michael J. Sandel, *Democracy's Discontent: America in Search of a Public Philosophy*, Cambridge, MA, Harvard University Press, 1996, pp. 133–39; Steven Mintz, "The First New Nation," in *Digital History*, Houston, University of Houston, 2003 (www.digitalhistory.uh.edu).

[8] Richard Hofstadter, *The American Political Tradition and the Men Who Made It*, New York, Vintage Books, 1958, p. 33.

the Federalists.[9] In the following years, Jefferson's Republicans would virtually eliminate the Federalists, but the opposition was reborn with the split of the remaining party into a Democratic and a Republican faction. American politics had become competitive and divided for good over the nature and meaning of democracy. The country's public opinion, wrote Alexis de Tocqueville in 1831, "is divided into a thousand minute shades of difference upon questions of detail," but the more we look at the contending parties, "the more do we perceive that the object of the one is to limit, and that of the other to extend, the authority of the people."[10]

At about the same time, in 1789, the French Revolution produced a more dramatic, sharper division over equality and democracy. The starting point, a hierarchical society composed of three distinct estates – the Church, the nobility, and the common people – was quite different from that of the United States. To create a democracy in such a context, the French had to make an even more radical break with the past. Politically, this break was realized through the creation of the National Assembly and the Declaration of the Rights of Man and the Citizen in 1789. Ideologically, it was accomplished most remarkably by the publication in the same year of *What is the Third Estate?* by Emmanuel Joseph Sieyès. The Third Estate, wrote Sieyès, is "everything;" even though so far it has been "nothing." Without the common people, the two other estates, and indeed the country, simply could not exist. Nothing would be produced or accomplished. Without the Church and the nobility, on the other hand, everything would work. Indeed the country would do better.[11] Equality was posed as the core issue from the outset. What was at stake was the very constitution of society, in social classes whose interests were seen as antagonistic. In a deeply hierarchical society, such an egalitarian vision could not prevail without a clash. Indeed, more than a hundred years of violent civil and international conflicts would be necessary to sort out the consequences of the French Revolution.

Political philosopher John Dunn summarizes these conflicts with the words of Filippo Michele Buonarroti, a Tuscan aristocrat who

[9] James MacGregor Burns, *The Deadlock of Democracy: Four-Party Politics in America*, Englewood Cliffs, NJ, Prentice-Hall, 1967, pp. 33 and 41.

[10] Alexis de Tocqueville, quoted in *ibid.*, pp. 57–58.

[11] Sieyès, quoted in Dunn, *Setting the People Free*, p. 108.

participated in the battles of the time. The French Revolution, explained Buonarroti, basically opposed the "order of egoism," focused on personal interests, commerce, and "the English doctrine of the economists," to the "order of equality," which sought to achieve genuine social equality.[12] In the short run, what Buonarroti called the "order of egoism" won, and a strong aristocratic impulse remained within the new democratic order. But the conflict was there to stay, and in fact it spread all over Europe. Everywhere on the continent, notes Dunn, democracy remained "a fiercely divisive political category."[13]

The struggles over democracy opposed revolutionaries and counter-revolutionaries, republicans and monarchists, the reds and the whites, and, increasingly, two sides seen as the left and the right. For many advocates of order, even representative democracy appeared suspect. By 1815, at the end of the Napoleonic wars, democratic advances had been defeated all over continental Europe, and authoritarianism prevailed everywhere.[14] Popular sovereignty and individual rights had to be established or re-established inch by inch, with a number of advances and retreats, well into the twentieth century.

Democracy as such, then, was the core issue. Movements and parties in favor of change mobilized against aristocratic, monarchist, or authoritarian forces, and they fought for the right to vote, the secret ballot, and accountable executives, as well as for national independence or unity.[15] Responsible government and universal suffrage were the emblematic issues of this long battle. At the turn of the nineteenth century, responsible government without suffrage qualifications was the main goal. In Britain, for instance, property, tax, or trade requirements restricted the vote to about 15 percent of adult males. In the United States and Canada, where landownership was less concentrated, similar rules entitled up to 80 percent of adult white males to vote.[16] In France, universal male suffrage and responsible government came together in 1877, at a time when the call for universal suffrage

---

[12] Buonarroti, quoted in *ibid.*, p. 124; Marc Ferro, *Histoire de France*, Paris, Odile Jacob, 2001, pp. 232–33.

[13] Dunn, *Setting the People Free*, p. 125.

[14] Tilly, *Contention and Democracy in Europe*, p. 212.

[15] *Ibid.*, p. 213; Dunn, *Setting the People Free*, p. 153.

[16] Dietrich Rueschemeyer, Evelyne Huber Stephens, and John D. Stephens, *Capitalist Development and Democracy*, University of Chicago Press, 1992, pp. 43, 123, and 133.

was becoming more forceful. Indeed, between 1877 and 1920, most countries of Western Europe removed the remaining barriers to universal male suffrage, under pressures from the rising working class, and against the wishes of conservative social forces and political parties.[17] At the beginning of the twentieth century, some democracies broke down and turned to authoritarianism, but in democracies the conflict over the right to vote continued, first to include women, and then other excluded groups. In most democracies, women acquired the vote around the time of the First World War, but the process was neither easy nor uniform. In Switzerland, for instance, one of the first democratic countries, this right was not established until 1971. Similarly, blacks in the United States were not allowed to exercise fully their right to vote until 1965.[18]

The object of the conflict was democracy, but the principle at stake was equality. It was indeed to achieve fully the political equality promised by liberalism that the left sought reforms, and its political success was closely tied to the actual equality that existed in a country.[19] On the other side, arguments were defined around the recognition of merit, the protection of property, the importance of traditions, and the risks of disorder and anarchy.[20] Through this basic opposition, the left and right as we now know them gradually took shape.

Peace and war

From the outset, this debate between the left and the right had international implications. The fight over democracy was also a conflict about the nature of the world order. On the left, proponents of equality and popular rule championed national sovereignty, cooperation among free peoples, and peace. On the right, defenders of the status quo preferred a stable international order governed by the most powerful states, by military strength, and, when necessary, by war.

---

[17] *Ibid.*, pp. 83, 90, and 140–41.   [18] *Ibid.*, p. 122.
[19] Pierre Rosanvallon, *Le sacre du citoyen: histoire du suffrage universel en France*, Paris, Gallimard, 1992, p. 18; Tilly, *Contention and Democracy in Europe*, pp. 211–12; Carles Boix, *Democracy and Redistribution*, Cambridge University Press, 2003, pp. 10–12.
[20] Geoff Eley, *Forging Democracy: The History of the Left in Europe, 1850–2000*, Oxford University Press, pp. 30–31.

Against absolutist monarchies claiming divine right, democrats opposed the idea of a state created by a social contract among free and rational men.[21] Anchored in reason and popular will, this new state would be much less likely to seek wars than the old regimes. "The spirit of monarchy is war and enlargement of dominion," wrote Montesquieu in 1748, "peace and moderation are the spirit of a republic."[22] Republics, explained German philosopher Immanuel Kant, favor peace because they are based on reason and popular consent. "If the consent of the citizens is required in order to decide that war should be declared," he argued in his *Project for a Perpetual Peace* (1795), "nothing is more natural than that they would be very cautious in commencing such a poor game, decreeing for themselves all the calamities of war.... But, on the other hand, in a constitution which is not republican, and under which the subjects are not citizens, a declaration of war is the easiest thing in the world to decide upon, because war does not require of the ruler, who is the proprietor and not a member of the state, the least sacrifice of the pleasures of his table, the chase, his country houses, his court functions, and the like."[23]

For the left, war was "rooted in the vested interests of the ruling classes."[24] As such, it would be difficult to vanquish, even though it appeared "inherently evil and often also foolish."[25] In a world marred by inequality and ruled by "the law of the strongest," noted Jean-Jacques Rousseau in his own *Project towards a Perpetual Peace* (1760), reason, justice, and peace would not prevail easily. Initiating a long intellectual and political tradition, Rousseau insisted that equality constituted a prerequisite for peace.[26]

These views about reason, equality, democracy, and peace were pre-eminent in revolutionary France. Threatened by the monarchies of Europe, the French Constituent Assembly did prepare for war, but the

[21] Torbjörn L. Knutsen, *A History of International Relations Theory*, Manchester University Press, 1992, p. 103.
[22] Charles de Secondat Montesquieu, *Spirit of the Laws*, quoted in Michael Howard, *War and the Liberal Conscience*, Oxford University Press, 1978, p. 25.
[23] Immanuel Kant, *Perpetual Peace: A Philosophical Sketch*, 1795 (www.mtholyoke.edu/acad/intrel/kant/kant1.htm).
[24] Howard, *War and the Liberal Conscience*, p. 27.
[25] Bernard Brodie, "The Continuing Relevance of *On War*," in Carl von Clausewitz, *On War*, ed. and trans. Michael Howard and Peter Paret, Princeton University Press, 1984, p. 48.
[26] Knutsen, *A History of International Relations Theory*, pp. 113–27.

aim was only to defend the revolution against its enemies. In May 1790, the Assembly proclaimed: "the French nation renounces the undertaking of any war with a view to making conquests, and it will never use its forces against the liberty of any people."[27] Initially, even the annexation of adjacent territories where there was strong popular support for the Revolution, such as Nice and Savoy, seemed objectionable to revolutionaries fearful of a policy of conquest. Gradually, however, the doctrine of France's "natural frontier" and the idea of granting "fraternity and aid to all peoples who wish to recover their liberty" displaced these initial doubts.[28] The French armies "saw themselves not as conquerors but as liberators, at the service of a universal ideal of liberty, equality, and fraternity," and in many regions of Europe they were indeed welcomed by republican forces.[29]

With Napoléon's *coup d'état* in 1799, this revolutionary impulse was stopped. Authoritarianism prevailed over democracy, liberation gave way to plunder and conquest, and reforms outside France were imposed rather than enabled.[30] By 1812, Napoléon had created an empire that covered most of Europe. Two years later, this overextended empire was defeated, and a new world order was fashioned, primarily by the United Kingdom, Austria, Prussia, and Russia.[31] From then on, the monarchies of Europe stressed the need to prevent revolution and disorder, and put forward their own worldview, anchored in the conventional notions of reason of state and balance of power. In 1830, Austria's State Chancellor, Metternich, succinctly summarized the dominant ideology of his times: "In no epoch of modern history has society been presented with more dangers than in the present, because of the upheaval in France. The true ... and last anchor left for the welfare of Europe lies in the understanding between

---

[27] Quoted in George Rudé, *Revolutionary Europe, 1783–1815*, London, Fontana Press, 1964, p. 208.

[28] *Ibid.*, p. 210.

[29] Robert Gildea, *Barricades and Borders: Europe 1800–1914*, third edition, Oxford University Press, 2003, p. 53.

[30] *Ibid.*, pp. 35–36; Michael Howard, *War in European History*, Oxford University Press, 1976, p. 82; Rudé, *Revolutionary Europe, 1783–1815*, pp. 214–15.

[31] G. John Ikenberry, *After Victory: Institutions, Strategic Restraint, and the Rebuilding of Order after Major Wars*, Princeton University Press, 2001, pp. 80–85.

the great powers, based on the conservative foundations of their happy and grand alliance."[32]

The worldview of the right rested less on abstract ideals than on pragmatic political considerations. It reflected, as well, a more skeptical view of human reason and democracy.[33] In this perspective, best articulated by Prussian military thinker Carl von Clausewitz, peace was merely the temporary absence of war. It was unlikely to last because political interests would always differ, and war was "a continuation of political intercourse, carried on with other means."[34] War was "part of man's social existence." It was a "clash between major interests, which is resolved by bloodshed – that is the only way in which it differs from other conflicts."[35] For Clausewitz, only military force could fashion the world order. At most, "attached to force" were "certain self-imposed, imperceptible limitations hardly worth mentioning, known as international law and custom, but they scarcely weaken it."[36] The German empire led by Chancellor Otto von Bismarck became the incarnation of this conservative, balance-of-power diplomacy, based on military strength, war readiness, and alliances. This realist approach was successful in so far as there were no major wars in Europe between 1871 and 1914.[37]

International affairs, argued conservative intellectuals, could not be governed by reason and morality because the world was an anarchical society where might made right. As Bismarck observed, the best way to preserve peace was to prepare for war. Politicians on the right, then, generally favored a strong military, and preferred to shield it as much as possible from the control of parliaments, always liable to reduce commitments and expenditures. In line with the right's belief in discipline and hierarchy, the military was also valued as a molder of fit and patriotic men, and as an anchor for social order.

The conservative politics of the nineteenth century could not prevent the rise of a vision of world order that was critical of the very idea of peace through force. Indeed, many strands of thought converged to

---

[32] Metternich, quoted in Jonathan Haslam, *No Virtue Like Necessity: Realist Thought in International Relations since Machiavelli*, New Haven, Yale University Press, 2002, p. 115.

[33] Knutsen, *A History of International Relations Theory*, pp. 143–45.

[34] *Ibid.*, p. 87.   [35] von Clausewitz, *On War*, p. 149.   [36] *Ibid.*, p. 75.

[37] Jean-Baptiste Duroselle, *L'Europe de 1815 à nos jours: vie politique et relations internationales*, Paris, PUF, 1964, p. 149.

update and reinforce the pacifist point of view initially defined by Rousseau and Kant. First, the progress of trade led many to believe, in Britain in particular, that commercial exchanges and prosperity would make war irrelevant and bring about international cooperation and peace. "Free Trade," emphasized Richard Cobden MP in the 1840s, "is God's diplomacy, and there is no other certain way of uniting people in bonds of peace."[38] Second, liberal and national principles made the primacy granted to power in international affairs increasingly dubious. Such principles were actively promoted by peace societies and the international peace movement that emerged in the first half of the nineteenth century.[39] These early social movements insisted that princes and autocrats, not peoples, were the ones who launched wars; that democratic choice, not secret arrangements among the great powers, should determine the destiny of nations; and that a world ruled by public opinion would most certainly be a peaceful world.[40] Third, if reason and freedom could bring about new regimes on a national scale, they could probably work the same way on a world scale. International law and institutions, in particular, should make a lasting peace possible. The creation of the League of Nations in 1919 was premised on this belief in rationality, law, and democracy.[41] The First World War cast doubt on the idea that citizens and workers would be reluctant to go to war against other citizens and workers, but the left's internationalist perspective nonetheless remained influential.

The left, wrote E. H. Carr, a man of liberal orientation who ended up writing a realist book during the inter-war period, believes in "reason." Unlike the right, Carr also contended, it is optimistic about human nature, the power of ideas, and the possibilities of international cooperation.[42] For the left, then, military power appeared much less appealing and necessary than it did for the right. First, from a democratic perspective, free citizens, not armies, should decide the fate of nations. Second, a just world should not grant privileges on the basis of force. If men were equal, then nations should also be equal,

---

[38] Richard Cobden quoted in Haslam, *No Virtue Like Necessity*, p. 147.
[39] Howard, *War and the Liberal Conscience*, pp. 40–41.
[40] E. H. Carr, *The Twenty Years' Crisis, 1919–1939: An Introduction to the Study of International Relations*, New York, Palgrave, 2001 (first edition 1939), p. 27.
[41] *Ibid.*, p. 29.   [42] *Ibid.*, p. 18.

whatever their size or military strength.[43] Third, as the incarnation of order and hierarchy, and often as the privileged realm of the aristocracy, the army was rarely a cherished institution on the left. Typically, progressives sought to reduce military expenditures, increase parliamentary control over the army, and democratize recruitment and promotions. Armies, remarked historian Alfred Vagts, "have seen their enemies on the Left, just as the Left has come to view them as foes."[44]

When threatened, a progressive regime would be best defended not by a traditional army, but by the nation itself. "The 'nation in arms'," stated French socialist Jean Jaurès in 1914, "represents the system best calculated to realize national defense."[45] As the expression of democracy, the "nation in arms" would pursue just ends and contribute to bring peace. The best approach, however, was still to avoid military engagement. Up to July 1914, Jaurès advocated a general strike to oppose France's entry into war. At the end of that month, however, the socialist leader was assassinated by a right-wing militant and, soon after, his party rallied to support the national war effort like the rest of the left in Europe.[46] In the 1930s, most on the left also accepted, albeit reluctantly, the necessity to fight Nazi Germany, a regime that embodied a radical form of right-wing authoritarianism, racism, and militarism. In parallel, in the Soviet Union, Stalin used the doctrine of "socialism in one country" to reconcile the internationalist roots of the revolution with the more proximate goals of consolidating the regime and preparing for total war, in a context of impending military threat.[47]

Overall, the inclination of liberals, social-democrats, and socialists remained to resist militarism and war, in opposition to parties of the

---

[43] *Ibid.*, p. 149.

[44] Alfred Vagts, *A History of Militarism: Civilian and Military*, New York, Free Press, 1967, p. 315.

[45] Jean Jaurès, quoted in Sigmund Neumann and Mark von Hagen, "Engels and Marx on Revolution, War, and the Army in Society," in Peter Paret (ed.), *Makers of Modern Strategy; From Machiavelli to the Nuclear Age*, Princeton University Press, 1986, p. 280.

[46] Eley, *Forging Democracy*, pp. 124–27.

[47] Condoleezza Rice, "The Making of Soviet Strategy," in Paret (ed.), *Makers of Modern Strategy*, pp. 660–63; Robert W. Cox, "'Real Socialism' in Historical Perspective," in Robert W. Cox, with Timothy J. Sinclair (eds.), *Approaches to World Order*, Cambridge University Press, 1996, pp. 212–15.

right, which were more fatalist. With the rise of socialism in the late nineteenth century, this pacifist standpoint was reinforced by a distinct understanding of the inherent unity of the international working class. War, argued the socialists, served only the interests of the bourgeoisie, and workers should oppose it, and go on strike if necessary.[48] By the turn of the century, socialism had become the dominant political stream on the left.

Capitalism and socialism

In the nineteenth century, the most important revolution was not political but economic. With the spread of democracy and the rise of liberal nationalism, there were undoubtedly major political upheavals, but nothing compared to the Industrial Revolution which originated in the United Kingdom. Throughout this period of buoyant expansion, unprecedented wealth was created and entire societies were restructured.

Between 1500 and 1820, the economy of the United Kingdom had grown faster than most economies in the world, at a rate of almost 1 percent a year (0.80 percent compared to a world average of 0.32 percent). From 1820 to 1870, this growth rate more than doubled to reach 2.05 percent per year, compared to a global rate of 0.93 percent.[49] On an annual basis, such an increase in growth may appear modest, but accumulated over five decades it produced major transformations. In fifty years, the per capita income of Britain almost doubled, rising from $1,706 to $3,190 (1990 dollars). By 1870, with 2.5 percent of the world's population, the United Kingdom accounted for 9 percent of world production.[50]

Science and technological innovations contributed significantly to this process of economic change, which gradually spread to Germany, France, and the United States. The steam engine, in particular, multiplied the productive capacity of a number of industries. Overall, however, the techniques in use remained relatively simple, and production continued to be predominantly labor-intensive. The revolution was in

---

[48] Peter Brock and Nigel Young, *Pacifism in the Twentieth Century*, University of Toronto Press, 1999, p. 116.

[49] Angus Maddison, *The World Economy. Volume I: A Millennial Perspective; Volume II: Historical Statistics*, Paris, OECD, 2006, p. 640.

[50] *Ibid.*, pp. 638–42.

fact less technological than social. It stemmed from the mobilization of large numbers of workers and machines in factories producing on a continuous basis for the market. A new society was thus born, defined by two classes, workers who owned nothing but the labor they could sell for wages, and capitalist employers driven to innovate and invest by competition and by the search for profit.[51]

Capitalism was triumphant and, with it, a political creed that came to occupy a central place in the vision of the right: *laissez-faire*. Introduced in the eighteenth century by the French physiocrats, the idea of *laissez-faire* was refined by Scottish political economist Adam Smith. In *The Wealth of Nations* (1776), Smith explained that generally, an individual "intends only his own gain, and he is in this, as in many other cases, led by an invisible hand to promote an end which was no part of his intention.... By pursuing his own interest he frequently promotes that of the society more effectually than when he really intends to promote it."[52]

As a reformist and moral philosopher, Adam Smith foresaw the tensions that could arise with the advent of a market society.[53] "Wherever there is great property," he observed, "there is great inequality...the affluence of the few supposes the indigence of the many." Following John Locke, Smith sided with the owner of valuable property, "which is acquired by the labour of many years, or perhaps of many successive generations" against the potential "injustice" of the poor, the owner's "unknown enemies." Still, Smith admitted that "civil government, so far as it is instituted for the security of property, is in reality instituted for the defence of the rich against the poor, or of those who have some property against those who have none at all."[54] Smith's followers, it must be said, tended to be less concerned by inequality. The Rev. Thomas Robert Malthus, for one, presented poverty as a necessary check to prevent population growth from exceeding nature's capacity to provide for food.

---

[51] Eric J. Hobsbawm, *Industry and Empire: From 1750 to the Present Day*, Harmondsworth, Penguin, 1968, pp. 56–68.

[52] Adam Smith, *An Inquiry into the Nature and Causes of the Wealth of Nations* (1776), London, Methuen, 1904, The Library of Economics and Liberty, Book 4, Chapter 2 (IV.2.9) (www.econlib.org/library/Smith/smWN.html).

[53] Albert S. Lindemann, *A History of European Socialism*, New Haven, Yale University Press, 1983, pp. 31–33.

[54] Smith, *An Inquiry into the Nature and Causes of the Wealth of Nations*, Book 5, Chapter 1 (V.1.45 and V.1.55).

In the nineteenth century, the *laissez-faire* approach became encompassing. Starting as an argument against the excessive interventions of the mercantilist state, it developed into a full-fledged vision of society, favorable to a free labor market, to a monetary system governed by the gold standard, and to free trade.[55] The promotion of a market for labor proved particularly critical because it concerned the very organization of society. Jean-Baptiste Say in France and David Ricardo in the United Kingdom advocated the "fair and free competition of the market" for labor, so that wages could rise and fall with demand and supply. If demand proved insufficient and wages fell below subsistence levels, some of the poor would "perish," but the labor supply would then decline and, as a consequence, wages would rise again. It is certainly "a great unhappiness to be poor," observed Say, "but it is an even greater unhappiness to be surrounded by people as poor as oneself."[56] In this perspective, it was in the interest of the poor to let the rich progress, since only the rich could employ them.

In 1834, the parliament of the United Kingdom adopted the Poor Law Amendment Act, which abolished previous forms of relief for the poor and left them with a choice between market wages and forced labor in workhouses. In 1844, the Bank Charter Act granted the Bank of England the exclusive power to issue banknotes and demanded that new banknotes be backed by gold, a measure that introduced an automatic, market-like mechanism for monetary regulation. In 1846, the Corn Laws were repealed, signaling the victory of free trade over protectionist arguments.[57] "By the middle of the nineteenth century," notes Eric Hobsbawm, "government policy in Britain came as near *laissez-faire* as has ever been practicable in a modern state."[58] Elsewhere in Europe, transformations were less radical but they proceeded along similar lines.

On the left, of course, industrial capitalism, *laissez-faire*, and the "invariable laws of nature" were not perceived as positively. Over a century, wages and working-class living standards would rise with

---

[55] Karl Polanyi, *The Great Transformation: The Political and Economic Origins of Our Time*, Boston, Beacon Press, 1944, pp. 135–36.

[56] Jean-Baptiste Say, *Cours complet d'économie politique* (1828–29), quoted in Michel Beaud, *A History of Capitalism 1500–1980*, New York, Monthly Review Press, 1983, p. 78.

[57] Polanyi, *The Great Transformation*, p. 138.

[58] Hobsbawm, *Industry and Empire*, p. 233.

economic growth but much misery was created in the process.[59] Work in the new industries was hard, unhealthy, and poorly paid. Women and children as well as men worked extremely long hours, often in cruel conditions. In a time when workers mostly walked to work, industrial life also brought families to dwell in miserable housing, packed into dense, dirty, polluted, and ill-equipped urban centers. "Every day that I live," wrote an American visitor in Manchester in 1845, "I thank Heaven that I am not a poor man with a family in England."[60] In 1832, the squalid conditions of British cities contributed to a cholera epidemic that killed around 31,000 persons. Between 1845 and 1850, famine killed up to a million people in Ireland, and brought two million more to leave for England, where they contributed to depress the lowest wages.[61]

Gradually, industrial workers were coming together and organizing, to protest such conditions. From the 1820s to the 1840s, riots, strikes, and protests multiplied in Britain and on the continent, and a number of working-class, trade unionist, and socialist movements emerged. Workers fought for better labor conditions, for the right to organize freely, and for the vote.[62] Intellectuals such as Henri de Saint-Simon, Robert Owen, and Pierre Proudhon proposed socialist objectives for this new age, based on the idea that all human beings were equal in worth and entitled to the same rights. In their view, only the replacement of capitalist exploitation by socialism could make it possible to fully realize social justice and equality.[63] These early socialists anticipated many of the conclusions that would soon be developed by Karl Marx and Friedrich Engels. Their standpoint, however, tended to be ethical and utopian more than analytical, and their politics hesitated between reformism and conspiracy. Marx and Engels broke with this tradition in both respects. They offered an elaborate explanation of the economic and social forces at work in a

---

[59] Robin W. Winks and Joan Neuberger, *Europe and the Making of Modernity, 1815–1914*, Oxford University Press, 2005, pp. 113–14.

[60] Quoted in Hobsbawm, *Industry and Empire*, p. 95.

[61] Christopher Harvie, "Revolution and the Rule of Law (1789–1851)," in Kenneth O. Morgan (ed.), *The Oxford Illustrated History of Britain*, Oxford University Press, 1986, pp. 445–51.

[62] Beaud, *A History of Capitalism 1500–1980*, pp. 102–5.

[63] Leszek Kolakowski, *Main Currents of Marxism: Its Origins, Growth and Dissolution. I. The Founders*, Oxford University Press, 1978, pp. 218–21.

modern capitalist economy, and they put forward an ambitious political strategy to bring about a revolution, based on the international organization of the working class.[64]

In *Capital* (1867), Marx argued, like Smith and Ricardo before him, that labor was the source of all value. For him, though, this reality implied that the capitalist appropriation of labor was inherently exploitative since wage earners necessarily lost the surplus they produced. "Capital is dead labour, that, vampire-like, only lives by sucking living labour, and lives the more, the more labour it sucks."[65] This exploitation was bound to expand, because it was driven by competition and the laws of accumulation. Capitalism transformed the world in an apparently unstoppable process: "The bourgeoisie cannot exist without constantly revolutionising the instruments of production, and thereby the relations of production, and with them the whole relations of society.... The need of a constantly expanding market for its products chases the bourgeoisie over the entire surface of the globe. It must nestle everywhere, settle everywhere, establish connexions everywhere."[66] In the end, however, capitalist accumulation would prove self-defeating. First, the laws of capital would engender increasingly severe economic crises, because competition and the use of capital-intensive technologies would tend to lower the rate of profit, concentrate property, and depress the demand for goods. Second, an increasingly united working class would revolt and bring about socialism and, later, communism. A confrontation between the bourgeoisie and the working class was indeed bound to come.[67] "The history of all hitherto existing society is the history of class struggles," wrote Marx and Engels in the *Communist Manifesto*. This vision of class conflicts clearly demarcated them from earlier socialists. Equality would not be achieved through education and reform, or through conspiracies, but rather through the organization of a broad and international working-class movement.

---

[64] *Ibid.*, pp. 222–24; Eley, *Forging Democracy*, pp. 38–40.
[65] Karl Marx, *Capital*, Volume I (1867), Moscow, Progress Publishers, 1887, Chapter 10, Section 1 (www.marxists.org/archive/marx/works/1867-c1/index.htm).
[66] Karl Marx and Friedrich Engels, *Manifesto of the Communist Party* (1848), Moscow, Progress Publishers, 1969, Section 1 (www.marxists.org/archive/marx/works/1848/communist- manifesto/index.htm).
[67] *Ibid.*

In 1864 in London, the International Workingmen's Association, later known as the First International, was founded. In the following decades, socialist parties progressed considerably, obtained the right to vote for male workers, and took up to 40 percent of the vote in national elections. Trade unions also grew remarkably, in the context of less repressive labor laws, and they organized into federations, often in association with socialist parties.[68] When the Second International was formed in 1889, it was less the expression of a variety of small radical movements than a federation of powerful parties.

As these parties gained ground, the key question became one of strategy. Should socialists participate in electoral politics and seek power through regular means? A victory seemed probable given the numerical importance of the working class, but would the bourgeoisie accept defeat, and let socialists abolish its privileges? Despite certain doubts, throughout Europe the parliamentarian strategy prevailed, often with much success. In Germany, Austria, Finland, Sweden, Norway, Denmark, and Belgium, social democrats became the dominant party between the beginning of the twentieth century and the 1930s.[69] The Soviet Revolution of 1917, however, brought the revolutionary strategy back to the forefront and soon opened a major schism on the left. Already divided by the First World War and unable to maintain the Second International, social democrats were further weakened by the creation of a Third International led by Moscow in 1919, and the emergence across Europe of new communist parties dedicated to revolution.[70] These divisions within the left did not prevent trade unions and socialist parties winning political concessions in the 1920s, and they did not alter either the basic nature of the conflict between the left and the right. The right advocated *laissez-faire* and the market economy, in spite of the Great Depression of the 1930s, while the left fought for socialism, whether through a reformist or a more radical road.

The rise of organized labor and the new threat represented by the Bolsheviks engendered a hardening on the right. In many countries, authoritarian governments restrained democracy in the name of

---

[68] Eley, *Forging Democracy*, pp. 66–70.
[69] Adam Przeworksi and John Sprague, *Paper Stones: A History of Electoral Socialism*, University of Chicago Press, 1986, pp. 27–28.
[70] Eley, *Forging Democracy*, pp. 176–78.

anti-communism and social order. More importantly, fascist regimes emerged in Italy and Germany that delineated a new and radical right-wing project, putting forward a previously unseen mix of conservative values, mass mobilization, aggressive nationalism, militarism, and racism. However extreme and criminal, this project remained an avatar of the right's fight against socialism. Without socialism, notes Hobsbawm, "there would have been no fascism."[71]

The colonial enterprise

The period between the American Revolution and the Second World War was also an age of worldwide Western expansion and domination. This expansion climaxed between 1880 and 1914, when most of the world outside Europe and the Americas was under the formal or indirect rule of fewer than ten states (namely the United Kingdom, France, Germany, Italy, the Netherlands, Belgium, the United States, and Japan). The entire Pacific and most of Africa were split into formal colonies of the great powers, most of Asia was divided into zones of influence, Latin America was in effect under American domination, and the main settlers' colonies (Canada, Australia, New Zealand) belonged to the British Empire.[72]

It has often been argued that imperialism and colonialism defied the left–right cleavage, because they stemmed from a broad consensus among the elites of the great powers. This is partly true. The idea that Western societies were more "civilized" and bound to lead the world was indeed common, and it often led political actors and thinkers, on both the left and the right, to accept colonialism. Even among European socialists and pacifists, notes Partha Sarathi Gupta, "a condescending attitude to non-European civilizations and an implicit assumption of leadership" generally cohabited with "an abhorrence of colonial wars."[73]

The full picture, however, requires nuances. First, in the era of the American and the French Revolutions, a strong anti-colonial current was already associated with the left's fight for democracy. Second,

---

[71] Eric J. Hobsbawm, *The Age of Extremes: The Short Twentieth Century, 1914–1991*, London, Abacus, 1994, p. 124.

[72] Eric J. Hobsbawm, *The Age of Empire: 1875–1914*, London, Abacus, 1987, pp. 56–59.

[73] Partha Sarathi Gupta, *Imperialism and the British Labour Movement, 1914–1964*, New York, Holmes & Meier, 1975, p. 8.

even when they supported colonialism, European socialists tended to do so for the sake of social progress more than in the name of an inherent inequality between races. Third, at the beginning of the twentieth century, it was the left that led the fight against colonialism.

In the eighteenth century, the philosophers of the Enlightenment proclaimed the unity of mankind, the moral equality of all humans, and the intrinsic value of the world's different cultures. They also opposed imperial rule and colonialism, as well as slavery. Jean-Jacques Rousseau, Denis Diderot, and Immanuel Kant were clear on that count, and so were thinkers such as Adam Smith and Edmund Burke.[74] The French revolutionaries referred to the ideal of equality when they debated the fate of the colonies. "Your interest, that of Europe and that of the world demands that you do not hesitate and sacrifice a colony rather than a principle," Dupont de Nemours told the National Assembly in 1791.[75] Pushed by revolts that shook the colonies, the National Convention abolished slavery in 1794, and it also ended colonial inferiority, making all inhabitants full French citizens. "Until now," said Georges Danton to the Convention, "we have decreed freedom selfishly and for us only. Today, we proclaim…universal freedom."[76] Napoléon reversed these advances and re-established slavery and colonialism, but the clock was not turned back entirely. Led by Toussaint Louverture and later by Jean-Jacques Dessalines, Haiti became the first black independent republic in 1804.

In the nineteenth century, this initial impulse against imperialism weakened and, in Europe at least, the necessity of colonialism became almost consensual. While denouncing its worst aspects, even liberals and socialists tended to approve the colonial entreprise. Many arguments seemed to justify imperial rule. First, with the development of communications and transportation, power politics increasingly took on a global dimension. Building an empire came to be seen as a direct corollary of a country's influence and prestige in the world. "The future is with the great Empires" declared British colonial secretary

---

[74] Sankar Muthu, *Enlightenment against Empire*, Princeton University Press, 2003, pp. 1–4; Jennifer Pitts, *A Turn to Empire; The Rise of Imperial Liberalism in Britain and France*, Princeton University Press, 2005, pp. 242–43.

[75] Dupont de Nemours, quoted in Gilles Manceron, *Marianne et les colonies: une introduction à l'histoire coloniale de la France*, Paris, La Découverte, 2003, p. 49. Our translation.

[76] Georges Danton, quoted in *ibid.*, p. 54. Our translation.

Joseph Chamberlain in 1902.[77] Expansion, said Cecil Rhodes, the British-born South African who gave his name to Rhodesia – now Zimbabwe – is everything, and a country "must take as many pieces of the world as possible."[78] Indeed, inaction would only lead to the occupation of a territory by a rival power. The politics of abstention, affirmed Jules Ferry, probably the politician who best articulated France's colonial ambition, could only lead to decay. France "must make its influence felt all over the world, and bring in everywhere possible its language, its way of life, its flag, its army, and its genius."[79]

Second, in an age of spectacular economic expansion, industrial nations felt the need to secure natural resources, markets for their goods, and opportunities for capital. At the turn of the twentieth century, J. A. Hobson noted that the word "imperialism" was "on everybody's lips," and that it had acquired a distinctly economic meaning.[80] On the right, imperialism was perceived as a commercial and economic necessity. "Colonial policy," explained Ferry, was "the daughter of industrial policy." On the left, the same evolution was understood more critically, but it remained seen as basically unavoidable. In his famous essay on imperialism, Lenin presented it as the "highest stage of capitalism."[81]

Third, colonialism was widely interpreted as a moral duty. The British referred to the "white man's burden" and the French to their "civilizing mission." At the 1884–85 Berlin Conference convened by European powers to regulate the division of Africa into colonies, European states insisted on the "preservation of the native tribes" and on the importance of "bringing home to them the blessings of civilization."[82] There was, of course, a paternalistic, even racist, dimension to this moral imperative, but the idea of bringing the

---

[77] Joseph Chamberlain, quoted in Winfried Baumgart, *Imperialism: The Idea and Reality of British and French Colonial Expansion, 1880–1914*, Oxford University Press, 1982, p. 72.

[78] Cecil Rhodes, quoted in Duroselle, *L'Europe de 1815 à nos jours*, p. 342. Our translation.

[79] Jules Ferry, quoted in Raould Girardet, *L'idée coloniale en France de 1871 à 1962*, Paris, La Table Ronde, 1972, p. 86. Our translation.

[80] J. A. Hobson, quoted in Hobsbawm, *The Age of Empire*, p. 60.

[81] Ferry and Lenin, quoted in Beaud, *A History of Capitalism*, pp. 137 and 140.

[82] General Act, Berlin West Africa Conference, quoted in Neta C. Crawford, *Argument and Change in World Politics: Ethics, Decolonization, and Humanitarian Intervention*, Cambridge University Press, 2002, p. 210.

benefits of progress to the peoples of the world was also, up to a point, genuine. The moral ambiguity of colonialism appeared clearly in the 1919 League of Nations Mandate system, which treated "peoples not yet able to stand by themselves" as "a sacred trust of civilization," but also opened the door to equality and self-determination.[83]

This ambiguity is best understood in light of the divergent readings the right and the left gave of imperialism, even at the peak of the colonial enterprise. On the right, the great powers seemed bound to dominate the world, because peoples were just too unequal. Why, asked French economist Paul Leroy-Beaulieu in 1874, should "the civilized people of the West ... leave perhaps half the world to small groups of ignorant men, who are powerless, who are truly retarded children dispersed over boundless territories, or else to decrepit populations without energy and without direction, truly old men incapable of any effort, of any organized and far-seeing action?"[84] The economic expansion of Europe, combined with what was interpreted as scientific evidence in favor of racism – such as the idea of the "survival of the fittest" derived from Charles Darwin's theory of evolution – tended to reinforce the right's notion of a fundamentally unequal world.[85] Typically, on the left, inequality was understood less as a natural condition than as an injustice, bound to be challenged in due time. Karl Marx, for instance, viewed England as an "unconscious tool of history," which was driven "by the vilest interests" and inflicted misery. But for him, colonialism also brought closer the day when a new Indian society would emerge, either when "in Great Britain itself the now ruling classes shall have been supplanted by the industrial proletariat, or [when] the Hindoos themselves shall have grown strong enough to throw off the English yoke altogether."[86]

It was this vision of human equality that inspired the fight against colonialism, which lasted for a good part of the twentieth century and was primarily led by the left. In the South, the decolonization

---

[83] Covenant of the League of Nations, quoted in Crawford, *Argument and Change in World Politics*, p. 261.

[84] Leroy-Beaulieu, quoted in Beaud, *A History of Capitalism*, p. 140.

[85] Pitts, *A Turn to Empire*, pp. 19–20.

[86] Karl Marx, "The British Rule in India," *New-York Daily Tribune*, June 25, 1853; and "The Future Results of British Rule in India," *New-York Daily Tribune*, August 8, 1853 (www.marxists.org/archive/marx/works/1853/06/25. htm and www.marxists.org/archive/marx/works/1853/07/22.htm).

movement was spearheaded by educated elites who sought national self-determination and modernization. They made some references to old values and cultural traits to obtain the support of traditional forces and to build new national identities, but their own orientation was secular, egalitarian, and, often, socialist.[87] Mustafa Kemal Atatürk, for instance, the founder and first president of the Republic of Turkey, favored a secular and modernist state, gender equality, and a culture more oriented toward Europe than the Islamic world, a preference clearly expressed in the replacement of arabic script by the roman alphabet. Mahatma Gandhi's fight for independence was likewise intimately connected to his desire to abolish the old caste system and transform Indian society. African leaders also defined their vision of pan-Africanism and national liberation in reference to socialism and communism.[88] In response to such developments, the initial indifference and paternalistic attitude of the Western left gradually gave place to an engagement in favor of decolonization. The final picture was not without contradictions, since many socialists clung to colonial views, but overall the liberation movements of the South found their best allies among socialists and communists, as well as within some humanitarian and Christian groups.[89]

In 1945, at the end of the Second World War, about a third of the world's population still lived in territories identified by the United Nations as "non self-governing." Three decades later, most of these territories had become independent countries and members of the UN General Assembly. "To go to the UN in 1962," explained a former Jamaican ambassador, "for Jamaica to stand before the world and claim the right to participate and for other countries to do so, this was extraordinary."[90] Today, less than two million people live in

---

[87] Hobsbawm, *The Age of Extremes*, pp. 201–02 and 208–09.

[88] Yves Person, "Le socialisme en Afrique noire," in Jacques Droz (ed.), *Histoire générale du socialisme, Tome 3: de 1919 à 1945*, Paris, PUF, 1977, pp. 620–24.

[89] Eric J. Hobsbawm, *Nations and Nationalism since 1780: Programme, Myth, Reality*, Cambridge University Press, 1990, pp. 148–50; Girardet, *L'idée coloniale en France de 1871 à 1962*, pp. 367–402; Gilles Manceron, "La gauche et la colonisation," in Jean-Jacques Becker and Gilles Candar (eds.), *Histoire des gauches en France. Volume 1: L'héritage du XIXᵉ siècle*, Paris, La Découverte, 2004, pp. 531–44; Gupta, *Imperialism and the British Labour Movement*, pp. 391–93.

[90] Don Mills, former Jamaican ambassador to the United Nations, quoted in Louis Emmerij, Richard Jolly, and Thomas G. Weiss, *Ahead of the Curve? UN Ideas and Global Challenges*, Bloomington, Indiana University Press, 2001, p. 25.

"non self-governing" territories, mostly small islands.[91] It may be too soon, however, to conclude, as did Tanzanian president Julius Nyerere in 1990, that colonialism has become "almost a thing of the past."[92] Indeed, the legacy of colonialism still lives within nation-states, in the unequal and difficult relationships between indigenous and non-native peoples.[93] This question, however, would come to light later in time. It is a story for another chapter.

Conclusion

As they defined their contending visions, the political forces of the left and of the right constructed the modern world together. They fought over the meaning of democracy, disagreed on the necessity of war and on the possibility of peace, debated the respective merits of capitalism and socialism, and diverged in their interpretations of colonization and decolonization. The right preferred hierarchy and order to equality and participation, and it looked favorably at peace through force, to capitalism and *laissez-faire*, and to the colonial enterprise. The left demanded a more inclusive democratic politics, opposed war and military interventions in most circumstances, and advocated various stripes of socialism. It also appeared more critical toward imperialism and more supportive of decolonization.

At times, this divide took violent, indeed extreme forms. Hitler was on the right, Stalin on the left. In many instances, however, the conflict between the left and the right was expressed in the language of democratic politics, through debates, popular actions, and electoral mobilizations. When this happened, the two sides often influenced one another to generate a new consensus. This was the case with the right to vote, with the creation of international organizations to sustain peace, with the development of social democracy as a compromise between *laissez-faire* and socialism, and with decolonization. Yet in due course every new consensus would give rise to different lines of opposition, consistent with the broader politics of equality delineated by the left and the right.

[91] United Nations, "The United Nations and Decolonization: History" (www.un.org/Depts/dpi/decolonization/history.htm).
[92] Julius Nyerere, quoted in Emmerij, Jolly and Weiss, *Ahead of the Curve?*, p. 25.
[93] Alan C. Cairns, *Citizens Plus: Aboriginal Peoples and the Canadian State*, Vancouver, UBC Press, 2000, pp. 19–46.

5 | The age of universality (1945–1980)

At the end of the Second World War, the United States was in a unique position. As the unchallenged global power, it controlled about half of the world's production, dominated in most technologies and resources, and disposed of a victorious and powerful army. "Today," wrote British scholar Harold Laski in December 1947, "literally hundreds of millions of Europeans and Asiatics know that both the quality and the rhythm of their lives depend upon decisions made in Washington."[1] The Americans would indeed play a central role in the shaping of a postwar order governed by new international norms and institutions. Many uncertainties and tensions remained, however, some inherited from the unresolved conflicts of the inter-war years, others from the new alignment of forces that emerged from the war.

Chief among these uncertainties was the challenge posed to the new hegemonic power by the rise and assertion of its former ally and now rival, the Soviet Union. "At the present moment in world history," President Harry Truman told a joint session of Congress in March 1947, "nearly every nation must choose between alternative ways of life...I believe that it must be the policy of the United States to support free peoples who are resisting attempted subjugation by armed minorities or by outside pressures."[2] The Cold War conflict Truman announced was profound and universal. It defined what Kemal Dervis, former Turkish Minister of the Economy and then head of the United Nations Development Programme (UNDP), aptly described as an enduring "global ideological battle." "On the right," explained Dervis, "there was, for want of a better word, 'capitalism,'

---

[1] Harold J. Laski, quoted in G. John Ikenberry, *After Victory: Institutions, Strategic Restraint, and the Rebuilding of Order after Major Wars*, Princeton University Press, 2001, p. 168.

[2] Harry S. Truman, "Address to Joint Session of Congress on Aid to Greece and Turkey," March 12, 1947, The Avalon Project at Yale Law School: Truman Doctrine (www.yale.edu/lawweb/avalon/trudoc.htm).

politically liberal or not, with a system of belief in private ownership, private entrepreneurship, and markets. On the left, there was Marxism, with rejection of private property of the means of production perceived as the source of exploitation and inequity, and the trust it placed in central planning as the best mechanism to allocate resources."[3]

In its most acute and dangerous form, this confrontation of "alternative ways of life" generated an arms race that literally put in the balance the "fate of the earth."[4] More generally, it gave rise to an East–West division that incorporated most other issues of international politics, and polarized positions on the right and on the left. Even decolonization and the birth of new states tended to be interpreted as battles in the war between communism and capitalism. In due course, however, the rise of poor nations and the question of development imposed their own logic, to define a distinctive North–South cleavage. Albeit in a different manner, this new conflict would also oppose progressives and conservatives.

In comparison, the domestic politics of the countries that were not directly on the fracture line between the East and the West appeared relatively quiescent. Various expressions were used to characterize this state of affairs. Some authors spoke of a Keynesian consensus, others of a stable compromise between capital and labor. Most agreed that the new welfare state had pacified social relations, at least in advanced democracies. John Gerard Ruggie used the notion of "embedded liberalism" to connect these domestic settlements to the establishment of an open world market ruled by the dollar, and to underline the fact that rich countries successfully consolidated international market rules by embedding them into a framework of state intervention and social protection at home.[5] Using a telling image borrowed from Joseph Schumpeter, German political scientists Elmar Rieger and Stephan Leibfried explained that just as fast cars could be designed once good brakes had been invented, an open trade regime became

[3] Kemal Dervis (with Ceren Özer), *A Better Globalization: Legitimacy, Governance and Reform*, Washington, DC, Center for Global Development, 2005, pp. 12–13.

[4] Jonathan Schell, *The Fate of the Earth*, New York, Knopf, 1982.

[5] John Gerard Ruggie, "International Regimes, Transactions, and Change: Embedded Liberalism in the Postwar Economic Order," *International Organization*, vol. 36, no. 2, Spring 1982, 379–415.

politically achievable once states knew how to guarantee social protection to their citizens.[6]

This being said, the consensual character of the postwar settlements should not be exaggerated. Even within the West, the gap between the left and the right remained important. In fact, when one looks attentively at the actual contours of embedded liberalism, what appears is less an encompassing consensus than further manifestations of the global ideological battle identified by Kemal Dervis. The terms of the debate were less extreme, but the dividing lines were basically the same. At home, political parties and social movements also fought over capitalism and socialism.

The real novelty of the era was less in a putative consensus than in the scope of the debate. For the first time, politics became truly global. International negotiations included independent states from every continent and drew an unprecedented web of cleavages. All human beings were also recognized as citizens, endowed with basic democratic and social rights. In 1948, the Universal Declaration of Human Rights formally established "the equal and inalienable rights of all members of the human family."[7] In principle at least, it was becoming increasingly difficult to exclude persons on the basis of nationality, ethnicity, status, or gender. In the West, the emergence of encompassing social programs gave a tangible meaning to this evolution, as it made universal social rights a core attribute of citizenship. This was indeed the age of universality. For almost four decades, the left and the right would debate the domestic and the international implications of this new vision, and argue over the mixed economy, the welfare state, the East–West conflict, and the North–South divide.

The mixed economy

The Great Depression of the 1930s shook the liberal order and radically undermined the *laissez-faire* doctrine. The dramatic fall of industrial production, the collapse of agricultural prices, and the lasting unemployment of up to a third of the labor force made the idea of an

---

[6] Elmar Rieger and Stephan Leibfried, *Limits to Globalization: Welfare States and the World Economy*, Cambridge, Polity Press, 2003, p. 6.

[7] United Nations, *Universal Declaration of Human Rights*, adopted and proclaimed by General Assembly resolution 217 A (III) of December 10, 1948 (www.un.org/Overview/rights.html).

efficient and self-regulating market increasingly hard to sustain. Lacking a clear understanding of the problem, governments intervened to shelter their producers from a market that no longer brought prosperity. Between 1931 and 1936, European and North American states regulated domestic markets, abandoned the gold standard, and raised tariff barriers. International trade and investments, which had grown steadily until then, fell drastically, and the idea of an open world market governed by *laissez-faire* simply collapsed.[8]

Beyond the adoption of defensive measures, three broad courses of action seemed plausible. First, communism along Soviet lines, an option that appeared to be reinforced by the capacity of the USSR to keep growing in a receding world economy. Second, fascism, an orientation that claimed to move beyond the old opposition between capitalism and socialism, and also seemed able to bring economic recovery, at least in Germany. Third, a reformed liberal economy that promised to better balance market rules and state intervention into a combination that would become known as the "mixed economy."

The war sealed the fate of fascism, and the Cold War contained the expansion of communism, leaving the idea of a mixed economy dominant in most countries. This idea, however, raised many questions. In the 1930s and 1940s, governments had experimented with economic regulation, planning, collective bargaining, and social security, but these reforms had been more improvised than designed. Both experts and the general public feared in fact that the end of the world conflict would bring back a severe recession.[9] Among the issues left unresolved by the war, the most fundamental concerned the rules that would govern international exchanges, the extent to which social equality should be achieved, the specific role of the state in the economy, and the place of the working class in society.[10] At the international level, a liberal trade regime rapidly prevailed, and domestically, as will be seen below, new welfare programs allowed states to combine the pursuit of economic growth with the quest for social justice. With respect to the state and the working class, two ideas also emerged that structured the debates between the left and the right: planning and collective bargaining.

---

[8] Eric J. Hobsbawm, *The Age of Extremes: The Short Twentieth Century, 1914–1991*, London, Abacus, 1994, pp. 88–95.

[9] *Ibid.*, p. 230.

[10] Charles S. Maier, "Nineteen Forty-Five: Continuity or Rupture?," *Europa: A Journal of Interdisciplinary Studies*, vol. 5, no. 2, 1982, 109–21, pp. 120–21.

The interest in planning predated the war, and it had many sources, some on the right, others on the left. Because planning supposed state intervention in the market, and because communist regimes governed their economy with five-year plans, the idea has in general been associated with the left. As Swedish economist Gunnar Myrdal noted, however, before the twentieth century there was little reference to this notion in the socialist tradition. Karl Marx, for one, had no use for the idea.[11] Planning only came of age with the new century, first in business and then in war.

In business, planning was introduced between the 1900s and the 1920s with Frederick W. Taylor's idea of scientific management. For Taylor, applied science and engineering could raise industrial productivity significantly and, in doing so, contribute to solve social conflicts over distribution. "What we need," explained one of his followers, "is not more laws, but more facts, and the whole question will solve itself."[12] In the United States, in particular, private corporations seemed large enough to implement by themselves and voluntarily this sort of "social efficiency." With its assembly line and mass production of a modest car for the average consumer, the Ford Motor Company pushed the logic a few steps further, and offered a fascinating model to European reformers of the left and of the right, captivated by what they called Fordism and Americanism. Meanwhile, during the First World War, German engineers and heads of industry, Walther Rathenau and Wichard von Moellendorf, successfully organized their country's production and distribution to sustain the war effort, thus broadening the scope of scientific management and planning to an entire society.

In revolutionary Russia, Lenin and his economic advisors took notice. The Soviet Union would emulate the Taylor system "and adapt it to our purposes."[13] In Europe, planning also appealed to the left, because its reliance on the power of the state seemed to push back

---

[11] Gunnar Myrdal, *Beyond the Welfare State: Economic Planning and Its International Implications*, New Haven, Yale University Press, 1960, pp. 4–8.

[12] Henry L. Gantt, quoted in Charles S. Maier, *In Search of Stability: Explorations in Historical Political Economy*, Cambridge University Press, 1987, p. 25.

[13] V. I. Lenin, quoted in James C. Scott, *Seeing Like a State: How Certain Schemes to Improve the Human Condition Have Failed*, New Haven, Yale University Press, 1998, p. 101.

laissez-faire and prepare the ground for socialism.[14] On the right there was more reluctance, but planning often seemed unavoidable. For instance, in Italy and Germany, the new fascist leaders promised to do away with state socialism and the planned economy, but they rapidly moved toward a command economy where the state effectively planned autarkic industrial development and war.[15] Elsewhere, many on the liberal right could not resist, either, a scientific approach that promised to settle threatening social conflicts.[16]

When the war ended, planning became the order of the day. The Great Depression had discredited *laissez-faire* and both the reforms of the New Deal period and the efficiency of war economies suggested that state intervention could work. John Maynard Keynes' new economic theory also supported the idea that enlightened macro-economic management could prevent damaging business cycles and sustain full employment and prosperity. The left and the right did not agree, however, on the extent of state intervention in the new mixed economy. Overall, the left wished to nationalize key industries and pursue extensive planning, and the right preferred as much market freedom as possible.

The American debate was a case in point. Before the war was even over, conservatives organized to prevent what they saw as excessive state intervention. Business leaders, Republicans, and Southern Democrats mobilized to defeat the ambitious reforms implemented by Northern Democrats and New Deal bureaucrats during the thirties. Now dominant in Congress, the right denounced "statism," and spoke of a looming "Communist state" that would eventually destroy "free enterprise" and the "American way of life."[17] "The United States," stressed Republican Congressman Jesse W. Wolcott of Michigan with an intriguing precision, was "now within 8 per cent of socialism."[18] In 1946, conservatives defeated a Bill that would have committed the American government to maintain full employment. A year later, they adopted the Taft-Hartley Act, which circumscribed in a number of ways the power of trade unions and made it more difficult for the

---

[14] Maier, *In Search of Stability*, p. 43.   [15] *Ibid.*, pp. 74 and 114.
[16] Hobsbawm, *The Age of Extremes*, pp. 96–97.
[17] Gary Mucciaroni, *The Political Failure of Employment Policy, 1945–1982*, University of Pittsburgh Press, 1990, p. 24.
[18] Jesse W. Wolcott, quoted in John Kenneth Galbraith, *American Capitalism: The Concept of Countervailing Power*, Boston, Houghton Mifflin, 1952, p. 5.

labor movement to progress and expand.[19] Planning would not become a public objective, except, as Charles Maier observes, "in a restricted sense," as a market-oriented managerial imperative to solve distribution problems by increasing productivity.[20] Even Keynesian demand management was interpreted in a minimalist fashion, without an institutional commitment to achieve high levels of employment.

The left, it must be said, was not always clear about the exact meaning of planning. In Britain, for instance, the Labour Party came to power in 1945 with a commitment to nationalize and plan, but little interest in Keynesian demand management.[21] Labour's idea of planning, however, remained vague and focused on short-term shortages, and it faced significant opposition from businesses, but also from trade unions and from a public tired of wartime controls. Planning soon gave way to a more limited commitment in favor of Keynesian and welfare policies.[22] Similarly, the French left came out of the war with a rather abstract idea of planning, and ended up focusing on nationalizations and social programs.[23] Intriguingly, it was the reformist right that salvaged the planning idea in France, to reconstruct it in a liberal and modernist perspective, as a sort of "conspiracy in the public interest between big business and big officialdom."[24] French planning, noted Peter Hall, "was designed to enhance the operation of the market rather than supersede it."[25] Likewise, in Japan "a conservative network of technologically advanced industry, finance, and the state bureaucracy [was] able to exploit the political exclusion of the

[19] Mark Blyth, *Great Transformations: Economic Ideas and Institutional Change in the Twentieth Century*, Cambridge University Press, 2002, pp. 79 86.

[20] Maier, *In Search of Stability*, pp. 129–30.

[21] Margaret Weir, "Ideas and Politics: The Acceptance of Keynesianism in Britain and the United States," in Peter A. Hall (ed.), *The Political Power of Economic Ideas: Keynesianism across Nations*, Princeton University Press, 1989, pp. 57, 67, and 80.

[22] *Ibid.*, pp. 74–75 and 80; Andrew Shonfield, *Modern Capitalism: The Changing Balance of Public and Private Power*, London, Oxford University Press, 1965, 89–99.

[23] Richard F. Kuisel, *Capitalism and the State in Modern France: Renovation and Economic Management in the Twentieth Century*, Cambridge University Press, 1981, pp. 175 and 201.

[24] Shonfield, *Modern Capitalism*, p. 128; Kuisel, *Capitalism and the State in Modern France*, pp. 248–52.

[25] Peter A. Hall, *Governing the Economy: The Politics of State Intervention in Britain and France*, Cambridge, Polity Press, 1986, p. 166.

left and organized labor" to plan in favor of business, at the expense of workers and consumers.[26]

Planning was thus dreamed by the left but implemented by the right, in a market-conforming manner. In the South, new nations were all encouraged by development economists and by the United Nations to plan for a mixed economy, and most of them did, usually with the stated objective of combining growth with social justice.[27] In practice, however, as Canadian economist Ozay Mehmet observed, international and domestic elites favored inequality, and planned for growth rather than for equity, for industrialization rather than for rural development, and for the benefit of asset-holding groups rather than for that of income earners.[28]

Similar oppositions between the left and the right manifested themselves in macro-economic management. John Maynard Keynes himself did not foresee these tensions. In British politics, Keynes was a Liberal, close to the center of the political spectrum. The economic approach he proposed distanced itself from both *laissez-faire* and socialism and, in his mind, was neither right nor left. The idea was to equip policy-makers adequately, with the right theory and the instruments necessary to regulate the business cycles and prevent both unemployment and inflation. Keynes' standpoint was that of the government, or more precisely that of the Treasury, and he never doubted that once understood, the best policies would prevail.[29]

[26] T. J. Pempel, "Japanese Foreign Economic Policy: The Domestic Bases for International Behavior," in Peter J. Katzenstein (ed.), *Between Power and Plenty: Foreign Economic Policies of Advanced Industrial States*, Madison, University of Wisconsin Press, 1978, pp. 141 and 183.

[27] Richard Jolly, Louis Emmerij, Dharam Ghai, and Frédéric Lapeyre, *UN Contributions to Development Thinking and Practice*, Bloomington, Indiana University Press, 2004, pp. 89–91; Ozay Mehmet, *Economic Planning and Social Justice in Developing Countries*, New York, St. Martin's Press, 1978, pp. 17 and 31.

[28] Mehmet, *Economic Planning and Social Justice*, pp. 31 and 271. For converging conclusions from quite distinct perspectives, see: Peter Evans, *Dependent Development: The Alliance of Multinational, State, and Local Capital in Brazil*, Princeton University Press, 1979, p. 288; and Robert H. Bates, *Markets and States in Tropical Africa: The Political Basis of Agricultural Policies*, Berkeley, University of California Press, 1981, p. 81.

[29] Gilles Dostaler, *Keynes et ses combats*, Paris, Albin Michel, 2005, pp. 166–88; Paul Diesing, *Science and Ideology in the Policy Sciences*, New York, Aldine, 1982, pp. 81–83.

Michal Kalecki, a Polish economist who was a contemporary of Keynes' and independently arrived at similar policy conclusions, was much more skeptical about governments. Time proved him right. In an article published in 1943, Kalecki argued that even though full employment would allow business to maximize profits, it would meet strong political resistance because it would also change the balance of power in society. First, the need for private investments would decrease and corporations would become less privileged or influential. Second, macro-economic management would generate public investments and enhance the role and prestige of the state. Third, a tight labor market would improve the bargaining position of workers and trade unions. In these circumstances, wrote Kalecki, we should expect less than optimal macro-economic policies, because business and conservative forces would call for restrictive policies as soon as the employment level rose, and only in true recessions would workers and the left succeed in obtaining policies favorable to growth.[30]

In the United States, this is precisely what happened after the Second World War. When he was elected president in 1952, Dwight D. Eisenhower stressed his belief in private initiative, and made lower taxes, a balanced budget, and the fight against inflation his utmost priorities. For eight years, the Republican president pursued these objectives relentlessly. Even with an inflation rate usually well below 2 percent, Eisenhower privileged restrictive budgetary policies, to the detriment of employment and economic growth.[31] Expansionary policies were only implemented after 1961, when the Democrats were back in strength in the White House and in Congress.[32]

The same pattern held in practically every country. Political parties of the right focused on low taxes, balanced budgets, and low inflation rates, at the expense of employment, and parties of the left favored income equality and redistribution, larger government budgets, and

[30] Michal Kalecki, "Political Aspects of Full Employment," in Thomas Ferguson and Joel Rogers (eds.), *The Political Economy: Readings in the Politics and Economics of American Public Policy*, New York, M. E. Sharpe, 1984, pp. 27–31.

[31] Anne Mari May, "President Eisenhower, Economic Policy, and the 1960 Presidential Election," *Journal of Economic History*, vol. 50, no. 2, June 1990, 417–27; Edward R. Tufte, *Political Control of the Economy*, Princeton University Press, 1978, pp. 15–18.

[32] Weir, "Ideas and Politics," p. 85.

high employment levels, rather than price stability.[33] In doing so, these parties were consistent with their basic ideological positions regarding equality. They also appealed to their core constituencies, unemployment being more threatening to income earners, more likely to be on the left, and inflation more disturbing for asset owners, usually closer to the political right.

In the long run, these partisan choices made a difference. Douglas A. Hibbs, who has studied the question extensively, noted that in countries where social-democratic parties governed most of the time between 1945 and 1969, average unemployment rates remained low and average inflation rates high, whereas a dominance of the right over the same period engendered higher unemployment and lower inflation rates.[34] In the end, however, the "structural unemployment" that increasingly characterized the labor market in countries where the left was weak did not even assure price stability. By the beginning of the 1980s, the nations with the worst employment records had also become the most inflation-prone.[35] This was the case because conservative governments were unable to build working compromises with organized labor.

By conviction and often through explicit alliances, parties of the left were favorable to trade unions, which represented workers and sought a more egalitarian distribution of income. They also supported collective bargaining, understood as a key social mechanism in a mixed economy. Parties of the right, on the contrary, remained suspicious of trade unions and saw collective bargaining as an impediment to the free functioning of the labor market, and as a source of unwarranted privileges and rents. Over time, these ideological preferences found their way into labor laws and shaped the regulation of industrial relations. In countries where the left dominated, a legislative and political framework conducive to unionization was put in place, and union membership rose; where the right was stronger, laws offered fewer opportunities, and in fact often raised obstacles, and union membership declined. In social-democratic Sweden, for instance, 78 percent of the workforce was unionized in 1973, and 94 percent in

[33] Tufte, *Political Control of the Economy*, p. 71.

[34] Douglas A. Hibbs, Jr., *The Political Economy of Industrial Democracies*, Cambridge, MA, Harvard University Press, 1987, pp. 299–301.

[35] David R. Cameron, "The Politics and Economics of the Business Cycle," in Ferguson and Rogers (eds.), *The Political Economy*, pp. 237–62.

1985. In the United States, these rates were only 25 percent in 1973, and down to 18 percent by 1985.[36]

These industrial relations orientations had macro-economic consequences. In countries where trade unions were strong and where the government remained committed to full employment, workers agreed to moderate their wage demands, so as to prevent inflation and avoid the use of restrictive policies that would have destroyed jobs. When unions were weak and confronted with recurrent recessions, on the other hand, organized labor used every occasion to push for immediate wage gains. This explains why countries governed by the left succeeded in consistently combining high employment levels with price stability, while those where the right prevailed ended up failing on both counts.[37]

Overall, the politics of the postwar years proved relatively favorable to planning and state intervention, to public investments and macro-economic management, and to trade unions and collective bargaining. The era of unbridled *laissez-faire* was over. The exact composition of the mixed economy nevertheless remained very much an object of contention between the left and the right. In the beginning, planning and nationalizations appeared most controversial. Soon, however, the debate shifted to the politics of macro-economic management and collective bargaining. Differences over these questions were serious and consequential. Debates often remained muted, though, because the issues involved often appeared technical or specialized. This was not so with another project that largely defined the era: the development of the welfare state.

The welfare state

In the beginning of the 1950s, hardly any country spent more than 10 percent of its gross domestic product on social welfare programs. Thirty years later, the average welfare effort of OECD countries had

---

[36] Bruce Western, *Between Class and Market: Postwar Unionization in the Capitalist Democracies*, Princeton University Press, 1997, pp. 17 and 24.
[37] David R. Cameron, "Social Democracy, Corporatism, Labour Quiescence and the Representation of Economic Interest in Advanced Capitalist Society," in John H. Goldthorpe (ed.), *Order and Conflict in Contemporary Capitalism: Studies in the Political Economy of Western European Nations*, Oxford University Press, 1984, pp. 143–78.

reached 20 percent of GDP, ranging from Sweden at 32 percent to Japan at 10 percent. The bulk of this transformation took place between 1960 and 1980, at a time when the economy itself was expanding rapidly.[38] Social transfers and services multiplied, coverage extended, and benefits improved, to provide the citizens of rich democracies with unprecedented social protection.

Economic prosperity undeniably contributed to this evolution. Between 1950 and 1973, the "golden age" of postwar capitalism, the world economy grew at an unprecedented rate of 2.9 percent a year, compared to 0.9 percent between 1913 and 1950, and 1.3 percent during the age of expansion and empire, between 1870 and 1913. In the West, progress was even more spectacular, with growth rates of around 4 percent a year in the United States and Europe, and around 8 percent in Japan.[39] Financial resources seemed readily available to improve social security, at a time when populations were relatively young and when well-paid and stable jobs were widely available. A new consensus had also emerged from the experience of worldwide depression and war, centered on an inclusive understanding of social citizenship. As stated in the Universal Declaration of Human Rights, all human beings deserved respect and dignity, and every citizen could claim social rights and expect some security. Concretely, this consensus was translated into national programs designed to protect the income of the standard household, a one-earner family headed by a male breadwinner.[40] This convergence around the idea of income security gave rise to a new debate though, on the nature and extent of social protection in an advanced democracy.

The welfare state did have antecedents, which went back to the nineteenth century. Interestingly, social insurance was first born as a conservative, indeed authoritarian project. Guided by Chancellor Otto

---

[38] Alexander Hicks, *Social Democracy and Welfare Capitalism: A Century of Income Security Politics*, Ithaca, Cornell University Press, 1999, pp. 153–55; Francis G. Castles, "The Dog That Didn't Bark: Economic Development and the Postwar Welfare State," in Stephan Leibfried (ed.), *Welfare State Futures*, Cambridge University Press, 2001, p. 40.

[39] Angus Maddison, *The World Economy. Volume I: A Millennial Perspective; Volume II: Historical Statistics*, Paris, OECD, 2006, pp. 126 and 138.

[40] Hugh Heclo, "The Social Question," in Katherine McFate, Roger Lawson, and William Julius Wilson (eds.), *Poverty, Inequality, and the Future of Social Policy: Western States in the New World Order*, New York, Russell Sage Foundation, 1995, pp. 667–75.

von Bismarck, German Emperor William I introduced health, industrial accident, and old age insurances in 1881, with the explicit objective
of undermining popular support for socialism. "The cure of social
ills," he then explained to the Reichstag, "must not be sought exclusively
in the repression of Social Democrats, but simultaneously in the
positive advancement of the welfare of the working classes."[41] Early
reforms were later implemented by Liberal-Labor coalitions and by
Catholic parties, but the major breakthrough came with the Great
Depression, when social programs definitively became associated with
the left. In the 1930s and 1940s, parties of the left and the center-left
introduced income security programs for the unemployed, the ill, and
the elderly in many countries of Europe and North America.[42] The
Second World War consolidated this evolution, and created the conditions for a full-fledged welfare state.

The report on social insurance presented at the end of 1942 by
British civil servant William Beveridge constituted a landmark in this
respect. Originally intended as a technical inquiry on social insurance,
the report captured the public imagination, in Britain and also abroad,
by delineating the contours of a comprehensive and universal social
protection regime. After the war, advocated Beveridge, the British
state should attack "five giants on the road of reconstruction": want,
disease, ignorance, squalor, and idleness. To do so, the government
should sustain full employment, provide family allowances, establish
a comprehensive health service, and, most importantly, design a
universal insurance system to protect all citizens from the main social
risks, from the cradle to the grave.[43] The scope and the universality of
Beveridge's proposal responded perfectly to the dominant preoccupations of the time. His report was discussed all over the world, and it
provided the conceptual foundations for what would become known
as the welfare state.

This vision of an inclusive world free of poverty was so powerful
and popular that all British political parties accepted its broad out-
lines. Important differences remained, however, over the meaning and

---

[41] Emperor William I, quoted in Hicks, *Social Democracy and Welfare
Capitalism*, p. 43.
[42] Hicks, *Social Democracy and Welfare Capitalism*, p. 82.
[43] Derek Fraser, *The Evolution of the British Welfare State: A History of Social
Policy since the Industrial Revolution*, third edition, Houndmills, Basingstoke,
Palgrave Macmillan, 2003, pp. 235–38.

implications of the idea. The Labour Party was most enthusiastic. It made a priority of implementing rapidly, in three years, the entire project outlined by Beveridge, and it insisted on the universality of social insurances. The Conservatives remained more reluctant, and tended to prefer gradualism and selective programs, aimed specifically at the poor. For the left, social insurance stood as a key instrument to promote equality and the emergence of a fair society. For the right, these programs appeared more as necessary expedients, which risked burdening the state budget, undermining market mechanisms, and penalizing individual success. Conservatives were willing to assist the poor but did not wish to equalize income or hinder private property. "We believe," stated a 1950 Conservative pamphlet that echoed the earlier preoccupations of Jean-Baptiste Say, in "the strong helping the weak rather than [in] weakening the strong."[44]

The worldwide postwar debate on social protection was thus set. Beyond the broad consensus over the welfare state, the left always pushed for universality, equality, and public intervention, while the right favored focused, selective, or contributory programs, and called for approaches that relied as much as possible on private and market mechanisms. The left was consistently quick to demand immediate relief for social ills and generous benefits for all. The right recurrently worried about excessive costs and potentially negative effects on individual morality and behavior.[45]

The impacts of these orientations on public policies were strong and durable. The comparative literature on the welfare state demonstrated clearly that countries governed by the left privileged universal rather than selective approaches, and spent more, and in a more egalitarian way, on social programs than countries where the right was stronger.[46] Partisan politics, concluded a recent study, "was the single most important factor that shaped the development of welfare states through

---

[44] *One Nation* (1950), quoted in Timothy Raison, *Tories and the Welfare State: A History of Conservative Social Policy since the Second World War*, Basingstoke, Macmillan, 1990, p. 27; Alan Sked and Chris Cook, *Post-War Britain: A Political History*, second edition, Harmondsworth, Penguin, 1984, pp. 38–39; Fraser, *The Evolution of the British Welfare State*, pp. 266–67.

[45] Hugh Heclo, *Modern Social Politics in Britain and Sweden: From Relief to Income Maintenance*, New Haven, Yale University Press, 1974, pp. 296–97.

[46] Francis G. Castles, *The Future of the Welfare State: Crisis Myths and Crisis Realities*, Oxford University Press, 2004, p. 94.

time."[47] By 1980, distinct models of social protection had indeed emerged. Long governed by social-democratic coalitions, the Scandinavian countries adopted universal programs that fostered equality and genuinely reduced poverty. In countries with a weak left, such as the United States, the welfare state remained residual and did not prevent high levels of inequality and poverty, even when employment and aggregate market incomes would have allowed better standards of living for all. When centrist or Christian-democratic coalitions prevailed, social protection became more generous but not as inclusive or egalitarian as in social-democratic regimes.[48]

By the middle of the 1970s, the postwar vision of a universal protection against the risks associated with unemployment, old age, and illness had been completed in most advanced democracies, with varying ambitions. The welfare state was now a solid, indeed almost immovable, institutional feature of democracy.[49] With this maturation, and in a more difficult economic context marked by rising unemployment and inflation, the debate between the left and the right began to change.

Without denying the benefits brought by encompassing social security and generous social services, the left increasingly criticized social policies as ineffective and bureaucratic. The welfare state was indeed unable to modify substantially the distribution of incomes and chances in a capitalist society, and it mostly compensated for the consequences of market inequality. No matter how well intended, social programs hardly dealt with the root causes of injustice. The new institutional arrangements were also bureaucratic, and at times repressive, and they imposed rigid social standards and norms of behavior, at the expense of personal autonomy or more ambitious visions of change. The right challenged, too, the welfare state as ineffective, and increasingly presented it as a disincentive to invest and

---

[47] Evelyne Huber and John D. Stephens, *Development and Crisis of the Welfare State: Parties and Policies in Global Markets*, University of Chicago Press, 2001, p. 1.

[48] Gøsta Esping-Andersen, *Social Foundations of Postindustrial Economies*, Oxford University Press, 1999, pp. 73–94; Robert H. Goodin, Bruce Headey, Ruud Muffels, and Henk-Jan Dirven, *The Real Worlds of Welfare Capitalism*, Cambridge University Press, 1999, pp. 240–58.

[49] Paul Pierson, "Coping with Permanent Austerity: Welfare State Restructuring in Affluent Democracies," in Paul Pierson (ed.), *The New Politics of the Welfare State*, Oxford University Press, 2001, p. 416.

work. In this perspective, well-intentioned social programs hindered economic growth, fueled inflation, and raised popular expectations to the point of making democracies almost "ungovernable." Yet, neither side had a clear alternative to propose. The left's progressive welfare state was allusive more than specific, and the right had not yet fleshed out what a modern economy with less, or different, social protection would be like.[50] This market-oriented alternative was about to emerge, however, and it would soon bring the left back to a nearly unconditional defense of the existing welfare state.

The East–West divide

On the world scene, the age of universality was dominated by the Cold War between the United States and the Soviet Union. Before it became an arms race, the East–West conflict was a fundamental clash of values, ideologies, and lifestyles. The United States and its allies defended freedom and capitalism, while the USSR and its "fraternal states" of Eastern Europe promoted equality through state socialism. In this confrontation, there was no great mystery as to the positions of the right and the left, at least within democratic countries.

After the defeat of fascism in 1945, the East–West division became the prism through which politicians and experts on the right analyzed global affairs. Every gesture of the Soviet Union stood as a proof that communism threatened the "free world." Erected in August 1961 to halt the flow of refugees trying to escape to the West, the Berlin Wall became a potent symbol in this respect. Perceived as "a standing insult to the West," the Wall demonstrated how the citizens of socialist countries were deprived of the most basic freedoms and were held as prisoners in repressive political regimes.[51]

Defending the free world against Soviet hegemonic ambitions meant maintaining an international order whose values and interests coincided with those of the West, and promoting the protection of individual freedoms. Against the backdrop of the reconstruction of Europe, such a task quickly became coterminous with the recognition of American

---

[50] Claus Offe, *Contradictions of the Welfare State*, Cambridge, MA, MIT Press, 1984, pp. 147–58.

[51] John Mander, *Berlin: Hostage for the West*, Harmondsworth, Penguin, 1962, p. 10.

political and military leadership. The founding of the North Atlantic Treaty Organization (NATO) in 1949 institutionalized this leadership, and provided the member states with the means "to safeguard the freedom, common heritage and civilisation of their peoples, founded on the principles of democracy, individual liberty and the rule of law."[52]

Starting with the Bandung Conference (1955) and the creation of the Non-Aligned Movement (1961), which resulted from an unprecedented Afro-Asian initiative, the defense of the free world was actively extended to developing countries. This broadening of the battle lines was a direct response to the anti-colonialism and opposition to all forms of international domination that defined the Non-Aligned Movement from its very inception. A number of conservative politicians and pundits, who viewed the ideology of non-alignment as a radical rejection of Western policies, maintained that the emerging North–South confrontation was just an outgrowth of the East–West conflict.[53] However reductive that interpretation may have been, it was not entirely baseless. For even though many Third World governments kept close ties with the West, the critique of the world order they articulated collectively was in many ways similar to the official discourse of the socialist countries.

For four decades, the rhetoric of the free world legitimized the West's hard line against communism and relative tolerance of right-wing dictatorships. In a famous 1979 article, Jeane Kirpatrick, who later became Ronald Reagan's first ambassador to the United Nations, explained that it was perfectly legitimate to be more aggressive toward communist regimes than toward traditional autocrats like Augusto Pinochet in Chile or Ferdinand Marcos in the Philippines.[54] After all, history had often witnessed the evolution of authoritarian states toward democracy, whereas until then there had not been a single example of a communist country making such a transition.

The two main instruments in the struggle against communism were nuclear deterrence and the policy of containment. Conservatives in both the United States and Western Europe pressed their political

---

[52] North Atlantic Treaty Organization, *The North Atlantic Treaty*, Washington, DC, April 4, 1949 (www.nato.int/docu/basictxt/treaty.htm).

[53] Rosemary Righter, *Utopia Lost: The United Nations and World Order*, New York, Twentieth Century Fund, 1995, p. 20.

[54] Jeane J. Kirkpatrick, "Dictatorships and Double Standards," *Commentary*, November 1979, 34–45.

leaders to invest whatever it took to prevent the Soviet Union from winning the arms race. Downplaying the possibility of mutually assured destruction (then known for its telling acronym: MAD), they considered it essential for the free world to maintain the technological advantage it had always held in the military sphere. As for containment, its purpose was "to confront the Russians with unalterable counter-force at every point where they show signs of encroaching upon the interests of a peaceful and stable world."[55] Conceived as a way of thwarting Soviet expansionism and a potential domino effect, the doctrine of containment relied more on military force than on political means. Yet for some, this doctrine did not go far enough. John Foster Dulles, for instance, who was President Eisenhower's Secretary of State, would have preferred to replace the containment of communism by a policy to actually liberate Eastern Europe from Soviet despotism.[56] In general, however, the right's realist view of international relations tempered its forceful opposition to communism.

Throughout the postwar period, conservatives defended capitalism and private property as institutions consistent with liberal principles and therefore morally superior. They also laid great stress on the unparalleled prosperity brought about by capitalism. The right attributed the remarkable growth of this "golden age" as much to the new arrangements of the mixed economies as to the spectacular rise of international trade. The expansion of trade was itself seen as a direct result of the liberalization orchestrated by the International Monetary Fund (IMF), the World Bank, and the General Agreement on Tariffs and Trade (GATT), three economic organizations established in the wake of the Bretton Woods Conference of 1944. It was pointed out that the Bretton Woods system, which the socialist countries had not joined, had made possible the reduction of tariffs and the convertibility of currencies that were necessary for the international development of business. Highly favorable to the opening of markets promoted by the GATT and the IMF, conservative politicians portrayed the economic approach of socialist governments as a lamentable failure. A repeated diagnosis put the blame for the poor productivity of East European

---

[55] George F. Kennan, "The Sources of Soviet Conduct," *Foreign Affairs*, vol. 25, July 1947, 566–82, p. 581.

[56] John Foster Dulles, "A Policy of Boldness," *Life*, vol. 32, no. 20, May 19, 1952, 146–60; Michael A. Guhin, *John Foster Dulles: A Statesman and His Times*, New York, Columbia University Press, 1972, p. 175.

countries on state ownership, centralized planning, and economic autarky. The persistence of the leaders of these countries in stubbornly following an unsuccessful course of action was presented as proof that the communist agenda was first and foremost "the product of ideology."[57]

The international situation was obviously viewed differently from the left of the political spectrum, although progressives, it must be acknowledged, proved far more divided than the right on the East–West conflict. Communists, Maoists, socialists, and social-democrats proposed divergent analyses of the Cold War, and they could not rally on a theme as strong as the defense of the free world was for conservatives. Nevertheless, the postwar progressive movement shared a number of common features, among which the most significant was undoubtedly the appeal of the Soviet model.

It is easy to forget, twenty years after the communist camp collapsed under the weight of its political and economic contradictions, that the Soviet Union was for decades a nuclear superpower, which played a potent role in defining the orientations of the global left. The influence of the USSR was especially strong in Eastern Europe, but its reach extended far beyond that part of the world. China and other developing countries where communists came to power (North Korea, Cuba, Mongolia, Vietnam, and Cambodia) were also part of the Soviet-led socialist system. The Soviet government also maintained close ties with non-ruling communist parties, as well as with numerous national liberation movements, many of which came to power. In 1962, the Sino-Soviet split demonstrated the limits of socialist solidarity, but the fact remains that at a certain time, about one third of humanity lived under the banner of Marxism-Leninism.

Communist orthodoxy as laid down by the Soviet authorities defined the postwar period as one of transition from capitalism to socialism. Within that process the East represented the forces of progress, and the West those of reaction. In accordance with the objective laws of social development, the crisis of imperialism and of state monopoly capitalism would inevitably engender a world revolution led by the working class. The decline of capitalism appeared unavoidable because the economic growth of the most advanced countries rested "upon

[57] Kennan, "The Sources of Soviet Conduct," p. 566.

the plunder of Asian, African and Latin American peoples, upon non-equivalent exchange, discrimination of female labor, brutal oppression of Negroes and immigrant workers, and also upon the intensified exploitation of the working people in those countries."[58] Believing itself invested with a historic mission, the USSR put forward popular democracy as an alternative that would liberate humanity "from social inequality...and the horrors of war."[59] The attraction of this communist ideology and its impact on the course of international relations were considerable. The case of Cuba, a small island located in the backyard of the United States, offered one of the most eloquent examples in this respect. At the outset, the revolutionary movement launched by young lawyer Fidel Castro and his middle-class *compañeros* had little to do with Marxism. Castro's alignment with the USSR came gradually, as his radical nationalism alienated him from the United States. That trajectory may have made Cuba look like "a piece on Moscow's political chessboard,"[60] but it also testified to the Soviet Union's willingness to side with the colonized and the underdogs in their opposition to the great powers and the rich.

The Western left was in fact more anti-American than pro-Soviet. Overall, it attributed less importance to the East–West division than did the right, and most progressives identified more readily with the interests of developing countries than with those of socialist countries. At the same time, both in Europe and North America, the left favored a strategy of openness toward the communist camp. The most notable manifestation of this openness was a more understanding attitude regarding the Soviet Union's desire to maintain its own zone of influence. In the wake of the 1956 Hungarian and 1968 Czechoslovakian crises, however, the left became ill at ease, and tried to square the circle by seeking to reconcile a call for moderation *vis-à-vis* Moscow with an indictment of Soviet military interventions. This balancing act was far from successful. The upshot was to embroil the progressive camp in deep dissensions.

---

[58] Communist Party of the Soviet Union, *Program of the Communist Party of the Soviet Union*, New York, Crosscurrents Press, 1961, p. 34.

[59] *Ibid.*, p. 10.

[60] W. Raymond Duncan, "Moscow and Cuban Radical Nationalism," in W. Raymond Duncan (ed.), *Soviet Policy in Developing Countries*, Waltham, Ginn and Company, 1970, p. 112.

In many ways, the liberal left viewed the United States as a greater threat than the Soviet Union. Much was done, therefore, to denounce the abuses of US policy. American sociologist C. Wright Mills interpreted Washington's behavior as essentially dictated by the political, economic, and strategic interests of a "power elite."[61] Crises and interventions in countries such as Guatemala, Cuba, Vietnam, and Chile lent weight to this interpretation of American foreign policy. Progressives also saw a "schizoid" dimension to the war on communism.[62] They severely condemned Senator Joseph McCarthy's witch-hunt in the United States, and deplored the tendency to see all Third World nationalist movements as infiltrated by communists, and all communist parties as puppets of Moscow.

In keeping with its anti-militarist tradition, the left also denounced the arms race as an irrational waste of resources. These criticisms were aimed above all at the American government, because the United States was at once the main producer and exporter of weapons. After Soviet overtures, such as the unilateral halting of nuclear testing in 1958 and the proposition made by Premier Nikita Khrushchev in 1959 at the UN to carry out a "general and complete disarmament,"[63] the West was frequently blamed for its unwillingness to seize peace opportunities.

Socialists finally showed some appreciation for the Soviet bloc's economic, technical, cultural, and athletic achievements. Although unquestionably poorer than the United States, it was the Soviet Union that set in motion the space age by launching the first Sputnik in 1957, to the Americans' great dismay. In 1961, Yuri Gagarin became the first man sent into orbit around the Earth. More generally, the international success of the scientists, artists, and athletes of the East appeared as proof that even though the citizens of socialist countries did not have access to the same consumer goods as their counterparts in capitalist countries, they nevertheless enjoyed a high standard of living and a good quality of life. In the 1970s, however, with the economic decline of the USSR and many revelations about the gulags, positive references to communism vanished almost entirely from the left's discourse.

---

[61] C. Wright Mills, *The Power Elite*, Oxford University Press, 1956.
[62] Hobsbawm, *The Age of Extremes*, p. 235.
[63] John G. Stoessinger, *The Might of Nations: World Politics in Our Time*, eighth edition, New York, Random House, 1985, p. 369.

The North–South conflict

With the acceleration of the decolonization movement in the 1960s, the North–South conflict was superimposed on the East–West divide, thus completing the geo-political construction of the postwar world. From the outset, this conflict was connected to the opposition between the left and the right. Because they emphasized the need for change, equality, and justice, the demands of the South were immediately associated with socialism and Marxism. Just as typically, governments of the North constantly called into question the legitimacy of the Third World's claims in the name of economic efficiency and market rationality. A similar polarization emerged among the public in developed countries: social groups who supported Third World demands usually identified with the left, while those who opposed them belonged to the right.[64]

Many arguments of the East–West debate were simply transposed into the North–South context. Conservatives, for instance, sought to convince developing countries that private enterprise opened the only practicable road to prosperity. Highly critical of the statist economic model favored by many Third World governments, they insisted that the strong expansion of the 1950s and 1960s was due to the free trade regime institutionalized by the GATT and the IMF. The right resigned itself to the United Nations' increased powers in the area of development and to the mushrooming of international agencies such as the United Nations Conference on Trade and Development (UNCTAD), the United Nations Development Programme (UNDP), and the United Nations Industrial Development Organization (UNIDO), but it always maintained loudly that the market approach of the Bretton Woods institutions was better able to deal with the challenges of poverty than the social-democratic and interventionist approach of the UN. For the right, the IMF and the World Bank also had the distinct advantage of being constitutionally controlled by the rich countries, an organizational trait that was said to ensure their sound management.

Moreover, from a conservative point of view, the postwar period had clearly improved global justice. As a result of decolonization, practically every nation now had a voice in international affairs, and

---

[64] David H. Lumsdaine, *Moral Vision in International Politics: The Foreign Aid Regime, 1949–1989*, Princeton University Press, 1993.

the world appeared more democratic than ever. Indeed, UN membership had risen from 51 countries in 1945 to 153 in 1980, due for the most part to the newcomers from the South.[65] International solidarity, it was felt, had grown as never before. The first display of that solidarity had come with the Marshall Plan, which, thanks to the leadership of the United States, had hastened the reconstruction of Western Europe. It continued with the aid regime established during the 1950s and the 1960s. In 1980, the developed countries were proud to claim that their generosity toward developing countries represented 0.37 percent of their GNP,[66] even though aid was by their own admission not devoid of self-interest. After all, it seemed only natural that priority should be given to friendly governments. To cite a cost-benefit analysis of that period, the key was to ensure that foreign assistance would generate more "utility" for the poor than "disutility" for the rich.[67]

Many also believed that the expansion of the world economy would have been even more spectacular if, instead of adopting an attitude of sterile confrontation, the governments of developing countries had accepted to follow the policies promoted by the North. The strategy of openness implemented by the newly industrializing countries of Asia (South Korea, Taiwan, Singapore) was far more appreciated than the inward-looking policies adopted by a majority of Southern states. Criticism of the Third World turned especially harsh in the 1970s, when the group of 77 (G-77) launched discussions on a new international economic order (NIEO) at the UN. Many conservatives felt that this coalition of countries – whose membership had quickly risen to more than a hundred states – was too heterogeneous to be credible. British journalist Rosemary Righter, for instance, concluded that the NIEO negotiations were nothing more than a form of "theater," driven by "the power of incantation."[68] Touching on questions as diverse as trade in primary commodities, control of transnational corporations, access to technology, and decision-making procedures in international

---

[65] Louis Emmerij, Richard Jolly, and Thomas G. Weiss, *Ahead of the Curve? UN Ideas and Global Challenges*, Bloomington, Indiana University Press, 2001, p. 59.

[66] OECD, *Twenty-five Years of Development Co-operation: A Review*, Paris, OECD, 1985, p. 335.

[67] OECD, *Development Co-operation: 1980 Review*, Paris, OECD, 1980, p. 63.

[68] Righter, *Utopia Lost*, pp. 114 and 117.

economic institutions, the demands of the South were considered utopian and too costly. Yet more fundamentally, the objectives of the developing countries were deemed incompatible with the workings of a market economy.

In the 1950s, neoclassical economists, earnestly involved in the political debate, defined development as a universal process directed toward industrialization and growth. The "underdeveloped" countries, later rechristened "developing," were defined in opposition to the "developed" countries. Although the connotations of "developing" seemed less pejorative than those attached to the notion of "underdeveloped," both adjectives ultimately expressed the same thought: poor nations simply lagged behind rich ones, and these showed the way ahead.[69] Formalized through the theory of modernization, this analysis couched the primary challenge of development in terms of progress from a traditional, rural economy to a modern, industrial economy characterized by technological development and high productivity.

In *The Stages of Economic Growth* – the cult text of modernization theory – Walt W. Rostow condensed the evolution of all societies under five headings: traditional society, preconditions for take-off, take-off, drive to maturity, and the age of high mass-consumption.[70] Inspired by the historical trajectory of the advanced capitalist countries, this interpretation identified modernization with Westernization and replicated in a pro-capitalist way the path to modernity envisioned by Marxism. Rostow's book was indeed subtitled *A Non-Communist Manifesto*. The author explicitly acknowledged the ideological nature of his work and presented it as "an alternative to Karl Marx's theory of modern history," in which "net human behaviour is seen not as an act of maximization, but as an act of balancing alternative and often conflicting human objectives."[71] According to modernization theory, the best strategy for promoting growth in poor countries was to open borders and integrate the world market. To use a terminology in vogue at the time, export promotion offered more economic potential than import substitution. In the field of finance, Third World countries

---

[69] Gilbert Rist, *The History of Development: From Western Origins to Global Faith*, London, Zed Books, 1997, p. 74.
[70] Walt W. Rostow, *The Stages of Economic Growth: A Non-Communist Manifesto*, third edition, Cambridge University Press, 1990.
[71] *Ibid.*, pp. 2 and 149.

were expected to first mobilize their own domestic savings. Yet they could also rely on foreign investment, the impact of transnational corporations on development being "on the whole...a favorable one."[72]

In sum, for the right, the formula for economic growth and development was invariable across time and space. The argument was proposed as a response to those on the left for whom colonialism explained both the development of the North and the underdevelopment of the South. For conservatives, the experiences of the United States, Canada, Australia, and the Scandinavian countries proved in fact that the lack of a colonial empire was not an obstacle to development. Noting that a number of former colonies had undertaken their economic take-off (Argentina, Brazil, and South Korea for instance), while territories that had never been colonized had remained underdeveloped (Ethiopia, Afghanistan, or Thailand), the right also argued that colonization was evidently not the chief determinant explaining poverty. History seemed to bear out the idea that what hampered development stemmed a good deal more from domestic than from external factors.

At the other end of the political spectrum, as progressives distanced themselves from communism, they strengthened their commitment to the Third World. According to a view that gradually gained ascendancy among socialists and social-democrats, widespread poverty posed a greater threat to global security than the arms race. Somewhat surprisingly, Pope Paul VI supplied the left with one of its most effective slogans when he declared in 1967 that development was "the new name for peace."[73]

The left often stressed the virtues of North–South interdependence. The 1980 report of the International Commission chaired by former social-democratic German Chancellor Willy Brandt, for instance, highlighted the degree to which the North and South shared mutual interests. The report's central thesis was that a global redistribution of resources would enhance political stability and economic growth for all.[74] Beyond this line of reasoning, the Brandt report also affirmed the

[72] Robert Gilpin, *The Political Economy of International Relations*, Princeton University Press, 1987, p. 248.
[73] Paul VI, *Populorum Progressio: Encyclical Letter of His Holiness Pope Paul VI*, March 26, 1967, p. 51 (www.ewtn.com/library/encyc/p6develo.htm).
[74] Independent Commission on International Development Issues (chaired by Willy Brandt), *North–South: A Program for Survival*, Cambridge, MA, MIT Press, 1980.

idea that the pursuit of international justice stood as a moral imperative. Motivated by an ethics that looked upon the inequitable sharing
of wealth as a barrier to human dignity, progressives considered that
the values of solidarity and democracy upheld in the developed world
had to be projected on a world scale.[75]

To counter the effects of relations based on sheer power, social-
democrats demanded that global rules and institutions be transformed. Just as they encouraged state intervention on the national
stage, they supported the intervention of international agencies in the
global arena. Planning, Keynesian policies, and the welfare state had
to be extended across borders in order to bring about a "welfare
world."[76] Advocating affirmative action, the left insisted on the idea
that the obligations of states ought to vary according to their different
levels of development. Whereas the free play of market forces might
be acceptable among rich countries, it could not be applied to relations between unequal partners. As Raúl Prebisch, the first Secretary-
General of UNCTAD, explained, the UN was no more obligated to
stay neutral in the face of underdevelopment than the World Health
Organization (WHO) was in the face of malaria.[77] Far from being
condemned to an illusory impartiality, international institutions were
duty-bound to narrow the gap between developed and developing
countries, a task that could not be carried out without the backing of
the governments of the North. To realize the principle of equal sovereignty proclaimed in the United Nations Charter, it was crucial that
the haves shoulder a larger share of responsibilities.

Despite the unavoidable disputes between reformists and radicals,
the bulk of the left rallied around a "structuralist" analysis of the
world order, according to which underdevelopment resulted not so
much from a society's culture or from the attitudes of current political
leaders as from the structure of the global economy. That structure, it
was argued, was shaped by an asymmetrical relationship between a

---

[75] Cranford Pratt, "Middle Power Internationalism and Global Poverty," in
Cranford Pratt (ed.), *Middle Power Internationalism: The North–South
Dimension*, Montreal and Kingston, McGill-Queen's University Press, 1990,
pp. 3–24.
[76] Myrdal, *Beyond the Welfare State*, p. 16.
[77] John Toye and Richard Toye, *The UN and Global Political Economy: Trade,
Finance, and Development*, Bloomington, Indiana University Press, 2004,
p. 212.

core of rich countries and a periphery of poor states: at the end of the 1970s, the North – 25 percent of the world population – received 80 percent of global income, while the South – 75 percent of the world population – lived on the remaining 20 percent.[78]

The left in no way denied that the postwar years had seen progress in the struggle for international equality. First, decolonization had allowed the peoples of the South to acquire political independence. Furthermore, the self-affirmation of the Third World – fostered by charismatic leaders such as Mao Zedong, Gamel Abder Nasser, Fidel Castro, and Salvador Allende as well as institutions like the Non-Aligned Movement and the G-77 – had created a momentum toward a reform of the international order. World events had also made clear that the status quo was not immutable. The Vietnam War, for instance, demonstrated that a small, poorly equipped state could defeat a superpower. The 1973 raising of oil prices by the Organization of the Petroleum Exporting Countries (OPEC) was also seen as a turning point, because for the first time a group of developing countries could impose a major economic decision on the developed countries. Above all, the postwar period had made possible the emergence of a body of development law that directly challenged traditional international law. The failure of the NIEO could not annul the fact that, out of a convergence between progressives of the North and the South, a new awareness of international economic disparities had arisen.[79]

These advances, however, were not sufficient to mitigate what Egyptian economist Samir Amin called "unequal development."[80] Noting that the political sovereignty of Third World countries had not brought about true economic sovereignty, scholars on the left proposed a new interpretation of the postwar order, which came to be known as dependency theory. While productivity and trade grew among the rich countries, the theory stated, Third World commodity exporters faced a steady deterioration of their terms of trade. Industrial

---

[78] Independent Commission on International Development Issues, *North–South*, p. 32.
[79] Richard Falk, *On Humane Governance: Towards a New Global Politics*, University Park, Pennsylvania State University Press, 1995, p. 28.
[80] Samir Amin and Brian Pearce, *Unequal Development: An Essay on the Social Formations of Peripheral Capitalism*, New York, Monthly Review Press, 1977. See also Andre Gunder Frank, "The Development of Underdevelopment," *Monthly Review*, vol. 18, no. 4, 1966, 17–31.

exports from developing countries were of little help because they remained subject to excessive protectionist barriers. In addition, transnational corporations established in the South exported their profits overseas, and parsimonious aid policies were tightly geared to the strategic and commercial interests of donors. In the wake of the International Commission for the Study of Communication Problems, otherwise known as the MacBride Commission, a number of observers commented that these combined trends nurtured "a form of cultural and economic domination."[81]

According to the overall analysis of the left, the main obstacles to development were not internal but external to the South. Two types of behavior on the part of the rich countries were explicitly denounced. First, the governments of the North refused to apply at the international level the interventionist policies that had proven effective nationally. Second, they persisted in wasting on armaments resources that would have easily sufficed to eradicate poverty in the developing world. During the 1960s and the 1970s, the left put forward numerous proposals to strike a new deal in North–South relations. These proposals gave rise to many debates – between those who favored increased economic integration and those who called for de-linking the South from the North, as well as between those advocating a productivist approach and those proposing a greener model of development – but a broad consensus was achieved around two basic positions: poor countries needed special treatment, and new international norms had to be introduced to rein in market forces.

A series of measures were thus proposed to make the trade and finance regimes as well as international economic institutions more equitable.[82] Typically, they were formulated by the developing countries, and then backed by the Soviet Union and the Western left. In trade, for instance, the Third World stressed the need to implement international agreements to control the price of commodities, and fought to secure trade preferences. Countries of the South also advocated the establishment of codes of conduct to facilitate their

[81] Sean MacBride, *Many Voices, One World: Towards a New More Just and More Efficient World Information and Communication Order*, Report by the International Commission for the Study of Communication Problems, London, New York and Paris, Kogan Page, Unipub, and UNESCO, 1980, p. 37.

[82] Jean-Philippe Thérien, *Une voix pour le Sud. Le discours de la CNUCED*, Paris and Montréal, L'Harmattan and Presses de l'Université de Montréal, 1990.

access to foreign technology and to regulate restrictive business practices. The generalized system of preferences, an agreement that fosters the export of industrial goods produced in developing countries, remains the only lasting outcome of these various reform projects.

In the financial sphere, the left concentrated most of its attention on development assistance. It fought for an increase in the volume of aid and for an improvement in the conditions of aid allocation. One of the left's few diplomatic victories, achieved in 1970 through a UN resolution, was to legitimize the idea that the rich countries should devote 0.7 percent of their GNP to development cooperation. Non-governmental organizations of the North and governments of the South also strove to get aid to respond more effectively to basic needs such as food, employment, and education, and to increase the multilateral component of aid funding. Aside from the overriding aid issue, the IMF was invited to adopt policies that were more expansionist and less geared to controlling inflation.

As for institutional matters, progressives felt that the economic circumstances of the developing countries could not improve without a massive makeover of international governance. They regarded the Bretton Woods institutions as anti-democratic and demanded a strengthening of the development role of the UN system. In addition to supporting the creation of a number of new UN bodies, the left also called for the merger of GATT and UNCTAD so as to place the goal of development at the heart of the trade regime. Overall, its strategy was largely centered on the power of law and diplomacy. This approach proved to be idealistic, for subsequent events made clear that majority rule rarely had any impact on the workings of the international order.

This overview would be incomplete if, in conclusion, it did not mention the left's silence during the postwar years when it came to the political and economic responsibility of Southern elites in relation to underdevelopment. The authoritarianism and corruption of many governments of the South were taboo subjects and remained largely unexamined. Vehemently denounced by the conservatives, this silence facilitated the right's offensive in the 1980s.

Conclusion

In many ways, the age of universality was a golden age for the left. The development of the mixed economy, the adoption of demand management policies, the rise of trade unions and collective bargaining, the expansion of the welfare state, the power and prestige of international socialism, and the rise of an autonomous and affirmative global South were all signs that the progressive vision of the world was influential and indeed ascendant. From 1945 to 1980, the right was often on the defensive. It resisted state intervention and redistribution, sought to contain socialism and communism, and battled to uphold the legitimacy and efficiency of market mechanisms to regulate international relations.

In a world defined by American hegemony and often ruled by conservative governments, in the 1950s notably, the right was certainly not powerless. In many countries, the policies that were actually implemented were decidedly conservative. The United States, for instance, adopted a "commercial" variant of Keynesianism and built its welfare regime around an extensive use of private social benefits.[83] Still, very often the left seemed to propose and the right to resist. The public ethos of the time was progressive. In the 1960s and 1970s, the demand for equality spread broadly to include women, blacks, native peoples, various ethnic groups, and sexual minorities. More educated and more prosperous than ever before, and more numerous as well, the youth of advanced democracies challenged most established rules and institutions, in the name of equality and freedom. Previously rock-solid standards regarding sexual behavior and family relations, and cultural norms in general, were cast aside one after the other. The tide, however, was about to turn. At the end of the 1970s, the political climate began to change.

---

[83] Theda Skocpol, "America's Incomplete Welfare State: The Limits of New Deal Reforms and the Origins of the Present Crisis," in Martin Rein, Gøsta Esping-Andersen, and Lee Rainwater (eds.), *Stagnation and Renewal in Social Policy: The Rise and Fall of Policy Regimes*, Armonk, NY, M. E. Sharpe, 1987, pp. 42–45; Jacob S. Hacker, *The Divided Welfare State: The Battle over Public and Private Social Benefits in the United States*, Cambridge University Press, 2002, pp. 7–20.

6 | *The triumph of market democracy (1980–2007)*

On November 8, 1989, a faltering East German government declared, in a context of mass protests and massive departures through Hungary and Czechoslovakia, that the Berlin Wall no longer stood as an obstacle to the free movement of its citizens. Crowds coming from the East and the West joined together in celebrations, and undertook to demolish the most offensive symbol of the Cold War. Less than a year later, the German Democratic Republic disappeared and Germany was reunified. Throughout Eastern Europe, communist regimes collapsed, and were replaced by electoral democracies committed to re-establishing market rules. In December 1991, the Soviet Union itself ceased to exist, to be replaced by a Commonwealth of Independent States, engaged in a process of democratization and liberalization.[1] In China, the ruling Communist Party resisted such attempts at democratization, killing several hundred students to crush a protest in Tiananmen Square. The regime nevertheless pursued a policy of economic liberalization that reintroduced market mechanisms in the world's largest communist country. Except for a few marginal cases – including North Korea, which became the first hereditary communist dictatorship – "really existing socialism" as a project of totally state-controlled, planned economy had ceased to exist.[2]

In the South, the 1980s and 1990s were also a triumphant era for both the market and liberal democracy. The turn to democracy started in Southern Europe in the late 1970s and in Latin America in the 1980s. The process was then more one of "re-democratization," most of these countries having experienced democracy in the past.[3] With

---

[1] Geoff Eley, *Forging Democracy: The History of the Left in Europe, 1850–2000*, Oxford University Press, 2002, pp. 443–45.

[2] Eric J. Hobsbawm, *The Age of Extremes: The Short Twentieth Century, 1914–1991*, London, Abacus, 1994, p. 497.

[3] Ruth Berins Collier, *Paths toward Democracy: The Working Class and Elites in Western Europe and South America*, Cambridge University Press, 1999, p. 13.

the 1990s, a genuine "explosion of democratization" took place, to reach several countries that had never been democracies, in Asia and Africa notably.[4] At the same time, just as communist countries were moving to capitalism, the governments of the South abandoned planning and reduced state intervention, in favor of markets and private enterprise.[5] These various changes, however, did not happen in a climate of benign international cooperation. On the contrary, developing countries had to face a continuing crisis because of a hostile external environment, and the gap between rich and poor states gradually emerged as "the most important line of division within the world order."[6]

The pro-market revolution actually started in the North, with the election of Margaret Thatcher in Britain in May 1979 and of Ronald Reagan in the United States in November 1980. A strong and confrontational conservative, Margaret Thatcher wanted to be remembered as one "[who] decisively broke with a debilitating consensus of a paternalistic Government and a dependent people; which rejected the notion that the State is all powerful and the citizen is merely its beneficiary; which shattered the illusion that Government could somehow substitute for individual performance."[7] In a similar perspective, Ronald Reagan inaugurated his first presidency by stating that "government is not the solution to our problem; government is the problem."[8] A conservative era had begun, which would redefine politics all over the world for at least two decades.

This chapter surveys the global right turn in favor of market democracy from the standpoints of domestic and international politics.

---

[4] Renske Doorenspleet, "Reassessing the Three Waves of Democratization," *World Politics*, vol. 52, no. 3, April 2000, 384–406, p. 399; Renske Doorenspleet, "The Structural Context of Recent Transitions to Democracy," *European Journal of Political Research*, vol. 43, no. 3, May 2004, 309–35, p. 330.

[5] Richard Jolly, Louis Emmerij, Dharam Ghai, and Frédéric Lapeyre, *UN Contributions to Development Thinking and Practice*, Bloomington, Indiana University Press, 2004, pp. 145–48.

[6] Anthony Payne, *The Global Politics of Unequal Development*, Basingstoke, Palgrave-Macmillan, 2005, p. 3.

[7] Margaret Thatcher (January 18, 1984), quoted in Dennis Kavanagh, *Thatcherism and British Politics: The End of Consensus?*, Oxford University Press, 1987, p. 252.

[8] Ronald Reagan, "Inaugural Address," Washington, DC, January 20, 1981 (www.reaganlibrary.com/reagan/speeches/speech.asp?spid=6).

Focusing on the rise of monetarism and neoliberalism, the first two sections consider the shift of advanced democracies from an ethos dominated by the search for equality through macro-economic management, collective bargaining, and the welfare state, to a new vision defined by a preference for competitiveness, budgetary austerity, and market mechanisms. The following sections then examine how this neoliberal vision was extended to development politics, and how forces of the right were able to transform the dynamics of North–South relations.

Monetarism

To understand the change of direction of the 1980s, it is useful to go back a few years, to see how new policy ideas were emerging on the right, in the heyday of the postwar "consensus." In the 1960s, conservative politicians rarely attacked head-on the Keynesian perspective or the welfare state project. Even Republican president Richard Nixon called himself a Keynesian in January 1971, as he looked toward his 1972 re-election bid.[9] Critiques of the approach mounted, however, among economists in particular. The attacks came from three sides. First, Keynesianism was criticized for failing to explain and solve creeping inflation and stagflation. Second, it was dismissed for its inadequate micro-foundations or, in other words, for its difficulty in accounting for the behavior of individual economic agents. Third, on more political grounds, Keynesianism and state intervention were challenged in the name of freedom, individual choice, efficiency, and morality.

Consider, first, the question of inflation. Milton Friedman, a University of Chicago economist who believed in free markets and distrusted state intervention, pioneered the offensive on this question. He started by reviving the old quantity theory of money, which suggested that a rise in the money supply necessarily increased prices, thus creating inflation. For Keynes, the connection was not so straightforward. Without denying the relevance of monetary factors, Keynes argued that in some cases, in a severe recession for instance, individuals

---

[9] Daniel Yergin and Joseph Stanislaw, *The Commanding Heights: The Battle Between Government and the Marketplace that Is Remaking the Modern World*, New York, Simon & Schuster, 1998, pp. 60–61.

simply would not use money, however abundant, to buy or invest. When such "liquidity traps" developed, the money supply proved irrelevant and monetary policy became ineffective. Governments then had to resort to fiscal policy – they could lower taxes or increase expenditures – to stimulate consumption and investment.[10]

In his study of the monetary history of the United States, conducted with Anna Schwartz, Friedman maintained on the contrary that deep recessions were primarily monetary phenomena, because they were always preceded by a significant fall of the quantity of money in circulation. The empirical demonstration was not without limitations and it was often contested, but it helped Friedman claim that money had more significance than the evolution of national income, and argue that policy-makers should design non-interventionist rules to guarantee a stable money supply. In a well-functioning market, a steady quantity of money would suffice to prevent both inflation and unemployment.[11]

The economics profession received these monetarist ideas coolly. The insistence on money, in particular, was seen more as an indication of the "zeal and exuberance" of "Friedman and his followers" than as a challenge that could undermine the Keynesian perspective.[12] For the monetarist interpretation to prevail, it would take two additional conditions. First, the view that inflation was an important problem had to arise in the public sphere. Second, the idea that monetarism offered the best diagnostic and the most satisfying remedies for inflation had to become the dominant view.[13]

Inflation did increase in the 1960s, but it was not yet perceived as a problem on par with unemployment. At the time, wrote Herbert Stein,

---

[10] David Smith, *The Rise and Fall of Monetarism*, Harmondsworth, Penguin, 1987, pp. 7–11.

[11] *Ibid.*, pp. 20–24; Michael Bleaney, *The Rise and Fall of Keynesian Economics: An Investigation of Its Contribution to Capitalist Development*, Basingstoke, Macmillan, 1985, pp. 135–39; Paul Krugman, *Peddling Prosperity: Economic Sense and Nonsense in the Age of Diminished Expectations*, New York, W. W. Norton, 1994, pp. 34–40.

[12] James Tobin, "The Monetary Interpretation of History," *American Economic Review*, vol. 55, no. 3, June 1965, 464–85, p. 481; Bleaney, *The Rise and Fall of Keynesian Economics*, pp. 137–39.

[13] Harry G. Johnson, "The Keynesian Revolution and the Monetarist Counter-Revolution," *American Economic Review*, vol. 61, no. 2, May 1971, 1–14, p. 7.

inflation "was rising in the hierarchy of national problems, simply because there was more of it," but "it was not an issue about which anyone felt deeply."[14] Scholars were nevertheless intrigued by the simultaneous persistence of both inflation and unemployment. Acknowledging this difficulty, British economist Alban Phillips suggested that there was in fact an imperfect trade-off between employment and inflation. In practice, governments that sought a very low level of unemployment had to accept some inflation.[15]

Characteristically, Friedman used the high visibility of his presidential address to the American Economic Association in 1967 to attack this standpoint, which made some inflation acceptable. The trade-off observed by Phillips, he argued, only worked in the short term. Economic agents soon realized that full-employment policies led to higher wages and prices, and they adjusted. With time, economic expansion could only be bought at the cost of increasingly high inflation rates: "there is no permanent trade-off," Friedman concluded.[16] This was the case because each society had a "natural" rate of unemployment, below which it was difficult to go. This "natural" rate, which later was more appropriately named the non-accelerating inflation rate of unemployment (NAIRU), was determined by social institutions and legislation, and it could only be reduced through structural reforms that enhanced market mechanisms. Reducing the minimum wage or the strength of trade unions, for instance, would lower the NAIRU and raise the non-inflationary level of employment better than any fiscal policy could.

This argument – which was simultaneously made in less flamboyant but more sophisticated terms by Columbia economist Edmund S. Phelps – proved extremely powerful, because it predicted the combined rise of unemployment and inflation that was about to come and that would be called "stagflation." The diagnostic suggested, too, a working policy response, something the Keynesian approach

---

[14] Herbert Stein, *Presidential Economics: The Making of Economic Policy from Roosevelt to Reagan and Beyond*, second revised edition, Washington, DC, American Enterprise Institute for Public Policy Research, 1988, p. 134.

[15] As we have seen earlier, this conclusion did not hold for countries that had maintained a firm commitment to full employment and succeeded in negotiating wage moderation. This comparative fact escaped most economists, who were focused on the Anglo-American situation.

[16] Milton Friedman, "The Role of Monetary Policy," *American Economic Review*, vol. 58, no. 1, March 1968, 1–17, p. 11.

could not do. For opponents, admitted Keynesian economist Alex Leijonhufvud, "it was a debacle."[17] "By 1980," added Alan Blinder, "it was hard to find an American academic macroeconomist under the age of 40 who professed to be a Keynesian."[18] Politicians on the right rapidly "latched on to Monetarist ideas as a way of attacking state expenditure and intervention for stoking inflation." For them, explained Michael Bleaney, "monetarism was to become the way to link popular dissatisfaction about taxation, public generosity and the suspicion that it was being abused by 'scroungers' with the other great source of anxiety, inflation."[19]

A second line of attack came from the study of individual economic agents by rational choice and rational expectations scholars. The rational choice approach, which emerged with the works of scholars like James Buchanan, Gordon Tullock, Anthony Downs, and Mancur Olson, analyzed political and social phenomena through the lenses of the utilitarian framework of neoclassical economics.[20] Individuals were portrayed as rational egoists unlikely to cooperate, voters as rational-ignorant and abstainers justified in not voting, bureaucrats and politicians as "maximizers" of budgets and votes, and groups and social movements as seekers of unwarranted privileges and rents. In this perspective, which updated the old conservative distrust of democracy and of the state, citizens could not expect much from the political process or even from cooperative social relations. The best they could hope for was to have as many social functions fulfilled by the market as possible, this mechanism being immunized by competition from power and rent seeking. A complementary explanation was offered by economists such as Robert Lucas, who studied what they called "rational expectations." The idea, here, was to challenge the Keynesian view of economic agents as acting in conditions of radical uncertainty, on the basis of "conventions," "motives," or even

---

[17] Alex Leijonhufvud (1983), quoted in Robert Heilbroner and William Milberg, *The Crisis of Vision in Modern Economic Thought*, Cambridge University Press, 1995, p. 54.

[18] Alan S. Blinder, "The Fall and Rise of Keynesian Economics," *Economic Record*, vol. 64, no. 187, December 1988, 278–94, p. 278.

[19] Bleaney, *The Rise and Fall of Keynesian Economics*, p. 141.

[20] Roger E. Backhouse, "The Rise of Free Market Economics: Economists and the Role of the State since 1970," in Steven G. Medema and Peter Boettke (eds.), *The Role of Government in the History of Economic Thought*, Durham, Duke University Press, 2005, p. 359.

"animal spirits." For persons acting in such uncertain conditions, economic signals from the government seemed precious, indeed indispensable. Lucas and his followers preferred to make the assumption that individuals and firms were fully aware of the structure of the economy and formed correct expectations about market events and government interventions. From this axiom, economists deduced that social actors would always foresee government interventions intended to manage the economy and discount their impact in advance, making them ineffective or even detrimental. This analytical proposition explained in micro-economic terms the stagflation predicted by Friedman, and it reinforced monetarist conclusions regarding the ineffectiveness of macro-economic management.[21] It also did much to break the Keynesian hold on the economics profession, because it offered an avenue to reunite the two disjointed sides of the discipline, micro- and macro-economics.

Finally, the attack on Keynesianism was also political. In *The Road to Serfdom*, published in 1944, Austrian-born economist Friedrich von Hayek had foreseen the key themes of the right-wing offensive, by associating planning, socialism, and collectivism with totalitarianism. Private property, argued Hayek, constituted "the most important guaranty of freedom, not only for those who own property, but scarcely less for those who do not."[22] Hayek's book was immediately influential, but for many years his views remained unheeded. John Maynard Keynes – who appreciated the book but wrote to its author that he would look less "like Don Quixote" if he conceded that "moderate planning" could be "safe" – proved more in tune with the times.[23] Hayek's line of thought nevertheless remained important on the right. Despite their disagreements on the role of the state and on monetary policy, Friedman himself contributed to reinvigorate Hayek's views, with the publication in 1962 of his *Capitalism and Freedom*. In this book, intended for a popular audience, Friedman similarly underlined

---

[21] Mark Blyth, *Great Transformations: Economic Ideas and Institutional Change in the Twentieth Century*, Cambridge University Press, 2002, pp. 90–94; Gary Mucciaroni, *The Political Failure of Employment Policy, 1945–1982*, University of Pittsburgh Press, 1990, pp. 142–43.

[22] Friedrich A. von Hayek, *The Road to Serfdom*, University of Chicago Press, 1944, pp. 103–104.

[23] John Maynard Keynes (1944), quoted in Hannes H. Gissurarson, "The Only Truly Progressive Policy...," in Norman P. Barry *et al.*, *Hayek's "Serfdom" Revisited*, London, Institute of Economic Affairs, 1984, p. 7.

the role of economic freedom as "a necessary condition for political freedom."[24] The economist once again made his case for legislated rules "instructing the monetary authority to achieve a specified rate of growth in the stock of money," and for a neutral fiscal policy designed "without any regard to problems of year-to-year economic stability."[25] Friedman also proposed the elimination of corporate taxes and of policies supportive of trade unions, and called for a flat income tax rate, contending that governments had done more harm than good in trying to redistribute revenues.[26] A liberal society, he concluded, should avoid "taking from some to give to others... on grounds of 'justice.' At this point, equality comes sharply into conflict with freedom; one must choose. One cannot be both an egalitarian, in this sense, and a liberal."[27]

It would take many years for these right-wing ideas to move out of the political margin and actually shape public policies. The occasion came in the 1970s, when the combined rise of unemployment and inflation undermined Keynesian economics and made the monetarist account plausible. The 1973 oil shock was a catalyst. In an already difficult economic context, marked as well by the end of the Bretton Woods system of fixed exchange rates, the decision of the leading members of the Organization of Petroleum Exporting Countries (OPEC) to cut production and raise prices had a dramatic impact. In a few months, the price of oil quadrupled and inflation rates jumped above 10 percent – the OECD average was 13.3 percent in 1974 – just as aggregate demand fell, because energy-buying countries lost some of their purchasing power to oil producers that had not yet started "recycling" their income back into the world economy.[28]

The first country to move toward monetarism was Germany. In a society where Keynesianism "never really took hold," and where a highly independent central bank always saw its primary task as preserving price stability, the turn toward a pragmatic form of monetarism came rather naturally. After the oil shock, the Bundesbank – Germany's

---

[24] Milton Friedman, *Capitalism and Freedom*, University of Chicago Press, 1962, p. 4.
[25] *Ibid.*, pp. 54 and 79.   [26] *Ibid.*, pp. 132 and 174–76.   [27] *Ibid.*, p. 195.
[28] Fritz W. Scharpf, "Economic Changes, Vulnerabilities, and Institutional Capabilities," in Fritz W. Scharpf and Vivien A. Schmidt (eds.), *Welfare and Work in the Open Economy. Volume I. From Vulnerability to Competitiveness*, Oxford University Press, 2000, pp. 27–29 and 340.

central bank – opted rapidly and unambiguously for a restrictive monetary policy to combat inflation, even though the federal government still pursued full employment.[29] Many European countries followed suit, because the European Exchange Rate Agreement (the "Snake") tied their currencies to the German mark and compelled them to a form of "imported monetarism."[30] This evolution went largely unnoticed, however, until 1979, when monetarist ideas began to be implemented with a "much more single-minded determination."[31]

Margaret Thatcher was the first political leader to be elected, in May 1979, with an avowedly monetarist program. Her government was committed to maintain rigid targets for the monetary supply, assuming this approach would stop inflation without increasing unemployment. The Conservative Party also promised to reduce the size of the state and enhance market mechanisms, to counter the power of trade unions, and to restore the authority of the government.[32]

Between 1979 and 1981, the British government adopted strict monetary policies, letting the short-term interest rate go as high as 16.6 percent in 1980. This course of action, combined with a steep increase in value-added taxes and national insurance contributions, contributed to the creation of a severe recession. By 1982, the unemployment rate had climbed above 12 percent, without lowering inflation, still around 8 percent.[33] On all sides, including among business leaders and within the cabinet, pressures mounted in favor of a more accommodative policy. Publicly, Thatcher resisted. She

[29] Fritz W. Scharpf, *Crisis and Choice in European Social Democracy*, Ithaca, Cornell University Press, 1991, pp. 132–33 and 202–207; Philip Manow and Eric Seils, "Adjusting Badly: The German Welfare State, Structural Change, and the Open Economy," in Fritz W. Scharpf and Vivien A. Schmidt (eds.), *Welfare and Work in the Open Economy. Volume II. Diverse Responses to Common Challenges*, Oxford University Press, 2000. p. 268; Kathleen R. McNamara, "Consensus and Constraint: Ideas and Capital Mobility in European Monetary Integration," *Journal of Common Market Studies*, vol. 37, no. 3, September 1999, 455–76, p. 466.

[30] Scharpf, "Economic Changes, Vulnerabilities, and Institutional Capabilities," pp. 32–33.

[31] John Smithin, *Macroeconomics after Thatcher and Reagan: The Conservative Policy Revolution in Retrospect*, Aldershot, Edward Elgar, 1990, p. 36.

[32] Kavanagh, *Thatcherism and British Politics*, pp. 12–13.

[33] *Ibid.*, pp. 225–33; Smithin, *Macroeconomics after Thatcher and Reagan*, p. 42–47 and 59; Peter A. Hall, *Governing the Economy: The Politics of State Intervention in Britain and France*, Cambridge, Polity Press, 1986, p. 120.

repeated that there was "no alternative" and stated in no ambiguous terms that "the lady's not for turning."[34] In reality, the Conservative government gradually abandoned its attempt to exercise a strict control over the money supply, which in effect was impossible, in favor of more pragmatic macro-economic orientations. Monetary and fiscal policy nevertheless remained tight, and inflation was eventually reduced, at the expense of a lasting increase in unemployment.[35]

In the United States, the monetarist turn actually preceded the election of Ronald Reagan. In the fall of 1979, in a last-minute attempt to demonstrate his determination to reduce a worryingly high rate of inflation, Jimmy Carter appointed Paul Volcker as chairman of the Federal Reserve Board. Volcker almost immediately adopted a strong monetarist stance, and contributed to an economic downturn that may have cost Carter the presidency. In 1980–81, with a new president who was more supportive of this stern orientation, interest rates climbed up to 15.9 percent and the United States experienced its worst recession since the 1930s.[36]

The case of Ronald Reagan was distinctive. In a country that had not lived through Britain's difficulties – in 1976, the Labour government of James Callaghan had to change its economic policies to obtain a much-needed loan from the International Monetary Fund – voters were not predisposed to support radical change.[37] To be elected, Reagan promised that inflation could be reduced without increasing unemployment, that taxes could be cut without incurring a deficit, and that spending could be lowered without injuring anyone. Traditional Republican "castor-oil economics," lamented economist Herbert Stein, was transformed into "the economics of joy," with the help of dubious notions associated with "supply-side economics."[38] In power,

---

[34] Margaret Thatcher, "Speech to the Conservative Party Conference ('The lady's not for turning')," Brighton, October 10, 1980 (www.margaretthatcher.org/speeches/displaydocument.asp?docid=104431).

[35] Smith, *The Rise and Fall of Monetarism*, p. 106; Hall, *Governing the Economy*, p. 118.

[36] Alberto Alesina and Geoffrey Carliner, "Introduction," in Alberto Alesina and Geoffrey Carliner (eds.), *Politics and Economics in the Eighties*, University of Chicago Press, 1991, p. 4; Douglass A. Hibbs, Jr., *The Political Economy of Industrial Democracies*, Cambridge, MA, Harvard University Press, 1987, pp. 163–90; Smithin, *Macroeconomics after Thatcher and Reagan*, p. 57.

[37] Hibbs, *The Political Economy of Industrial Democracies*, pp. 176–82.

[38] Stein, *Presidential Economics*, pp. 236–37.

Reagan implemented important tax cuts but did not reduce spending as much, which contributed to an "unprecedented increase in the budget deficit" and set the stage for a lasting debate on the limits of public intervention.[39] The new president also increased military spending, curtailed programs for the poor, undermined trade unions, and weakened the enforcement of health, safety, and environmental regulations.

The world economy was severely hit by the American and British recessions of 1981–82, and even governments still committed to full employment had to adjust. In an increasingly integrated capital market with high interest rates, the use of expansionary monetary and fiscal instruments had become difficult and costly, and most governments, including social-democratic ones, adopted anti-inflation, austerity policies.[40] The evolution of France was emblematic. Here was a country that, in May 1981, after twenty-three years of uninterrupted rule by the right, elected a socialist president, François Mitterrand, who was allied with the communists and promised profound transformations. In its first year in power, the Mitterrand government did pursue an expansionary economic policy, increasing public spending just as the rest of the world was responding to the recession with austerity measures. In this unfavorable context, France soon faced a balance of payments crisis and strong pressures on its currency. In June 1982, after a year in power, the French socialists changed course. The franc was devalued and a severe austerity plan was adopted. "Keynesianism in one country" had been proven unsustainable.[41]

Neoliberalism

The pure monetarist doctrine gradually faded away, because it was too simplistic to govern economic policy. The Keynesian commitment

---

[39] Alesina and Carliner, "Introduction," p. 13; Krugman, *Peddling Prosperity*, pp. 152–53; Paul Pierson, "The Deficit and the Politics of Domestic Reform," in Margaret Weir (ed.), *The Social Divide: Political Parties and the Future of Activist Government*, Washington, DC, The Brookings Institution, 1998, pp. 126–27.

[40] Scharpf, "Economic Changes, Vulnerabilities, and Institutional Capabilities," p. 51; Torben Iversen, "Decentralization, Monetarism, and the Social Democratic Welfare State," in Torben Iversen, Jonas Pontusson, and David Soskice (eds.), *Unions, Employers, and Central Banks: Macroeconomic Coordination and Institutional Change in Social Market Economies*, Cambridge University Press, 2000, pp. 205–06 and 217.

[41] Hall, *Governing the Economy*, pp. 192–201.

to full employment, however, had been displaced, in favor of a stronger stance against inflation and public deficits, and a clear preference for market mechanisms. More generally, the public policies of the 1980s and 1990s privileged privatization, deregulation, lower taxes, and a leaner state, usually in the name of international competitiveness. The term neoliberalism was used to encompass these different dimensions, and to underline the novel character of this policy package, even though politicians and experts on the right often disapproved of the label.

Consider, for instance, the fate of the civil service. Historically, the right has always distrusted state intervention and bureaucracy, and favored modest governments. The neoliberal movement of the 1980s and 1990s prolonged but also renewed this perspective, by advocating not only a leaner state, but also a government that would be run like a business. Some functions would be abandoned, others would be privatized or contracted out, assets would be sold, and employees would be released. Canada's conservative prime minister Brian Mulroney, for instance, promised to give "pink slips and running shoes to bureaucrats."[42] What remained of the public service would find its inspiration from the private sector, public administration being reinvented as public management. Citizens would become "clients" and public services would be autonomous, empowered, and efficient. The new "public managers" would focus more on results than on rules and process. Many years later, it remained unclear how successful this movement really was in transforming complex public administrations primarily designed to be accountable to authorities, but the "new public management" certainly defined the debate for over two decades.[43]

The turn toward markets was general. Financial institutions were deregulated, industrial policies were practically abandoned, and labor market rules and institutions were made more "flexible." When it came to the welfare state, however, the right faced stronger resistance. For conservatives, generous social programs created four basic problems. First, they pushed taxes up and discouraged investments. Second,

---

[42] Donald J. Savoie, *Thatcher, Reagan, Mulroney: In Search of a New Bureaucracy*, University of Pittsburgh Press, 1994, p. 4.

[43] *Ibid.*, pp. 172–99 and 256–72; Geert Bouckaert, "Modernising Government: The Way Forward – A Comment," *International Review of Administrative Sciences*, vol. 72, no. 3, 2006, 327–32.

they acted as disincentives to work and, in monetarist terms, contributed to increase the "natural" rate of unemployment. Third, they grew increasingly costly, and appeared hard to maintain without serious reforms. Fourth, they undermined core social values, and encouraged "dependency," marital breakdown, and teenage pregnancies among the poor.[44] Thatcher, for instance, insisted on giving choices to individuals and on the importance of work and merit, and she often pleaded in favor of the "Victorian virtues."[45] Reagan accepted in principle to help the "truly needy," but believed that most social programs actually reached citizens who did not need or did not deserve public support – such as the Chicago "welfare Queen" he liked to denounce in 1976 – and that social assistance injured rather than helped the poor.[46]

The welfare state, however, continued to be extremely popular. Most citizens benefited, in one way or another, from social programs, and they remained supportive of arrangements that were also anchored in well-established institutions and guarded by organized and committed interest groups. Taking away benefits, noted Paul Pierson judiciously turned out to be much more difficult than extending them.[47]

Thatcher and Reagan, for instance, succeeded in cutting some of the benefits aimed at the poor – always a weak constituency – but only touched at the margin the larger social programs that constituted middle-class entitlements.[48] More generally, across affluent democracies

---

[44] Fred Block, "Rethinking the Political Economy of the Welfare State," in Fred Block, Richard A. Cloward, Barbara Ehrenreich, and Frances Fox Piven (eds.), *The Mean Season: The Attack on the Welfare State*, New York, Pantheon, 1987, p. 113; Barbara Ehrenreich, "The New Right Attack on Social Welfare," in Block *et al.* (eds.), *The Mean Season*, p. 178.

[45] Timothy Raison, *Tories and the Welfare State: A History of Conservative Social Policy since the Second World War*, Basingstoke, Macmillan, 1990, p. 107; Sylvia Bashevkin, *Welfare Hot Buttons: Women, Work, and Social Policy Reform*, University of Toronto Press, 2002, p. 35.

[46] Bashevkin, *Welfare Hot Buttons*, pp. 22–23; Gareth Davies, "The Welfare State," in W. Elliot Brownle and Hugh Davis Graham (eds.), *The Reagan Presidency: Pragmatic Conservatism and Its Legacies*, Lawrence, University Press of Kansas, 2003, p. 209.

[47] Paul Pierson, "Coping with Permanent Austerity: Welfare State Restructuring in Affluent Democracies," in Paul Pierson (ed.), *The New Politics of the Welfare State*, Oxford University Press, 2001, pp. 411–13.

[48] Paul Pierson, *Dismantling the Welfare State: Reagan, Thatcher, and the Politics of Retrenchment*, Cambridge University Press, 1994, pp. 114–115; Carles Boix, *Political Parties, Growth and Equality: Conservative and Social Democratic*

between 1980 and 1998, the average growth of social expenditures went down compared to the previous two decades, but it did not become negative. In other words, welfare states continued to expand, albeit at a slower pace.[49] One of the factors behind this continued expansion of social programs was the steady rise of market inequality, which meant that states had to intervene more to obtain the same distributive results.[50]

This does not imply that nothing changed. First, in some countries, such as the United Kingdom and New Zealand, there were significant retrenchment efforts that truly reduced social protection.[51] Second, many programs were modified in a neoliberal perspective. While not affecting aggregate levels of spending, these modifications altered important features of the welfare state and probably opened the way for further reforms in the future.

In health care, most countries made efforts to contain costs in the 1980s and 1990s, and they also reduced the public share in total health expenditures (by increasing the role of private insurances or the proportion of co-payments, for instance).[52] With respect to public pensions, admittedly the most difficult programs to modify, governments generally implemented reforms meant to reduce generosity and contain costs. A common trend was also to move gradually from pay-as-you-go to funding systems, the latter being more sustainable in the long run, but also less redistributive, at least in principle, and more consistent with a market logic.[53]

    Economic Strategies in the World Economy, Cambridge University Press, 1998, pp. 192–94; John A. Ferejohn, "Changes in Welfare Policy in the 1980s," in Alesina and Carliner (eds.), *Politics and Economics in the Eighties*, pp. 138–39.

[49] Francis G. Castles, *The Future of the Welfare State: Crisis Myths and Crisis Realities*, Oxford University Press, 2004, p. 45.

[50] Lane Kenworthy and Jonas Pontusson, "Rising Inequality and the Politics of Redistribution in Affluent Countries," *Perspectives on Politics*, vol. 3, no. 3, September 2005, 449–71, p. 450.

[51] Evelyne Huber and John D. Stephens, *Development and Crisis of the Welfare State: Parties and Policies in Global Markets*, University of Chicago Press, 2001, pp. 300–01; Jonas Pontusson, *Inequality and Prosperity: Social Europe vs. Liberal America*, Ithaca, Cornell University Press, 2005, p. 202.

[52] Pontusson, *Inequality and Prosperity*, pp. 187–88; Jacob S. Hacker, "Dismantling the Health Care State? Political Institutions, Public Policies, and the Comparative Politics of Health Reform," *British Journal of Political Science*, vol. 34, no. 4, October 2004, 693–724, pp. 699–700.

[53] Giuliano Bonoli, *The Politics of Pension Reform: Institutions and Policy Change in Western Europe*, Cambridge University Press, 2000, pp. 23–24.

The evolution of programs for the unemployed, a central worry for conservatives, proved particularly striking. Between 1985 and 1999, the net income replacement rate for persons out of work was reduced practically everywhere in the OECD, and cuts were most severe where parties of the right were in power.[54] Conditions were also tightened. In country after country, governments tried to better link income support to the labor market, to help, encourage, or compel the unemployed to go back to work. Where the right was in power, these conditions tended to be stricter, and at times punitive, shading into workfare. Where the left remained stronger, the measures adopted were more likely to be voluntary and focused on training and social inclusion.[55]

Throughout this period marked by neoliberalism, the distinction between the right and the left often appeared muted, and to some almost irrelevant. Indeed, the right was prevented from going as far as it would have wished by the unflinching popularity of the welfare state; and the left was compelled to accept austerity measures by persistently high levels of unemployment.[56] Both sides were thus forced to adjust the welfare state at the margins, slowing its growth and gradually transforming its mission. The way they did so, however, proved quite different.

Parties of the right wanted to reinforce market mechanisms and to reduce state intervention and redistribution. They were thus more likely to advocate important cuts to the welfare state and indeed they often succeeded. Conservatives also believed, in monetarist fashion, that the best way to adjust to globalization and reduce unemployment was to keep taxes low and deregulate the labor market, so as to maintain competitive wages. Parties of the left did accept that monetary and fiscal policies had become blunt tools, and they also turned to the supply side, but they did so with distinct priorities. Rather than lowering taxes and wages, they sought to use public investment to enhance education and training, which they saw as the best foundations

---

[54] Pontusson, *Inequality and Prosperity*, pp. 191–92; James P. Allan and Lyle Scruggs, "Political Partisanship and Welfare State Reform in Advanced Industrial Societies," *American Journal of Political Science*, vol. 48, no. 3, July 2004, 498–512.

[55] Neil Gilbert, *Transformations of the Welfare State: The Silent Surrender of Public Responsibility*, Oxford University Press, 2004, pp. 62–63.

[56] Huber and Stephens, *Development and Crisis of the Welfare State*, p. 305.

for a competitive, high-wage, knowledge economy. These differences manifested themselves in the public policies of the period. Parties of the left taxed more and more progressively than parties of the right, and they used the additional revenues to invest in education and training as well as in programs to sustain competitiveness. Conservatives, on the other hand, lowered tax rates and labor costs, and relied more on private investments.[57] Even though both sides were influenced by neoliberalism and accepted austerity, only the left combined welfare state retrenchment with public investments in new programs favorable to equality.[58]

The marginalization of the North–South debate

In world politics, the 1980s and 1990s also saw the triumph of conservative forces.[59] Communism was defeated and the East–West division abolished. Only the North–South cleavage remained, but this conflict was less and less defined by the demands of the South for redistribution and global reforms. Actively promoted by the governments of the North, the major international economic agencies, and the business community, a neoliberal view of development came to prevail, to the point of becoming accepted by most as something like "common sense."[60]

The historical backdrop to this evolution very much coincided with the circumstances that led to the rise of the right in affluent democracies. Indeed, the actors and events involved were largely the same that brought about monetarism and welfare state retrenchment. It was quite natural for leaders such as Margaret Thatcher and Ronald Reagan to extend their political views to world affairs. As she wanted to herald the beginning of a new era, Thatcher, for example, insisted that the very idea of a North–South bipolarity had to be discarded: "The term 'North–South,' implying as it does a simple division of needs and interests," contended the British prime minister, "is an

---

[57] Boix, *Political Parties, Growth and Equality*, pp. 39 and 99–101.
[58] Castles, *The Future of the Welfare State*, p. 109.
[59] Robert Gilpin (with the assistance of Jean M. Gilpin), *Global Political Economy: Understanding the International Economic Order*, Princeton University Press, 2001, p. 309.
[60] Jan Aart Scholte, *Globalization: A Critical Introduction*, second edition, New York, Palgrave-Macmillan, 2005, p. 39.

inadequate and often misleading description of the complex inter-relationship that now exists between countries in a wide variety of economic circumstances."[61] Her administration, like an increasing number of governments in the North, was simply not ready to support a structural reform of the global economic system.

Conservatives considered that the developing countries were too ideological in their approach to international economic issues. This attitude, it was argued, had engendered a shopping list of contra-dictory demands whose only rationale was the need to please as many Third World leaders as possible. The South's confrontational strategy was also denounced on the grounds that a number of the governments who backed it were corrupt and undemocratic, and therefore not in a position to lecture others on matters of morality. For the right, the developing countries had no choice but to become more realistic and pragmatic. In calling for more pragmatism, conservatives sought pri-marily to have the poor nations give up the notion that the imbalances of the global economy could be corrected through the adoption of an international treaty. They also aimed to convince the Third World that, despite its acknowledged importance, justice had to remain subordinate to order in the hierarchy of international values. The momentum generated in the 1970s by the negotiations on a new inter-national economic order and by the creation of the Brandt Commis-sion was thus gradually lost. On the right, this turn of events was viewed in a positive light, as it put an end to a diplomatic enterprise that was considered a huge waste of energy. On the left, it was seen as a major setback, and the beginning of a "lost decade" for development.

Nothing illustrated the marginalization of the North–South debate more pointedly than the failure of the Cancún Summit in 1981.[62] Following up on the Brandt Commission's report, this summit brought together twenty-two heads of state of the North and the South, for discussions on four interrelated topics: food, trade, energy, and finance. The developing countries hoped that, with its informal setting, the

[61] Margaret Thatcher, "Response to the Brandt Report," in Friedrich Ebert Foundation (ed.), *International Responses to the Brandt Report*, London, Temple Smith, 1981, p. 105.
[62] Jean-Philippe Thérien, "The Brandt Commission: The End of an Era in North–South Politics," in Ramesh Thakur, Andrew F. Cooper, and John English (eds.), *International Commissions and the Power of Ideas*, Tokyo, United Nations University Press, 2005, pp. 27–45.

summit would serve as a launching pad for global negotiations on international economic issues. The meeting, however, yielded only results which observers judged "insubstantial and disappointing."[63] No agreement was reached on the opening of global negotiations and, more tellingly, the participants even rejected the idea of institution-alizing their forum.

The road to the Cancún Summit was already unpromising, with the newly elected Ronald Reagan only reluctantly agreeing to participate. The American president was on the whole more concerned with domestic economic problems than international affairs and, to the extent that he was interested in foreign affairs, East–West issues remained in his view far more important than North–South questions. In Cancún, Reagan argued that through its trade and aid policies the United States already contributed more than any other country to Third World development, and he reaffirmed his confidence in the market economy and in existing international economic institutions. With the world's foremost power taking such a stance, the summit could hardly produce a program of substantial reforms.

Even the most optimistic, who, like Willy Brandt, maintained that Cancún had produced some new consensus, had to admit there was a "setback" in North–South relations after the Summit.[64] The problem was confirmed by the little attention paid to the second Brandt report, published in 1983, and by the gradual disappearance of any allusion to the new international economic order from the discourse of inter-national institutions. In 1990, the South Commission – an independent body created in 1987 to promote views from the South – complained that North–South diplomacy had "virtually collapsed."[65] The failure of Cancún had indeed been a turning point. It would take until 2002, with the holding of the Monterrey Summit on development financing, for such a high-level meeting to address again the problems of poor nations in a "holistic manner."[66]

[63] Charles A. Jones, *The North–South Dialogue: A Brief History*, New York, St. Martin's Press, 1983, p. 115.

[64] Independent Commission on International Development Issues (chaired by Willy Brandt), *Common Crisis. North–South: Co-operation for World Recovery*, Cambridge, MA, MIT Press, 1983, p. 4.

[65] South Commission, *The Challenge to the South: The Report of the South Commission*, Oxford University Press, 1990, p. 18.

[66] Nitin Desai, "Preface," in United Nations, *Financing for Development: Building on Monterrey*, New York, United Nations, 2002, p. vii.

The global rise of the right led to profound transformations in development diplomacy. The UN, in particular, lost ground throughout the 1980s and 1990s, at the expense of the Bretton Woods institutions, which became central in the management of relations between rich and poor countries. The declining influence of the UN – previously the North–South forum *par excellence* – was not simply a by-product of a change in priorities. It came following a forceful conservative campaign, led by Washington and London, against the organization and its mission.[67]

Among the charges leveled at the UN, the most fundamental denied its legal authority to reform international trade and finance, on the grounds that these questions were under the jurisdictions of the GATT, the IMF, and the World Bank. In addition, the UN's understanding of economic processes was presented as basically wrong. The organization was notably reproached for promoting "a socialist path to development," and for displaying little concern for freedom and individual rights.[68] Pointing to the numerous votes where countries of the North had found themselves isolated because of the "automatic majority" of the South, conservative politicians also denounced the anti-Western bias of the UN, a prejudice that was in their view all the more objectionable since the organization was funded primarily by the governments of developed nations. The right also indicted the UN for suffering from the same bureaucratic problems that afflicted public institutions worldwide.

The anti-UN crusade was spearheaded by the United States. The American government resisted the temptation to leave the organization outright, as some on the right would have liked, but it deployed a wide range of intimidation tactics. Two decisions in this long wrestling match were especially significant. First, in 1984, the United States withdrew from the United Nations Educational, Scientific and Cultural Organization (UNESCO) to protest against the politicization

---

[67] Craig N. Murphy, *International Organization and Industrial Change: Global Governance since 1850*, New York, Oxford University Press, 1994, pp. 258–59; and Jacques Fomerand, *Mirror, Tool, or Linchpin for Change? The UN and Development*, Waterloo, Academic Council on the United Nations System, 2003, p. 42.

[68] Joshua Muravchik, *The Future of the United Nations: Understanding the Past to Chart a Way Forward*, Washington, American Enterprise Institute for Public Policy Research, 2005, p. 71.

of that body, which, the American government felt, had culminated in the debate on a new world information and communication order. This punitive measure, which Great Britain also adopted in 1985, was not lifted until 2003, when the United States finally rejoined UNESCO. The second decision was the implementation in 1985 of the American administration's policy of delaying the payment of its contribution to the UN regular budget.[69] Since the United States was the UN's main financial contributor, this strategy quickly succeeded in modifying the organization's behavior to Washington's liking. As these episodes demonstrate, hostility toward the UN – expressed more recently in the discussions on the International Criminal Court, the Kyoto Protocol, and the war in Iraq – has been a key component of US foreign policy for an entire generation.

The pressures brought to bear during the 1980s put the UN on the defensive and produced many changes within the organization. The UN endeavored to shift the focus of its activities toward security issues, while in the field of development it assumed a much lower profile. The very idea of overhauling the world economic order was dropped, along with plans to stabilize commodity prices or regulate technology transfers. It is also noteworthy that when the UN initiated a comeback in the area of development in the 1990s, it adopted an approach that was plainly less ambitious than before. As they dealt with topics such as children (1990), the environment (1992), human rights (1993), women (1995), habitat (1996), or racism (2001), the UN major conferences of that decade opened new paths for dialogue, but they deliberately stayed away from the alternative global approach that was put forward during the 1970s. As the years passed, the UN increasingly fell into line with the prevalent orthodoxy, according to which development policies had to rely on the market, with domestic impediments to growth outweighing the constraints associated with the external environment.[70]

---

[69] Margaret P. Karns and Karen A. Mingst, *International Organizations: The Politics and Processes of Global Governance*, Boulder, Lynne Rienner, 2004, pp. 253–54; United Nations Association of the United States of America, "United Nations Funding: FY2007 Budget Request", UNA-USA factsheet, May 2006 (www.unausa.org/site/pp.asp?c=fvKRI8MPJpF&b=667579).

[70] Robert W. Cox (with Michael Schechter), *The Political Economy of a Plural World: Critical Reflections on Power, Morals and Civilization*, London, Routledge, 2002, p. 86.

As the UN watched its political influence wane, the IMF, the World Bank, and the GATT – which became the World Trade Organization (WTO) in 1995 – saw theirs wax considerably. In two decades, these bodies were able to establish themselves as the main "globalizers."[71] For the right, two main reasons justified the realignment of forces within the multilateral system. To begin with, the economic expertise of the Bretton Woods institutions was deemed unquestionably superior to that of the UN. Specifically, the mainstream, neoclassical approach of these institutions appeared better able to address the needs of poor countries. Second, conservatives believed that the strengthening of the Bretton Woods institutions would improve the cohesion of the international system by allowing the rich countries to play a more important political role. Indeed, the voting power of member-states in the IMF and the World Bank is directly proportional to their economic power. The United States, in particular, occupies a dominant position in both institutions, since no major decision can be made without its consent. At the GATT–WTO, decision-making procedures are formally more democratic but they remain *de facto* "weighted...in favour of the major developed countries."[72] By acknowledging more frankly the link between wealth and political authority, the new multilateral setup seemed to provide the governance of development with a more rational operational framework.

The Third World debt crisis of the early 1980s strongly contributed to the rising influence of the IMF and the World Bank. It should be recalled that in the North, this crisis was often said to jeopardize the very foundations of the international financial system. The governments of the G7 thus felt compelled to urge the international financial institutions to be stricter with borrowing states. This new approach led to the inception of structural adjustment programs, which over the years imposed a series of stringent economic and political conditions on nearly a hundred debtor countries. The GATT–WTO, for its part, was able to become a potent political force because of two converging factors. For one thing, the adjustment policies advocated by the international financial institutions always favored free trade and

[71] Ngaire Woods, *The Globalizers: The IMF, the World Bank and Their Borrowers*, Ithaca, Cornell University Press, 2006.

[72] Margaret P. Karns and Karen A. Mingst, *The United Nations in the Post-Cold War Era*, second edition, Boulder, Westview, 2000, p. 130.

extolled the spirit of GATT rules. In addition, conservatives and the business community actively pushed the GATT–WTO to extend the liberalization of the world economy beyond the exchange of manufactured goods.

On the strength of their rising authority, the Bretton Woods institutions managed, in a few years, to redefine development politics. The "Washington consensus" became the emblem for the neoliberal reforms promoted jointly by the IMF, the World Bank, the GATT–WTO, and the governments of the North. The term became fashionable to a degree that dismayed John Williamson, the British economist who had coined it, with a narrower meaning in mind. Once it had slipped out of the control of experts, the idea of a "Washington consensus" served as a shorthand reference to the proximity, both geographic and intellectual, of the main strongholds of development-related international power. As Ngaire Woods reminds us, the policies implemented in the name of this "consensus" were in fact challenged on both sides of the political spectrum.[73] These challenges, however, were hardly symmetrical: the opposition to the "Washington consensus" mobilized a major portion of the left, but only a small part of the right. Overall, it was truly a conservative "counter-revolution"[74] that the Bretton Woods institutions piloted as of the 1980s.

A new development agenda

Fostered by the political right, the rearrangement of North–South relations brought a redefinition of development objectives. The new agenda was based on the axiom "that there is only one economics, and that economics is a universal science equally applicable to all societies."[75] With the failure of the socialist experiment and the difficulties faced by Keynesianism, the notion that there might exist a distinct discipline called "development economics" – more open to state intervention – was increasingly called into question. British economist John Toye relates that in the mid-1980s the US representative to the Asian Development Bank flatly declared, "the United

---

[73] Woods, *The Globalizers*, p. 1.
[74] John Toye, *Dilemmas of Development: Reflections on the Counter-Revolution in Development Economics*, second edition, Oxford, Blackwell, 1993.
[75] Gilpin, *Global Political Economy*, p. 311.

States completely rejects the idea that there is such a thing as 'development economics'."[76] The premise that the economic policies valid for rich countries were also valid for poor ones did a great deal to advance the movement from the old development agenda toward a new set of priorities.

The World Bank encapsulated this shift by describing the 1980s as a period that "downplayed distribution and poverty and insisted on re-establishing market mechanisms to promote economic growth."[77] The priority of economic governance, according to a popular catch-phrase, was "to get prices right." This approach was incorporated in the policies of the IMF and the World Bank, for whom the prime responsibility of governments was to ensure that markets were propped up by a sound macro-economic framework. Structural adjustment programs, which were in effect monetarist recipes for the South, pushed developing countries to adopt high interest rates in order to curb inflation, to devalue their currencies to stimulate exports, and to introduce rigorous budgetary measures to improve public finances. Within this cocktail of prescriptions designed to stabilize the balance of payments, the reduction of government expenditures was regarded as especially warranted, on the grounds that markets were more efficient than states in allocating resources. Accordingly, adjustment policies often involved the deregulation of the price of goods and services that had until then been publicly supported, and the privatization of state-owned enterprises. Initially, these reforms were presented as transition measures on the road back to a financially sound environment. Over time, however, they increasingly became understood as elements of a "permanent discipline."[78]

In conjunction with structural adjustment, two other objectives shaped the policies designed by the international institutions and the governments of the developed countries in the 1980s and 1990s: trade liberalization and the promotion of foreign direct investment. The two objectives stemmed in fact from a common assumption, that the opening of borders was good for development.

[76] Toye, *Dilemmas of Development*, p. 94.
[77] James D. Wolfensohn and François Bourguignon, *Development and Poverty Reduction: Looking Back, Looking Ahead*, Washington, DC, World Bank, 2004, p. 3.
[78] Payne, *The Global Politics of Unequal Development*, p. 12.

Free trade became promoted as never before. For conservatives, there was a natural step from recognizing the benefits of markets at the domestic level to advising Southern countries to become more open to international trade. Trade was seen as a powerful engine of economic growth, because exports created jobs, while imports prompted local businesses to enhance the quality and the diversity of their products. Resolutely supportive of this way of thinking, the WTO declared in 2002 that the elimination of all tariff and non-tariff barriers could increase the income of Third World countries by $370 billion.[79] Conservatives also embraced the idea that growth helped the poor. Citing such examples as China, India, Vietnam, or Uganda, they asserted that the countries that had best succeeded in reducing poverty were those with the highest growth rates.[80] The full reasoning was straightforward: since trade was good for growth, and growth good for the poor, then trade was necessarily good for the poor. This line of argument, ultimately, summarized the neoliberal stance on the benefits of globalization for developing countries.

The Uruguay Round negotiations (1986–94), the creation of the World Trade Organization (1995), and the launching of the Doha Round (2001) contributed to integrating the South in a trade regime that remains by and large defined and shaped by the North. Governments of the North, indeed, drafted new norms for services, intellectual property, and investment, in line with their own national interests. Although developing countries did make some gains in recent trade talks, their historical concerns regarding the acceptance of import substitution policies, the promotion of self-reliance, the possibility of special and differential treatment, and the reform of decision-making structures were for the most part put aside. To this day, it is still unclear whether Third World countries, starting with giants such as India and Brazil, ended up joining the game of international competition willingly. Be that as it may, in the trade negotiations of the past two decades the poor conceded more than the rich, and the WTO often

---

[79] World Trade Organization, "To Doha and Beyond: A Roadmap for Successfully Concluding the Doha Development Round," remarks by Mr. Mike Moore, Director-General, WTO, Montreux, April 12, 2002 (www.wto.org/english/news_e/spmm_e/spmm83_e.htm).

[80] World Bank, *Globalization, Growth, and Poverty: Building an Inclusive World Economy*, Washington, DC, World Bank, 2002, p. 6.

took the part of an instrument in the service of "an old-fashioned form of realist power politics."[81]

As for the promotion of foreign direct investment, it was an integral component of the vast movement in favor of the private sector and the globalization of markets. The United Nations Conference on Trade and Development (UNCTAD) estimated that between 1991 and 2002, 95 percent of all government measures dealing with foreign investment encouraged greater liberalization.[82] With the countries of the South taking an active part in this international trend, foreign direct investment began to play a much bigger role than before in development financing. Between 1980 and 2004, flows of foreign direct investment to the Third World grew 28-fold, surging from $8 billion to $230 billion.[83]

International institutions were instrumental in rehabilitating foreign investment and in getting the developing countries to display a new openness toward transnational corporations. The leadership role played by the WTO was in this respect decisive. The Agreement on Trade Related Aspects of Intellectual Property Rights that was negotiated during the Uruguay Round represented a particularly significant innovation, as it gave large corporations increased protection for their patents. At the same time, the structural adjustment programs imposed by the IMF and the World Bank systematically required the governments of the South to relax their restrictive policies toward foreign investors. As for the UN, whose previous hostility toward multinational companies was well known, it effected "a change of 180 degrees."[84] After the early 1990s, instead of advocating greater control over transnational corporate activities in the Third World, the organization took on the mandate of actively promoting foreign investment. This ideological shift was aptly summarized by then Secretary-General Kofi

[81] Payne, *The Global Politics of Unequal Development*, pp. 118 and 170.

[82] UNCTAD, *Development and Globalization: Facts and Figures*, New York, UNCTAD, 2004, p. 36.

[83] *Ibid.*, p. 33; UNCTAD, "Surge in Foreign Direct Investment in Developing Countries Reverses Global Downturn," press release, Geneva, September 29, 2005 (www.unctad.org/templates/webflyer.asp?docid=6334&intItemID=3369&lang=1).

[84] G. C. A. Junne, "International Organizations in a Period of Globalization: New (Problems of) Legitimacy," in Jean-Marc Coicaud and Veijo Heiskanen (eds.), *The Legitimacy of International Organizations*, Tokyo, United Nations University Press, 2001, p. 204.

Annan, when he described the goals of the UN – promoting peace and development – and the goals of business – creating wealth and prosperity – as "mutually supportive."[85]

It is still difficult to assess precisely the impact of the new economic approaches that have been introduced in the South over the past twenty years. Whereas these policies were put in place to foster economic growth, there is some evidence that they have led to a growing concentration of wealth and to an increase in inequality. What is perfectly clear, at all events, is that the advancement of structural adjustment, free trade, and foreign investment was in close harmony with the values and principles of an assertive global right.

This neoliberal reshaping of development objectives was accompanied by a transformation of development assistance policies. In 1980, foreign aid represented 0.37 percent of the developed countries' GNP. By 1997, this proportion had reached a historic low of 0.22 percent.[86] To the satisfaction of conservatives – and thanks in large part to the US administration's ceaseless efforts – the international target of 0.7 percent, which the governments of the South and NGOs recalled at every opportunity, had lost its sacred aura. Revealingly, Denmark, Norway, Sweden, and the Netherlands – four states where social-democracy and the left have historically been strong – were the only rich countries to constantly display an aid contribution above 0.7 percent. The predictions of those who foresaw the possible end of foreign aid proved unwarranted, however. In the wake of the 2002 Monterrey meeting, and boosted by debt relief operations, development assistance went up to 0.33 percent of the developed countries' GNI and totaled over $100 billion by 2005. Yet, according to preliminary OECD estimates, aid is likely to fall back in the late 2000s.[87] Overall, the relative weight of aid in Northern countries' foreign policy has been on the decline over the past quarter-century.

Numerous reasons explained the drop of development assistance. More often than not, governments of the North justified their decreased generosity by the need to put their public finances in order. The

---

[85] United Nations, "Cooperation Between United Nations and Business," press release, SG/2043, February 9, 1998.

[86] OECD, *Development Co-operation Report 2002*, Paris, OECD, 2003, p. 229.

[87] See OECD, "Development Aid from OECD Countries Fell 5.1 Percent in 2006," (www.oecd.org/document/17/0,2340,en_2649_34447_38341265_1_1_1_1,00.html)

reduction in aid budgets was presented as part of a larger effort to limit government spending, and as the price to pay to ensure the long-term sustainability of development assistance programs. An "aid fatigue" among the public of donor countries was also evoked, and attributed to the apparent failure of past policies. In Africa, it was often said, the allocation of vast resources had not succeeded in pushing back poverty. Conservatives also argued that it was unacceptable to continue to subsidize inefficient governments, which rejected market mechanisms and stubbornly held on to state-centered development strategies.[88] At the end of the 1990s, the World Bank fueled such criticisms when it concluded that developing countries with "mediocre" policies received more financial aid than those with "good" policies.[89] As aid agencies understandably sought to reverse this trend, slashing development assistance budgets was increasingly legitimized by the need to fight against waste and corruption.

Although this was rarely admitted publicly, there is no doubt that the end of the Cold War also contributed to the decline of aid. Until the end of the 1980s, the struggle against communism and the desire to prevent Third World countries from aligning themselves with the USSR pushed Western governments to maintain relatively generous development assistance policies. From the moment the Soviet Union converted itself to a market economy, that strategic motivation vanished. In addition, as former territories of the Soviet bloc became themselves aid recipients, they drained a share of the total resources available to the poorest countries.

In keeping with the neoliberal approach, the rise of private financing was presented as minimizing the need for aid in the fight against poverty. Many on the right contended that the quality of aid was a good deal more crucial than its volume. Following the precepts of the "new public management," aid agencies increasingly tried to make their organizational culture more "results-oriented."[90] This new philosophy had a significant impact on the design of development assistance

---

[88] David K. Fieldhouse, *The West and the Third World*, Oxford, Blackwell, 1999, p. 243.

[89] World Bank, *Assessing Aid: What Works, What Doesn't, and Why*, New York, Oxford University Press, 1998, pp. 23–25.

[90] Hyun-sik Chang, Arthur M. Fell, and Michael Laird (with the assistance of Julie Seif), *A Comparison of Management Systems for Development Co-operation in OECD/DAC Members*, Paris, OECD, 1999, p. 97.

programs. For much of the 1980s, aid was thus adapted to the imperatives of adjustment policies, either to hasten their implementation
or to compensate for their negative social effects.[91] In the 1990s, the
donor community then shifted its objectives to promote good governance. This catch-all concept served at times to strengthen the rule
of law – a result welcomed by all – but it was also often used to ease
the adoption of policies favoring market expansion. It was, for
example, in the name of good governance that governments of the
South were asked to privatize public services and foster public–private
partnerships.

   More recently, the conservative influence on aid policies has made
itself felt through the emphasis put on the fight against terrorism.
The inclusion of this issue in the aid regime – due, of course, to the
September 11, 2001 attacks and to the subsequent war on terrorism –
was made official by donor countries in 2003.[92] The struggle against
terrorism then justified a redirection of aid resources toward certain
countries (Afghanistan, Iraq, and Pakistan notably) in response to
geo-political interests. In 2005, for instance, debt forgiveness grants
to Iraq amounted to nearly $14 billion. More generally, the fight
against terrorism led to an increasing overlap between development
and security financing. Highly critical of this tendency toward a
"securitization of development aid,"[93] the left has constantly repeated
that the defeat of terrorism is impossible in the absence of a war on
poverty; these arguments, however, have been to little avail.

Conclusion

In the last two decades of the twentieth century, the global right
gained the upper hand. Communism was no longer a threat, democracy
was on the rise around the world, and social-democratic prescriptions
for state intervention seemed less convincing than the new breed of

[91] Olav Stokke, "Foreign Aid: What Now?," in Olav Stokke (ed.), *Foreign Aid
    towards the Year 2000: Experiences and Challenges*, London, Frank Cass,
    1996, pp. 73–74.
[92] OECD, *A Development Cooperation Lens on Terrorism Prevention: Key Entry
    Points of Action*, DAC Guidelines and References Series, Paris, OECD, 2003.
[93] Ayodele Aderinwale, "The Securitization of Development Aid," in The Reality
    of Aid Management Committee, *The Reality of Aid 2006: Focus on Conflict,
    Security and Development*, Quezon City and London, IBON Books and Zed
    Books, 2006, pp. 88–106.

market-oriented policies associated with monetarism and neoliberalism. Most countries made a priority of fighting inflation, even at the cost of increasing unemployment, and practically every public policy was reconsidered in order to reduce cost and enhance market flexibility. The market logic was extended to almost every social undertaking: even the state was to be "run like a business."

In the international arena, the demands of the poorer countries for a more equitable world were also displaced by strong calls for structural adjustment policies and for trade and investment rules suitable for an integrated global market. The affluent democracies reduced their contributions for development assistance, but they nevertheless felt justified in assessing the governments of the South for their good governance. This stance conveniently ignored the fact that when a country was poor, governance was also likely to be poor. "The problem," noted Jeffrey Sachs, was "not that poorly governed countries get too much help, but that well-governed countries get far too little."[94]

Culturally, the triumph of market democracy also facilitated the ascent of individualism. In a context where competitiveness became an all-encompassing objective, indeed almost a value, personal success was readily celebrated. Individual rights and identities became central political concerns, and citizens increasingly looked to the courts to adjudicate disputes. Conservatives were ambivalent about these trends, some applauding any expression of individualism, others being more concerned by the potential decline of traditional values. On the left, reactions were mixed as well, the politics of rights and identity being perceived as progress by some, and as a distraction from the search for equality by others. In a sense, the lines appeared to be blurring. As the left adjusted to a neoliberal world, the possibility of a new configuration for the long-lasting debate between the left and the right was increasingly evoked.

[94] Jeffrey Sachs, *The End of Poverty: How We Can Make It Happen in Our Lifetime*, Harmondsworth, Penguin, 2005, pp. 269 and 312.

7 | Twenty-first-century rapprochement

On May 1, 1997, Tony Blair and his New Labour Party won the British general election with 43.2 percent of the vote, against 30.7 percent for the Conservatives and 16.8 percent for the Liberal Democrats. Coming from a distance, the Labour Party won more seats than ever in its history. It progressed in every region and in most social groups, among the less fortunate and the young in particular.[1] After eighteen years in opposition, the British left was finally able to form a strong and legitimate majority government. This was, however, a new left. A New Labour government, Blair had promised, would define a new course, away "from the solutions of the old left and those of the Conservative right," and focused on "what works."[2]

Tony Blair was not alone. A few years earlier, in 1992, Democrat Bill Clinton was elected president of the United States with a commitment to "reinvent government" and restore the responsibility of citizens and a sense of community. "The change I seek and the change that we must all seek," Clinton had explained in October 1991, "isn't liberal or conservative. It's different and it's both."[3] In October 1993, Canadians replaced the Conservatives, in power since 1984, with the centrist Liberal Party, led by Jean Chrétien. In continental Europe, social-democrats were also coming to power, in one country after the other. At the June 1997 European summit in Amsterdam, ten out of fifteen member-states sent social-democratic or socialist prime ministers (Austria, Denmark, Finland, France, Greece, Italy, the Netherlands,

---

[1] David Butler and Dennis Kavanagh, *The British General Election of 1997*, Basingstoke, Macmillan, 1997, pp. xi, 244, and 255.
[2] Tony Blair, "Britain Will Do Better with New Labour," Introduction to *New Labour Because Britain Deserves Better*, New Labour Manifesto, 1997 (www.labour-party.org.uk/manifestos/1997/1997-labour-manifesto.shtml).
[3] Bill Clinton (1991), quoted in Jon F. Hale, "The Making of the New Democrats," *Political Science Quarterly*, vol. 110, no. 2, Summer 1995, 207–32, p. 226.

Portugal, Sweden, and the United Kingdom).[4] Among the few countries still governed by conservatives, Germany was also about to turn left, with the election of Gerhard Schröder in October 1998. Like Clinton and Blair before him, Schröder offered a reformed set of progressive policies, conceived to please voters, described as "*Die Neue Mitte*," the new center.[5]

The left was back, and it was back with a new message, which claimed to define a distinctive path – a "Third Way" – between the traditional left and the neoliberal right. In the meantime, the right also softened up. After two Reagan mandates, presidential candidate George H. W. Bush promised in 1988 a "kinder, gentler America."[6] Succeeding Margaret Thatcher in 1990, John Major offered continuity, but in a pragmatic, less abrasive fashion.[7] This milder conservatism was often described as "Thatcherism with a grey face."[8] In Mexico, center-right president Vicente Fox, who came to power after a historic election in 2000, often stressed that he was not a neoliberal – "*yo no soy neoliberal*" – but simply interested in improving the income and quality of life of his country's families.[9] Just as social-democratic parties were constrained by pressures to maintain competitive tax rates and a balanced budget, conservatives had to face the unflinching

[4] Philip Manow, Armin Schäfer, and Hendrik Zorn, *European Social Policy and Europe's Party-Political Center of Gravity, 1957–2003*, MPIfG Discussion Paper (Max-Planck-Institut für Gesellschaftsforschung Köln), 04/6, October 2004, p. 29 (www.mpi-fg-koeln.mpg.de/pu/mpifg_dp/dp04-6.pdf).

[5] Russell J. Dalton, "Germany's Vote for a 'New Middle'," *Current History*, vol. 98, no. 627, April 1999, 176–79.

[6] Fred I. Greenstein, "The Prudent Professionalism of George Herbert Walker Bush," *Journal of Interdisciplinary History*, vol. 31, no. 3, Winter 2001, 385–92, p. 388.

[7] Philip Norton, "The Conservative Party: 'In Office But Not in Power'," in Anthony King, Iain McLean, Pippa Norris, Philip Norton, David Sanders, and Patrick Seyd (eds.), *New Labour Triumphs: Britain at the Polls*, Chatham, NJ, Chatham House, 1998, pp. 96–97; Christopher Stevens, "Thatcherism, Majorism and the Collapse of Tory Statecraft," *Contemporary British History*, vol. 16, no. 1, Spring 2002, 119–50, pp. 135–36.

[8] Martin Rhodes, "Restructuring the British Welfare State: Between Domestic Constraints and Global Imperatives," in Fritz W. Scharpf and Vivien A. Schmidt (eds.), *Welfare and Work in the Open Economy. Volume II. Diverse Responses to Common Challenges*, Oxford University Press, 2000 p. 62.

[9] "Conversación que sostuvo el Presidente Fox con el periodista José Gutiérrez Vivó," Mexico, July 4, 2001 (http://fox.presidencia.gob.mx/actividades/?contenido=1374).

popularity of the welfare state, as well as growing worries about inequality and poverty.[10]

The end of the 1990s was also marked by a major downturn in the world economy. The East Asian financial and economic crisis that started in July 1997 was indeed the most important global crisis since the Great Depression. Spreading rapidly through Asia and then to Russia and Latin America, the crisis shook confidence in multilateral economic institutions and raised serious questions about the neoliberal policies associated with the "Washington consensus." Meant to foster economic growth and stability, these policies had indeed been legitimated by the success of the East Asian "models."[11] Amidst debates on the causes and on the significance of the Asian debacle, critical voices began to be heard and alternative policies, more favorable to state intervention and redistribution, were put forward.[12]

In world as in domestic politics, the distance between the right and the left seemed to narrow. Politicians and diplomats began to speak of a growing consensus on development and of the need to combat global poverty.[13] Mark Malloch Brown, who was then head of the United Nations Development Programme (UNDP), put the matter succinctly:

I believe we are at a pivotal moment in global development – an international equivalent of the contemporary domestic debates about welfare reform that are in different ways preoccupying countries from the United States to France to Germany – where the right has realized that the case for doing

---

[10] Carles Boix, *Political Parties, Growth and Equality: Conservative and Social Democratic Economic Strategies in the World Economy*, Cambridge University Press, 1998, pp. 203–211.

[11] Charles Gore, "The Rise and Fall of the Washington Consensus as a Paradigm for Developing Countries," *World Development*, vol. 28, no. 5, 2000, 789–804, p. 799; Joseph E. Stiglitz, *Globalization and Its Discontents*, New York, W. W. Norton, 2002, pp. 89–132.

[12] Barry Eichengreen, "The Global Gamble on Financial Liberalization: Reflections on Capital Mobility, National Autonomy, and Social Justice," *Ethics & International Affairs*, vol. 13, no. 1, March 1999, 205–26, pp. 205–7.

[13] In 2003, the OECD referred to an emerging "global anti-poverty consensus." Ida McDonnell, Henri-Bernard Solignac Lecomte, and Liam Wegimont, "Introduction – The Global Anti-Poverty Consensus: Driving the Reform of International Co-operation," in Ida McDonnell, Henri-Bernard Solignac Lecomte, and Liam Wegimont (eds.), *Public Opinion and the Fight against Poverty*, Paris, OECD, 2003, p. 11; Alain Noël, "The New Global Politics of Poverty," *Global Social Policy*, vol. 6, no. 3, December 2006, 304–33, pp. 304–306.

something is now too powerful to hide behind past failures, and the left –
recognizing those failures – is taking a much tougher approach to performance and results.[14]

This chapter explores this rapprochement between the left and the
right. The story starts with the transformation of the left in the 1990s,
which brought progressive forces around the world to accept some
aspects of the neoliberal agenda. The following two sections consider
the tangible consequences of this evolution, and ponder in particular the significance of "Third Way" politics and of what has been
deemed the "new development consensus." The last section underlines
the continuing relevance of the left–right cleavage, in a context where
the search for equality continues to be a defining division, in global as
well as in domestic politics.

A renewed left

In the 1990s, the left was confronted with two challenges, which
pulled it in opposite directions. On one hand, a host of new movements
emerged, to question established parties and organizations and voice
additional demands, which were not met readily by traditional socialist
or social-democratic approaches. On the other hand, the political
success of the right forced progressives to revise their orientations,
accept more openly the market economy, and design policy options
that were more attuned to the requirements of global competition.

Consider, first, the rise of new social movements. Between the end
of the Second World War and the 1980s, economic growth, the
expansion of the service sector, high levels of employment, and the
welfare state literally transformed affluent democracies. Manufac-
turing workers declined in numbers compared to service employees,
which became the dominant category in post-industrial economies.[15]
Many of these service employees were little qualified, poorly paid, and
poorly protected. They found themselves on the losing side of modernization. Numerous others, however, ended up on the winning side,

---

[14] Mark Malloch Brown, "Meeting the Millennium Challenge: A Strategy for
Helping Achieve the United Nations Millennium Development Goals," address
by the Administrator of the UNDP, Berlin, June 27, 2002, p. 1.

[15] Donald Sassoon, *One Hundred Years of Socialism: The West European Left in
the Twentieth Century*, New York, The New Press, 1996, pp. 651–52.

and occupied skilled and professional positions, in both the public and the private sector. Political conflicts increasingly pitted the new middle class, formed by these winners who were more educated and guided by post-materialist values, against established elites and groups, anchored in traditional values. Social demands became less focused on production and distribution than on consumption, lifestyle, and social risks, and they were voiced by a host of movements speaking in the name of the young, women, or different ethnic, cultural, or sexual minorities. New causes were also promoted, to protect the environment, ban nuclear energy, bring world peace, or defend local neighborhoods. These emerging conflicts were fought using innovative modes of operation that privileged participation, local and global networking, and direct actions. The aim was not only to influence political decisions, but also to change the very democratic procedures that presided over these decisions.[16]

Parties of the left were in retreat in the 1980s, and these new movements tended to fill the void. Local and national actions were undertaken on a broad variety of issues, and they pushed leftist politics in uncharted territory. Faced with rapid changes in the political environment, particularly well illustrated by the rise of green parties, social-democrats tried to adjust, sometimes by distancing themselves from what some called the "loony left," but more often than not by renewing their own programs.[17] For its part, the right had to deal with the emergence of radical parties on its side, which articulated a populist, and at times racist, defense of the losers in post-industrialism. Being in power, however, it usually did so more easily – at least for a time – with symbolic gestures and piecemeal legislation that displayed toughness against criminals, welfare recipients, or illegal immigrants.[18]

Challenged on their right as well as on their left, social-democrats also had to rethink their policy orientations to take into account the power of the neoliberal agenda. The first adjustments in this respect

[16] Hanspeter Kriesi, "Movements of the Left, Movements of the Right: Putting the Mobilization of Two New Types of Social Movements into Political Context," in Herbert Kitschelt, Peter Lange, Gary Marks, and John D. Stephens (eds.), *Continuity and Change in Contemporary Capitalism*, Cambridge University Press, 1999, pp. 399–406; Herbert Kitschelt, *The Transformation of European Social Democracy*, Cambridge University Press, 1994, pp. 3–6.

[17] Geoff Eley, *Forging Democracy: The History of the Left in Europe, 1850–2000*, Oxford University Press, 2002, pp. 467–78.

[18] Kriesi, "Movements of the Left, Movements of the Right," p. 420.

were mostly defensive. Whether in opposition or in government, parties of the left basically felt compelled to fall in line with the imperatives of a neoliberal world. Controlling inflation became a priority, higher levels of unemployment were accepted, and the welfare state was preserved rather than expanded. Policy options remained, and differences between the left and the right persisted – in labor market, family, or education policies, for instance – but progressives, who had always considered that history was on their side, were no longer guided by a clear vision of a socialist or social-democratic future.[19] Governing affluent democracies came to appear as a lackluster exercise in managing as fairly as possible a situation of "permanent austerity."[20] In the South, strong neoliberal pressures and serious internal difficulties also pushed leftist governments toward prudent, adaptive policies.[21] At the end of the 1990s, however, most parties of the left had begun to change, to define their own, more positive synthesis of social-democracy and neoliberalism, under the umbrella of the "Third Way." A telling expression of this evolution came from the Indian state of West Bengal, when the world's longest-running democratically elected communist government, led by Marxist Buddhadeb Bhattacharya, had to admit that there were benefits to foreign investments. Bhattacharya summarized the transformation of his party, re-elected for a seventh consecutive term in 2006, in stark terms: "It's either reform or perish."[22]

A similar shift took place in world politics, with the combined rise of new social actors and new policy orientations. The growth of global social movements was particularly spectacular. In 1973, the

[19] Eley, *Forging Democracy*, p. 482; Andrew Glyn, "Aspirations, Constraints, and Outcomes," in Andrew Glyn (ed.), *Social Democracy in Neoliberal Times: The Left and Economic Policy since 1980*, Oxford University Press, 2001, p. 19.

[20] Paul Pierson, "Coping with Permanent Austerity: Welfare State Restructuring in Affluent Democracies," in Paul Pierson (ed.), *The New Politics of the Welfare State*, Oxford University Press, 2001, pp. 411–13.

[21] Richard Sandbrook, Marc Edelman, Patrick Heller, and Judith Teichman, *Social Democracy in the Global Periphery: Origins, Challenges, Prospects*, Cambridge University Press, 2007, p. 7.

[22] Erich Inciyan, "Libéralisme et capitalisme n'effarouchent plus le gouvernement communiste du Bengale Occidental," *Le Monde*, June 26, 2004, p. 4; United Kingdom, Department for International Development, "Reform or Perish, says Buddhadeb Bhattacharya," June 10, 2004 (www.dfidindia.org/news/coverage/2004/2004_6_10nk.htm).

world had fewer than 200 transnational social movements organizations (TSMOs), which could be defined as organizations that brought
participants from various countries to work together toward political
change on issues such as human rights, the environment, peace,
women's rights, development, and global justice. By 2000, the total
was close to a thousand. Greenpeace and Amnesty International, for
instance, had become thriving TSMOs that stood at the forefront of
the global progressive movement.[23] Likewise, Jubilee 2000, a broad
international coalition calling for the cancellation of Third World debt,
was able to gather more than 24 million signatures from 166 countries
in 2000, to produce the largest petition in history.[24] International
non-governmental organizations (NGOs) more broadly defined – to
include a wide variety of private, voluntary groups – also progressed,
to rise to more than 25,000 by 2004, with the number of local and
national NGOs even larger.[25] Some of these NGOs remained apolit-
ical or even closer to the political right, but overall those who leaned
toward the left were more numerous and more vocal.

TSMOs and NGOs actively participated in the global upsurge of
civil society that took place in the 1990s and early 2000s. As was the
case domestically, this upsurge first expressed a critique of globalization and of triumphant neoliberalism. The main targets were the
WTO, the IMF, the World Bank, and the G-8, and the participants in
a rising wave of protests came from diverse backgrounds, including
trade unions, student associations, environmental groups, and human
rights coalitions.[26] Gradually, this global movement took a more pur-
poseful orientation, and sought to define a globalization compatible

---

[23] Jackie Smith, "Globalization and Transnational Social Movement
Organizations," in Gerald F. Davis, Doug McAdam, W. Richard Scott, and
Mayer N. Zald (eds.), *Social Movements and Organization Theory*, Cambridge
University Press, 2005, pp. 231–38.

[24] Jubilee 2000, *The World Will Never Be the Same Again*, London, Jubilee 2000
Coalition, 2000, p. 17 (www.jubileeresearch.org/analysis/reports/J2REPORT.
pdf); John D. Clark, *Worlds Apart: Civil Society and the Battle for Ethical
Globalization*, Bloomfield, CT, Kumarian Press, 2003, p. 99.

[25] Union of International Associations, *Yearbook of International Organizations:
Guide to Global and Civil Society Networks, Edition 42, 2005–2006.
Volume 5: Statistics, Visualizations and Patterns*, Munich, K. G. Saur, 2005,
p. 3; Commission on Human Security, *Human Security Now*, Washington, DC,
Communications Development, 2003, p. 88.

[26] Sidney Tarrow, *The New Transnational Activism*, Cambridge University Press,
2005, pp. 72–73.

with social justice. The anti-globalization label gave way to the notion of another globalization, or alter-globalization. The rapid evolution of alternative summits was telling in this respect. Initiated in the 1980s as relatively quiet parallel summits that challenged the restrictive character of the formal gatherings of the world's elites, leftist meetings soon developed into genuine counter-summits that brought protesters to the streets. This more militant form of action culminated at the WTO Seattle meeting in 1999, which constituted something like the high-water mark of the anti-globalization movement. At about the same time, in the wake of a counter-summit to denounce the 1999 World Economic Forum in Davos, a truly alternative summit was conceived, the World Social Forum, which first met in Porto Alegre in January 2001. A more affirmative purpose then emerged, to replace the sheer protest against globalization by a commitment to define and promote global justice from a progressive perspective.[27]

The general idea became to improve rather than merely to reject global capitalism. To a large extent, the moderate stance that prevailed was the one defended by civil society organizations in UN-sponsored conferences as of the beginning of the 1990s. The political strategy advocated by these organizations had always privileged negotiation rather than confrontation. In terms of objectives, their approach centered on the need to put the fight against poverty at the heart of international development policies. Besides fostering growth and justice, they claimed, the reduction of poverty would contribute to attenuate a whole range of threats, including interethnic conflicts, terrorist violence, environmental degradation, crime, racial hatred, and pandemics.

The global left thus entered the twenty-first century more united and more assertive than it had been in two decades. As old references to socialism or to collective and national self-reliance more or less vanished, progressives strove instead for a "fair" world economy.[28] Fairness, in this perspective, implied closing the widening gap between the richest and the poorest, and addressing the "inequality predicament" that prevented "social justice and better living conditions

---

[27] *Ibid.*, pp. 130–31.
[28] World Commission on the Social Dimension of Globalization, *A Fair Globalization: Creating Opportunities for All*, Geneva, International Labour Office, 2004; Joseph E. Stiglitz and Andrew Charlton, *Fair Trade for All: How Trade Can Promote Development*, Oxford University Press, 2005.

for all."[29] In this connection, the left increasingly criticized the double standard of the economic policies of the North. By imposing on the South trade rules and norms that they did not have to respect during their own industrialization process, countries of the North were indeed seen as "kicking away the development ladder."[30] More sensitive than before to the logic of liberalism, the left also embedded its social concerns within a human rights approach.[31] Social movements presented the promotion of human rights as the paramount responsibility of governments, and defined development as a process whose ultimate goal was the realization of the political, economic, social, and cultural rights of individuals.

Finally, the left paid more attention to the democratization of global governance. The internationalization of production and finance networks, it was argued, had not been accompanied by an equivalent internationalization of social institutions.[32] Markets had become global, but political power continued to be exercised within the framework of national sovereignty. To better anchor market processes in universally shared values, progressive movements called for a new global social contract. This was another way to pursue the long-fought battle for multilateral reforms that would give the South more say in the management of the world economy. In a somewhat more innovative vein, compatible with the new left emphasis on democratic procedures, civil society organizations also asserted that the governance of development could not be entrusted to states alone, and that poverty reduction could not move ahead without citizen involvement. Convinced that real democracy went beyond the holding of free elections, NGOs worked to make social groups better heard by national governments and international organizations. Global democracy remained a long way off, but these movements did help to

[29] United Nations, *The Inequality Predicament: Report on the World Social Situation 2005*, New York, United Nations, 2005, p. 1.
[30] Ha-Joon Chang, *Kicking Away the Ladder: Development Strategy in Historical Perspective*, London, Anthem Press, 2002.
[31] Richard Jolly, Louis Emmerij, Dharam Ghai, and Frédéric Lapeyre, *UN Contributions to Development Thinking and Practice*, Bloomington, Indiana University Press, 2004.
[32] John Gerard Ruggie, "Taking Embedded Liberalism Global: The Corporate Connection," in David Held and Mathias Koenig-Archibugi (eds.), *Taming Globalization: Frontiers of Governance*, Cambridge, Polity Press, 2003, pp. 93–129.

involve a greater number of citizens from the North and the South in the development debate.

To sum up, progressive forces may have been slow to respond to the rise of neoliberalism in the early 1980s, but after the end of the Cold War, the collaboration forged among TSMOs, NGOs, international organizations, and some national governments gradually transformed world politics. The global left fashioned a new discourse, which was consistent with the emerging domestic preoccupations of social-democrats, and was heard everywhere, from the corridors of major international institutions to the slums of Third World cities. The primary concerns of this renewed global left were constructed around the idea of a fair world economy, and included the fight against poverty, gender equality, debt cancellation, the promotion of fair trade and sustainable development, increases in foreign aid, and the empowerment of civil society. At home, just as parties of the left were accepting some of the tenets of neoliberalism, social movements also adopted new causes and identities and, more broadly, fought for what British sociologist Anthony Giddens called "the democratizing of democracy."[33]

The Third Way

In April 1999, Bill Clinton organized a meeting in Washington with Tony Blair, Gerhard Schröder, and Dutch and Italian social-democratic prime ministers Wim Kok and Massimo D'Alema. The five leaders decided to launch a new international center-left alliance, the Progressive Governance movement, which would meet annually, starting with a conference in Berlin in June 2000. A few months after the Washington meeting, Blair and Schröder released a joint paper, to present their center-left ideas for the future of Europe.[34] The social-democratic left was now in power, and in a position to define and implement its own vision for the coming years.

The Third Way and *Die Neue Mitte*, explained Blair and Schröder, were the labels used in British and German politics to capture a new

---

[33] Anthony Giddens, *Beyond Left and Right: The Future of Radical Politics*, Stanford University Press, 1994, pp. 16 and 113.

[34] Anthony Giddens, *The Third Way and Its Critics*, Cambridge, Polity Press, 2000, pp. 4–6; Policy Network, "Progressive Governance Network" (www.progressive-governance.net/aboutus/index.aspx?id=58).

social-democratic perspective, which was faithful to the perennial values of the left but also in tune with the demands of "today's world." In the past decades, the two leaders wrote, the left had focused too much on "equality of outcome" and not enough on the importance of "rewarding effort and responsibility"; it had favored solutions that were often bureaucratic and expensive, and forgotten that "social conscience cannot be measured by the level of public expenditures"; it had put more weight on rights than on responsibilities; and it had undervalued "the importance of individual and business enterprise to the creation of wealth."[35] The world, however, had changed, and the left could no longer let itself be trapped in an "ideological straitjacket" inherited from the past.

Modernization, globalization, and technological evolution made products, capital, and labor markets more fluid and required flexible rules. Changed gender roles, new family structures, and longer life expectancy imposed a revision of welfare programs just as the level of public expenditures "more or less reached the limits of acceptability." And unprecedented threats with respect to the environment, crime, and poverty had to be addressed. To do so, social-democrats needed to bet on "a new entrepreneurial spirit at all levels of society." They had, in particular, to foster the development of a qualified and well-paid workforce, through a social security system that encouraged "initiative." Progressives also needed to accept private enterprise and partnerships of all kinds more readily, and aim for a leaner state, which "should not row, but steer."[36] In policy terms, these orientations translated into a "new supply-side agenda for the left" premised on: a market framework favorable to competition; streamlined and lower income and business taxes; flexible social and labor market policies to encourage rapid transitions from school, unemployment, or welfare to work; strong investments in education and training; and sound public finances. These choices might appear to some rather close to those of the conservatives, but for Blair and Schröder this was a mistaken view. "Modern social democrats," they explained, were "not laissez-faire neo-liberals," because they believed in "an

---

[35] Tony Blair and Gerhard Schröder, "Europe: The Third Way/Die Neue Mitte," Appendix in Bodo Hombach, *The Politics of the New Centre*, Cambridge, Polity Press, 2000, pp. 159–62.
[36] *Ibid.*, pp. 163–65.

active state" whose "top priority" was "investment in human and social capital."[37]

Anthony Giddens, who was a close advisor to Tony Blair and certainly the most prominent advocate of the Third Way, similarly differentiated this new vision from both "classical" social democracy and neoliberalism. Classical social-democracy, Giddens wrote, favored a strong state, a mixed economy, Keynesian demand management, full employment, comprehensive welfare programs, egalitarianism, and internationalism in the context of a bipolar world. Neoliberalism, on the other hand, privileged a minimal state, unrestricted markets, monetarism, price stability, a welfare state acting merely as a "safety net," less egalitarian objectives, and a nationalist and realist stance in a still bipolar world. Breaking with these antinomies, Third Way politics proposed instead a more democratic state relying on an active civil society, a new mixed economy of state-society and private-public partnerships, a notion of equality centered on social inclusion, a welfare state understood as a social investment instrument, and a more cosmopolitan view of the world.[38] It remained unclear, however, what exactly would be the distinctive macro-economic policy of the Third Way. The focus was more general, and referred to a less interventionist state, which would conceive its expenditures as social investments and seek to facilitate the inclusion of all citizens in the market economy.

Not surprisingly, many on the left considered that Third Way advocates and politicians were basically a kinder and gentler sort of neoliberal. Few critics put the matter as bluntly as Oskar Lafontaine, who was Schröder's rival in the German social-democratic party and his finance minister until he quit in March 1999. In the book he published after his resignation – *Das Herz schlägt links* (*The Heart Beats to the Left*) – Lafontaine stated that "the Third Way was no way at all" ("*Der dritte Weg ist ein Holzweg*").[39] In the same vein, British political scientist Mark Wickham-Jones contended that Blair's Third Way discourse amounted to an "abandonment of social democracy"

---

[37] *Ibid.*, p. 169.
[38] Anthony Giddens, *The Third Way: The Renewal of Social Democracy*, Cambridge, Polity Press, 1998, pp. 7–8 and 70.
[39] Oskar Lafontaine (1999), quoted in Giddens, *The Third Way and Its Critics*, p. 14; Mark Leonard, "Introduction," in Hombach, *The Politics of the New Centre*, pp. xxv–xxvii.

in favor of a politics of resignation that offered no more than remedial responses to the failures of neoliberalism.[40]

In Europe, most social-democratic politicians avoided the Third Way label, and positioned themselves at a distance from Blair and Schröder.[41] Some were openly critical, like French socialist prime minister Lionel Jospin, who struggled to keep together his "plural left" governing coalition (*"gauche plurielle"*). Claiming to lead the most leftist government in the Western world, Jospin regularly denounced Blair as a neoliberal.[42] In practice, however, these different social-democratic governments evolved along similar lines, close to Third Way orientations. They modified legislations and incentives to stimulate employment growth without using expansionary fiscal policies, sought to contain public expenditures, and invested in education, training, and employability programs, in a social investment perspective.[43] Did they all succumb to what Andrew Glyn called the "remorseless pressure" of neoliberalism?[44] Or was the Third Way a genuine center-left alternative to the conservative policies of the 1980s and 1990s?

A good way to address these questions is to look at the conception of equality put forward by proponents of the Third Way. Ideas about equality, after all, stand at the heart of the left–right division. If the Third Way broke with the tradition of the left, it certainly was not because it accepted market mechanisms or sought to limit the growth of social spending. Indeed, social-democrats have for many decades accepted the market – usually with less enthusiasm than Tony Blair, though – and they have long understood that the fight for social justice was not primarily a conflict about the level of social expenditures.[45]

---

[40] Mark Wickham-Jones, "From Reformism to Resignation and Remedialism? Labour's Trajectory through British Politics," in Erwin C. Hargrove (ed.), *The Future of the Democratic Left in Industrial Democracies*, University Park, Pennsylvania State University Press, 2003, p. 36.

[41] Giuliano Bonoli and Martin Powell, "One Third Way or Several?," in Jane Lewis and Rebecca Surender (eds.), *Welfare State Change: Towards a Third Way?*, Oxford University Press, 2004, pp. 53–54.

[42] *Ibid.*, p. 54; David S. Bell, "French Socialists: Refusing the 'Third Way'," in Hargrove (ed.), *The Future of the Democratic Left*, pp. 57 and 62–63.

[43] Bonoli and Powell, "One Third Way or Several?," pp. 56–61.

[44] Glyn, "Aspirations, Constraints, and Outcomes," p. 20.

[45] Christoffer Green-Pedersen, Kees van Kersbergen, and Anton Hemerijck, "Neo-liberalism, the 'Third Way' or What? Recent Social Democratic Welfare Policies in Denmark and the Netherlands," *Journal of European Public Policy*,

The left consistently sought, however, to advance social equality, whereas parties of the right accepted inequality as an unavoidable and, in truth, rather positive fact of life.

What about the Third Way? Did it remain on the left or move to the right with respect to equality? If one takes Giddens as representative, the Third Way certainly stood on the left. "The pursuit of equality," he wrote, "has to be at the core of third way politics" and "the recipe 'take from the rich to give to the poor' should remain a cornerstone of centre-left policy."[46] In other writings, Giddens referred explicitly to Norberto Bobbio in agreeing that the question of equality was a defining one for the left, and thus for the Third Way. He insisted, too, on the importance of going beyond a mere equality of opportunity, such a "meritocratic" conception being insufficient as a goal and unsustainable in the long run, since inheritance necessarily made opportunities unequal.[47] Some ambiguity nevertheless remained. Blair, notably, spoke more easily of an equality of opportunity than of a more demanding notion of equality, and Giddens himself sometimes seemed in two minds on this count.[48]

In part, these tensions could be linked to a transformation in the prevailing conceptions of equality, whereby equality was less and less understood as "income equality here and now," which did not seem feasible or desirable, and more and more as a fair "distribution of life chances over the life course." The prudence of Third Way politicians in this respect was also tied to their perception of important political and economic constraints that seemed to preclude strong egalitarian orientations.[49] One should note, however, that the Third Way discourse about redistribution evolved over time, starting closer to neo-liberalism in the 1990s and gradually moving in a more leftist and

vol. 8, no. 2, April 2001, 307–25, p. 321; Gøsta Esping-Andersen, *The Three Worlds of Welfare Capitalism*, Princeton University Press, 1990, p. 21.

[46] Anthony Giddens, "Introduction," in Anthony Giddens (ed.), *The Global Third Way Debate*, Cambridge, Polity Press, 2001, p. 8.

[47] Giddens, *The Third Way*, pp. 38–39 and 101–105; Giddens, *The Third Way and Its Critics*, pp. 38–39.

[48] Stuart White, "Welfare Philosophy and the Third Way," in Lewis and Surender (eds.), *Welfare State Change*, pp. 34–35; Giddens, *The Third Way and Its Critics*, pp. 85–86.

[49] Green-Pedersen, van Kersbergen, and Hemerijck, "Neo-liberalism, the 'Third Way' or What?," p. 322; White, "Welfare Philosophy and the Third Way," p. 43.

egalitarian direction in the 2000s. In the 1990s, the right was still largely dominant and the left first had to re-establish itself as a credible alternative. The British Labour Party, in particular, had to demonstrate its capability to govern, in a policy context shaped by almost two decades of Thatcherism.[50] To do so, New Labour leaders devised a program that downplayed many of the left's traditional preoccupations, including its preference for equality. In power, the Blair government nevertheless implemented important redistributive measures, to reduce child and pensioner poverty in particular, as well as to improve the income of low-paid workers. This "redistribution by stealth" did not lower inequalities, but it prevented a further increase in after-tax inequalities – which would have happened if the conservative tax-benefit system had not been changed – and it contributed to a reduction in poverty.[51] In France, the Jospin government rejected the Third Way and placed more emphasis on the search for equality, but it adopted relatively similar reforms, which made social protection more market-oriented and, in a favorable economic context, also helped reduce poverty.[52]

With or without the label, Third Way politics defined a moderately progressive course tinged with neoliberalism, which allowed the left to govern and, after a time, put the question of social justice back on the agenda. Poverty and inequality, in particular, once again became important political preoccupations. In 2000, for instance, a European Council dominated by social-democratic leaders adopted a new encompassing objective that combined economic growth with social development. The aim was to make the European Union "the most competitive and dynamic knowledge-based economy in the world capable of sustaining economic growth with more and better jobs and greater social cohesion." At the same Lisbon meeting, the Council

---

[50] David Sanders, "The New Electoral Battleground," in King *et al.* (eds.), *New Labour Triumphs*, pp. 227–28.

[51] Wickham-Jones, "From Reformism to Resignation and Remedialism?," pp. 37–38; Kitty Stewart, "Equality and Social Justice," in Anthony Seldon and Dennis Kavanagh (eds.), *The Blair Effect, 2001–5*, Cambridge University Press, 2005, pp. 329–30 and 334–35.

[52] Bruno Palier, *Gouverner la sécurité sociale: les réformes du système français de protection sociale depuis 1945*, Paris, PUF, 2002, pp. 400–06; Observatoire national de la pauvreté et de l'exclusion sociale, *Rapport 2003–2004*, Paris, La documentation française, 2004, pp. 27–37 (http://lesrapports. ladocumentationfrancaise.fr/BRP/044000149/0000.pdf).

made the reduction of poverty and social exclusion an explicit and operational objective, to be achieved through National Action Plans and the open method of coordination.[53] A year later, the Council commissioned a report on a "new architecture for social protection" in Europe.[54] Initiated by a renewed social-democratic left but also accepted by a right that had moved toward the center, a new consensus seemed to be emerging on the need to combine economic objectives with institutions and policies that protected social cohesion and fostered social justice.

The new development consensus

In world politics, at the turn of the century, North–South negotiations also gave way to a remarkable rapprochement between the left and the right, to the point that UN Secretary-General Kofi Annan could speak in 2005 of an "unprecedented consensus" on how to manage relations between rich and poor countries.[55] Using the term "consensus" to describe development diplomacy was perhaps too optimistic, but the concept nonetheless resonated among experts, who referred in turn to a post-Washington consensus, a Copenhagen consensus, a Monterrey consensus, or a Sao Paulo consensus, to capture the changing dynamics of North–South relations.

The multilateral system provides the best vantage point from which to examine how global development was debated by conservatives and progressives. For over half a century, the market-oriented approach of the Bretton Woods institutions had indeed stood in sharp contrast to the social-democratic approach of the United Nations and its agencies.[56] At the end of the 1990s, the ideological gulf between these

[53] Noël, "The New Global Politics of Poverty," p. 305.
[54] Gøsta Esping-Andersen, with Duncan Gallie, Anton Hemerijck, and John Myles, *Why We Need a New Welfare State*, Oxford University Press, 2002, p. xxv.
[55] Kofi A. Annan, *In Larger Freedom: Towards Development, Security and Human Rights for All*, Report of the Secretary-General, New York, United Nations, 2005, p. 7 (www.un.org/largerfreedom).
[56] Richard Jolly, Louis Emmerij, and Thomas G. Weiss, *The Power of UN Ideas: Lessons from the First 60 Years*, New York, United Nations Intellectual History Project, 2005; Richard Jolly, Louis Emmerij, Dharam Ghai, and Frédéric Lapeyre, *UN Contributions to Development Thinking and Practice*; Bob Deacon (with Michelle Hulse and Paul Stubbs), *Global Social Policy: International Organizations and the Future of Welfare*, London, Sage, 1997,

two groups of international organizations narrowed considerably, and the dialogue between them became more intense than ever. This left–right dialogue stemmed, to a large extent, from the more nuanced vision of globalization adopted by each side. As the Director-General of the International Labour Office (ILO) noted in 2005, all came to accept that globalization was "neither the answer to every problem nor the cause of every evil."[57] While UN agencies increasingly agreed that an integrated world economy offered "great opportunities" for poor countries,[58] the Bretton Woods institutions acknowledged for their part that globalization also engendered losers and that, in some instances, it "reinforced the strong ones and weakened those that were already weak."[59]

In September 2000, the new development consensus was solemnly endorsed, when the United Nations General Assembly adopted the Millennium Declaration, a statement that recognized that the "benefits" of globalization were "very unevenly shared," and committed the international community to reduce world poverty by half before 2015.[60] Other "Millennium Development Goals" (MDGs) included achieving universal primary education, promoting gender equality, reducing child mortality, improving maternal health, halting the spread of infectious diseases, ensuring environmental sustainability, and developing a global partnership for development. For the first time, a coherent set of quantified and time-bound targets was established for development policies. The importance of the MDGs was reiterated at the Monterrey Conference on Financing for Development in 2002 as well as at the UN World Summit in 2005. The Monterrey Declaration

pp. 57–90; and Mahbub ul Haq, Richard Jolly, Paul Streeten, and Khadija Haq (eds.), *The UN and the Bretton Woods Institutions: New Challenges for the Twenty-First Century*, New York, St. Martin's Press, 1995.

[57] Juan Somavia, "Address by the Director-General of the International Labour Office to the High-Level Segment of the United Nations Economic and Social Council," New York, June 29, 2005, p. 2.

[58] Kofi A. Annan, *"We the Peoples:" The Role of the United Nations in the 21ˢᵗ Century*, New York, United Nations, 2000, p. 6 (www.un.org/millennium/sg/report).

[59] Pascal Lamy, "Humanising Globalization," address by the Director-General of the World Trade Organization, Santiago, January 30, 2006, p. 1. (www.wto.org/english/news_e/sppl_e/sppl16_e.htm).

[60] United Nations General Assembly, "United Nations Millennium Declaration," UN Resolution A/RES/55/2, New York, September 18, 2000 (www.un.org/millennium/declaration/ares552e.htm).

proposed to make the twenty-first century "the century of development for all," while the World Summit emphasized the need "to galvanize efforts towards poverty eradication."[61]

The convergence between the UN agencies and the Bretton Woods institutions had been clearly manifested in June 2000 when the IMF, the World Bank, the UN, and the OECD jointly signed *A Better World for All*.[62] This groundbreaking document, itself the result of decisions adopted at various UN conferences held throughout the 1990s, laid the foundations for the Millennium and the Monterrey Declarations. After its publication, as Louis Pauly noted, collaboration between the UN and the Bretton Woods institutions became routinized.[63] A global version of Third Way politics then seemed to be emerging.

The Bretton Woods institutions began to attribute more importance than before to the social dimension of development. The World Bank and the IMF, for instance, advocated higher levels of foreign aid and "pro-poor" economic growth. This change of direction was particularly notable at the Bank, which redefined its official mission as "working for a world free of poverty."[64] Under the leadership of James Wolfensohn (1995–2005), the organization also broadened its understanding of poverty beyond traditional income measures, to include dimensions such as health, education, the environment, and political participation.[65] The following president of the Bank, Paul Wolfowitz, maintained this anti-poverty orientation, even though his association with American neoconservatism did not predispose

[61] United Nations, *Monterrey Consensus on Financing for Development*, New York, United Nations, 2003, p. 5 (www.un.org/esa/ffd/Monterrey/Monterrey%20Consensus.pdf); and United Nations, "2005 World Summit Outcome," Resolution Adopted by the General Assembly, A/RES/60/1, New York, October 24, 2005, p. 3 (www.unfpa.org/icpd/docs/2005summit_eng.pdf).

[62] IMF, OECD, UN, and World Bank, *A Better World for All*, Washington, DC, Communications Development, 2000 (www.paris21.org/betterworld/home.htm).

[63] Louis W. Pauly, "The United Nations in a Changing Global Economy," in Steven Bernstein and Louis W. Pauly (eds.), *Global Liberalism and Political Order: Toward a New Grand Compromise?*, Albany, SUNY Press, 2007, p. 105.

[64] See www.worldbank.org.

[65] James D. Wolfensohn and François Bourguignon, *Development and Poverty Reduction: Looking Back, Looking Ahead*, Washington, DC, World Bank, 2004, pp. 3–4 (www.worldbank.org/ambc/lookingbacklookingahead.pdf).

him to do so. At the IMF, Managing Director Horst Köhler described poverty as "the greatest challenge to peace and security in the 21st century."[66] The Fund's Enhanced Initiative for Highly Indebted Poor Countries (HIPC), established in 1999, and its Multilateral Debt Relief Initiative, set up in 2005, helped to substantially reduce the debt load of Southern governments. Moreover, the introduction by the IMF of the Poverty Reduction Strategy Papers (PRSPs) increased the borrowing countries' ownership of their economic policies, while encouraging more civil society participation in economic decision-making.

In trade, the failure of the 1999 Seattle conference prompted the WTO to engage more closely with developing countries. Significantly, the negotiation round initiated in Doha in 2001 was deemed the "Development Round." At the outset, the South took advantage of more transparent negotiation procedures to make gains on issues such as technical cooperation and the implementation of the Uruguay Round. Later on, the WTO confirmed the poor countries' right to buy generic drugs, and agreed to lift trade restrictions on 97 percent of the least developed countries' exports to the North. The WTO does not see itself as a development agency, but in the wake of the Seattle debacle it admitted that spreading prosperity more widely stood as a "moral imperative."[67] WTO authorities thus became far more vigorous in denouncing the rich countries' protectionism, especially in the agricultural sector. Director-General Pascal Lamy spoke of "humanizing globalization," and recognized that the WTO had to do its share to achieve the MDGs. In an untypical critique of the market economy, Lamy even suggested that at times "the 'invisible hand' itself needs to be taken by the hand."[68]

[66] Horst Köhler, "Working for a Better Globalization," remarks by the IMF Managing Director at the Conference on Humanizing the Global Economy, Washington, DC, IMF, January 28, 2002, p. 2 (www.imf.org/external/np/speeches/2002/012802.htm).

[67] Supachai Panitchpakdi, "Why Trade Matters for Improving Food Security," speech delivered by the Director-General of the WTO at the FAO High-Level Round Table on Agricultural Trade Reform and Food Security, Rome, April 13, 2005, p. 6 (www.sarpn.org.za/documents/d0001560/Trade-matters_food-security_April2005.pdf).

[68] Pascal Lamy, "Trade Can Be a Friend, and Not a Foe, of Conservation," address by the Director-General of the WTO at the WTO Symposium on Trade and Sustainable Development within the Framework of Paragraph 51 of the Doha Ministerial Declaration, Geneva, October 10–11, 2005, p. 1 (www.wto.org/English/news_e/sppl_e/sppl07_e.htm).

Meanwhile, the UN development paradigm became more market-friendly. Faced with steady criticisms from developed countries, the UN gradually abandoned its old "anti-business prejudice,"[69] a turn reinforced by Bill Gates and Ted Turner's generous support for UN activities. The change was particularly remarkable within the Secretariat and at the UNDP. In *A Better World for All*, for example, UN Secretary-General Kofi Annan agreed that Third World countries had "to lower their tariffs and other trade barriers and streamline their systems for the flow of imports, exports and finance," a position traditionally defended by the IMF.[70] In Doha, Annan went still further, and stated that opening markets was "even more important for developing countries and transition economies than for the rest of the world."[71] The willingness of the UN Secretariat to accept market forces was best demonstrated by the Global Compact launched in 2000. The Compact created a multistakeholder network that in 2006 involved over 2,500 businesses from ninety countries, along with labor organizations, NGOs, and the UN. Its objective was to induce the private sector to adopt good practices, based on ten internationally approved principles in the areas of human rights, labor, the environment, and the prevention of corruption.[72] Sometimes caricatured as a pact between the UN and the devil, the Global Compact was rooted in the notion that the promotion of corporate social responsibility through voluntary measures constituted one of the best ways to correct the downsides of globalization.

The UNDP also worked hard after 2000 to build a more business-oriented organizational culture.[73] Shifting to new forms of results-based management, the UN agency endeavored to make its services

---

[69] Sidney Dell, *The United Nations and International Business*, Durham and London, Duke University Press and UNITAR, 1990, p. ix.

[70] IMF, OECD, UN, and World Bank, *A Better World for All*, p. 22.

[71] Kofi A. Annan, "Message of the UN Secretary-General of the United Nations at the Doha Ministerial Conference of the WTO," November 9, 2001, p. 1.

[72] Jean-Philippe Thérien and Vincent Pouliot, "The Global Compact: Shifting the Politics of International Development?," *Global Governance*, vol. 12, no. 1, 2006, 55–75.

[73] See Craig N. Murphy, *The United Nations Development Programme: A Better Way?*, Cambridge University Press, 2006, pp. 299–308; Kemal Dervis, "Statement by the Administrator of the UNDP at the Executive Board of the UNDP/UNFPA," New York, January 24, 2006, p. 17 (http://content.undp.org/go/newsroom/january-2006/statement-dervis-undp-unfpa-20060124.en?categoryID=349463).

"more competitive," and it emphasized performance in the design of its assistance programs.[74] The UNDP also played an active role in the implementation of the PRSPs sponsored by the IMF and the World Bank, and it became much more attentive than before to economic growth and trade.[75] Through programs like the Growing Sustainable Business Initiative and the United Nations Capital Development Fund, the UNDP emerged as one of the linchpins in the new strategy of collaboration between the UN and the private sector.

A number of factors may explain this evolution toward a more consensual vision of development. The new attitude of the Bretton Woods institutions can be attributed, in particular, to the lessons drawn from the Asian crisis, which was "deeper, longer and harder" because of the austerity policies pursued by the IMF.[76] With their credibility tarnished, the international financial institutions became less arrogant. Their stance was also influenced by the coming to power of many center-left governments in Europe and North America at the end of the 1990s. Leaders of these governments were more favorably disposed than their predecessors toward international development objectives.

On the other side, the UN system was strongly influenced by the success of developing countries that had liberalized their economy. Observing that "the past 25 years have seen the most dramatic reduction in extreme poverty that the world has ever experienced," the UN came to the conclusion that markets and globalization could be hugely beneficial to development.[77] On the left, some have argued that this change of attitude resulted in fact from a "widespread mood of resignation" engendered by two decades of pro-market "global intellectual hegemony."[78] Whatever the case, the evolution of development

---

[74] UNDP, *Development Effectiveness: Review of Evaluative Evidence*, New York, Evaluation Office of the UNDP, 2001, p. 12 (www.undp.org/eo/documents/der2001.pdf).

[75] Murphy, *The United Nations Development Programme*, p. 310; Mark Malloch Brown, "Statement by the UNDP Administrator at the Conference on the Review of Poverty Reduction Strategy Papers," Washington, January 16, 2002, p. 3 (http://content.undp.org/go/newsroom/january-2002/mmb-conference.en; jsessionid=axbWzt8vXD9?categoryID=593045&lang=en).

[76] Joseph E. Stiglitz, "The Insider: What I Learned at the World Economic Crisis," *New Republic*, April 17–24, 2000, 56–60, p. 60.

[77] Annan, *In Larger Freedom*, p. 11.

[78] "Jordan Valley Declaration: Time for Mobilizing the South," South Centre High Level Policy Forum, Dead Sea, Jordan, 14–15 January 2003, Geneva, South Centre, 2003, p. 3 (www.southcentre.org/info/southbulletin/

diplomacy was in phase with the worldwide left–right convergence that took place at the turn of the century.

Faced with the limitations of past policies, the left and the UN became more aware of the importance of markets, economic growth, and performance. Confronted with their own failures and with the criticisms articulated by the South, by civil society organizations, and by dissenting experts, the right and the Bretton Woods institutions, for their part, were prepared to accept that the state had a role to play, and integrated poverty and equity concerns into their policies. From this two-sided process emerged a common language giving pride of place to the notions of effectiveness and partnership. The new development consensus, however, remained a fragile outcome of power relationships, and it did not erase the fundamental differences between the global left and the global right.

Still the left and the right

In the first round of the French presidential election, in April 2002, Lionel Jospin's "plural left" coalition splintered into its various components and many dissatisfied voters abstained, allowing the head of the far-right National Front, Jean-Marie Le Pen, to end up with more votes than the socialist leader and to qualify for the second round against center-right candidate Jacques Chirac. Around Europe, wrote an Italian newspaper, political circles were "hit by a thunderbolt."[79] The event, however, was not without precedent. In 2000, the far-right party of Joerg Haider had been included in an Austrian coalition government, creating quite a stir in the European Union. A year before, the Italian left had been defeated by the center-right coalition of Silvio Berlusconi, which also included far-right elements. A month after the French shock, the Dutch far-right, whose leader – Pim Fortuyn – was assassinated during the electoral campaign, obtained spectacular results, and helped bring about the victory of a center-right coalition. Even Denmark and Norway had turned to the right in the previous months.

---

bulletin49-50/bulletin49-50-01.htm); Branislav Gosovic, "Global Intellectual Hegemony and the International Development Agenda," *International Social Science Journal*, vol. 52, no. 166, December 2000, 447–56.

[79] Barnaby Mason, "The Rise of the European Right," BBC News, World Edition, April 22, 2002 (http://news.bbc.co.uk/2/hi/europe/1944157.stm).

Five years after Blair's victory, the European social-democratic left was losing ground to center-right parties that capitalized on economic insecurity and on fears about globalization, national identity, and immigration. These parties maintained their neoliberal orientations, but blended them with more populist and nationalist arguments, borrowed from far-right parties they had roundly denounced until then. When necessary, mainstream conservatives even accepted formal alliances with the far-right, to form broad government-winning coalitions.[80] In the United States, the Republicans also regained control of both the presidency and Congress, and they moved determinedly to the right, to implement tax cuts that undermined the federal government's capacity to fund Medicare, social security, education, and debt reduction, and disproportionately benefited the richest one percent of Americans.[81]

Social-democrats, admitted Giddens, faced a critical juncture. Their situation was not uniformly bad. For one thing, they were still in power in many countries of Western Europe, and making progress in Eastern Europe and Latin America. Moreover, the comeback of the right appeared somewhat superficial, because it was more opportunistic than anchored in a strong and appealing vision of the future. Often, center-right parties simply "normalized" the themes of the far-right to take advantage of popular anxieties about immigration, multiculturalism, and crime. Still, the left had "a good deal of rethinking to do" to adjust to a new, more competitive political reality.[82]

For Giddens, it no longer seemed necessary to speak of a Third Way. This label, he explained, had proven useful to specify what the new center-left was not, and to differentiate it from unreformed

---

[80] Tim Bale, "Cinderella and Her Ugly Sisters: The Mainstream and Extreme Right in Europe's Bipolarising Systems," *West European Politics*, vol. 26, no. 3, July 2003, 67–90; Anthony Mughan, Clive Bean, and Ian McAllister, "Economic Globalization, Job Insecurity and the Populist Reaction," *Electoral Studies*, vol. 22, no. 4, December 2003, 617–33.

[81] Jacob S. Hacker and Paul Pierson, *Off Center: The Republican Revolution and the Erosion of American Democracy*, New Haven, Yale University Press, 2005, pp. 1, 25–47, and 58–65.

[82] Anthony Giddens, "Is Three Still the Magic Number?," *Guardian*, April 25, 2003 (http://politics.guardian.co.uk/progressive/comment/0,,943358,00.html).

social-democracy.[83] This positioning, however, was now accomplished, and the left could assume power and govern on the basis of its core historical values. With a populist right back in power, it became in fact more important to stress again the opposition between the left and the right, or between social-democracy and neoliberalism, rather than insisting once more on the distinctive character of the contemporary center-left. The Third Way was no longer necessary and the social-democratic identity could come back.

This reaffirmation of the traditional left–right division implied as well a return to the core concern of left–right politics: equality. In a book published in 2005, Giddens and his co-authors made "the case for a new egalitarianism," and deplored the growing inequalities brought by decades of neoliberalism.[84] By contrast, during his 2007 electoral campaign, rightist French president Nicolas Sarkozy argued unabashedly against egalitarianism and in favor of order, authority, work, and merit, a discourse that had been shunned by the country's center-right until then.[85] In recent years, American politics also displayed a strong left–right polarization over cultural values and redistribution.[86]

More spectacularly, the turn of the twenty-first century gave rise to a strong resurgence of the democratic left in Latin America, with the election of Hugo Chávez in Venezuela (1998), Luiz Inácio "Lula" da Silva in Brazil (2002), Néstor Kirchner in Argentina (2003), Tabaré Vásquez in Uruguay (2005), Evo Morales in Bolivia (2006), Michelle Bachelet in Chile (2006), Rafael Correa in Ecuador (2006), and Daniel Ortega in Nicaragua (2006). The new Latin American left sometimes proved populist and controversial, as in Venezuela and Bolivia, but often it chose a prudently reformist course, close to the spirit of the Third Way, as in Chile and Uruguay. In either case, the left benefited from a widespread desire for more social justice, in countries where

---

[83] Anthony Giddens, "Introduction: Neoprogressivism. A New Agenda for Social Democracy," in Anthony Giddens (ed.), *The Progressive Manifesto: New Ideas for the Centre-Left*, Cambridge, Polity Press, 2003, p. 6.

[84] Anthony Giddens, "Introduction," in Anthony Giddens and Patrick Diamond (eds.), *The New Egalitarianism*, Cambridge, Polity Press, 2005, p. 1.

[85] Philippe Ridet, "La victoire de Sarkozy est 'une revanche de la droite qui ne s'est reconnue ni dans Giscard, ni dans Chirac'," *Le Monde*, May 4, 2007 (www.lemonde.fr/web/chat/0,46-0@2-823448,55-905246@51-906165,0. html).

[86] Hacker and Pierson, *Off Center*, pp. 43–44.

democratization and market reforms had failed to reduce profound inequalities and enduring poverty. Populist leaders deployed an anti-American, anti-globalization discourse and experimented with nationalization and strong-armed interventions, but they also invested in social programs and in redistributive measures, in a more or less clientelistic manner. More orthodox with respect to the market, public administration, and the world order, reformist governments also undertook to improve social programs and income distribution.[87] Across the continent, the politics of left and right became alive, and was very clearly defined around the question of equality.

In Taiwan and Korea, similar debates on democratization and neoliberalism took place but, in these cases, it was leftist social movements that moved non-programmatic political parties to adopt redistributive and welfare state reforms.[88] In South Africa, achieving effective redistribution proved difficult and the African National Congress may even have failed in this respect, but political debates were also consumed by equality and by the possibilities of social justice in a neoliberal world.[89] In the Kerala state of India, the social-democratic Left Democratic Front defeated the neoliberal right by a landslide in 2006, building on its previous success in alleviating poverty, in a region with a very low aggregate income.[90] In the democracies of the different continents, then, the long historical debate between the left and the right was reaffirmed through competing visions of equality.

The same dividing lines manifested themselves in world politics, as the new development consensus rapidly showed its limits. This consensus, indeed, always remained imperfect. Reflecting their distinct

[87] Jorge G. Castañeda, "Latin America's Left Turn," *Foreign Affairs*, vol. 85, no. 3, May/June 2006, 28–43, pp. 30 and 35; Michael Shifter, "In Search of Hugo Chávez," *Foreign Affairs*, vol. 85, no. 3, May/June 2006, 45–59, pp. 50–51.

[88] Joseph Wong, "Democratization and the Left: Comparing East Asia and Latin America," *Comparative Political Studies*, vol. 37, no. 10, December 2004, 1213–37, pp. 1219–23; Sandbrook, Edelman, Heller, and Teichman, *Social Democracy in the Global Periphery*, pp. 18 and 235.

[89] Nicoli Nattrass and Jeremy Seekings, "Democracy and Distribution in Highly Unequal Economies: The Case of South Africa," *Journal of Modern African Studies*, vol. 39, no. 3, September 2001, 471–98; Patrick Bond, *Talk Left, Walk Right: South Africa's Frustrated Global Reforms*, second edition, Scottsville, University of KwaZulu-Natal Press, 2006, pp. 14–15 and 179–89.

[90] Sandbrook, Edelman, Heller, and Teichman, *Social Democracy in the Global Periphery*, pp. 85 and 91.

mandates, constituencies, and values, the UN agencies and the Bretton Woods institutions continued to differ, the former insisting on social justice, the latter placing more emphasis on economic growth.[91] These divergent priorities were anchored in conceptions of equality that were clearly delineated by the left–right opposition.

Inequality, it should be recalled, was a major issue on the UN agenda of the early days. The issue was "marginalized" with the failure of the new international economic order negotiations of the 1970s, but in the wake of the Millennium Summit, the UN became increasingly attentive to the exacerbation of global inequality.[92] The organization presented the persistence of inequality between countries as a huge barrier preventing the achievement of the MDGs and the promotion of international security. Estimating that "about 70% of global income inequality is explained by differences in incomes between countries," the UN insisted on placing the reduction of inequality at the core of development policies.[93] In a comprehensive perspective, the UN promoted simultaneously a greater equality of rights, of opportunity, and of living conditions.

While they had recently accepted the need to combat poverty, the Bretton Woods institutions proved more reluctant to talk about inequality. In fact, the very logic of markets and competition that underpinned the neoliberal model of development advocated by these organizations demanded a certain degree of tolerance toward inequalities. Traditionally more open to progressive ideas than the IMF or the

---

[91] John Gerard Ruggie, "The United Nations and Globalization: Patterns and Limits of Institutional Adaptation," *Global Governance*, vol. 9, no. 3, 2003, 301–21, pp. 303–05; and Jean-Philippe Thérien, "Beyond the North-South Divide: The Two Tales of World Poverty," *Third World Quarterly*, vol. 20, no. 4, 1999, 723–42.

[92] Richard Jolly, Louis Emmerij, and Thomas G. Weiss, *The Power of UN Ideas*, p. 56. See also UNDP, *Human Development Report 2005: International Cooperation at a Crossroads: Aid, Trade and Security in an Unequal World*, New York, Oxford University Press, 2005; United Nations, *Report on the World Social Situation 2005: The Inequality Predicament*, New York, United Nations, 2005 (http://daccessdds.un.org/doc/UNDOC/GEN/N05/418/73/PDF/N0541873.pdf?OpenElement); United Nations, *World Economic and Social Survey 2006: Diverging Growth and Development*, New York, United Nations, 2006 (www.un.org/esa/policy/wess/wess2006files/wess2006.pdf); and United Nations, *Social Justice in an Open World: The Role of the United Nations*, New York, United Nations, 2006 (www.un.org/esa/socdev/IFSD/documents/SocialJustice.pdf).

[93] United Nations, *World Economic and Social Survey 2006*, p. vi.

WTO, the World Bank did come to acknowledge that inequality undermined economic inefficiency and aggravated social conflicts. Revealingly, however, its policy conclusions remained in line with the Bretton Woods orthodoxy.[94] For one thing, the Bank focused on the inequality of opportunities and paid little attention to the inequality of outcomes. Also, while admitting that international inequalities were more pronounced than internal inequalities, the Bank continued to concentrate on the domestic constraints to development, in keeping with its contention that "developing countries hold the keys to their prosperity."[95]

Fundamentally, the UN and the Bretton Woods institutions maintained their contrasting approaches toward globalization and governance. The Bretton Woods institutions' oft-repeated view that "growth is the tide that lifts all boats" was openly contested by the UN Secretary-General, who reiterated his belief that "no rising tide in the global economy will lift all boats."[96] For UN agencies, globalization and growth could have positive effects only if they were "grounded in a human-rights approach and the human empowerment concept of development."[97] This outlook, however, carried little weight with the IMF, the World Bank, and the WTO, who simply did not consider the promotion of human rights to be part of their mandate.[98] From their perspective, global economic integration not only increased "the size of the cake," but it also responded to an innate human desire "for expanded horizons and freedom of

[94] See World Bank, *World Development Report 2006: Equity and Development*, New York, Oxford University Press, 2005, pp. 9 and 57–66.

[95] *Ibid.*, p. 206.

[96] Rodrigo de Rato, "A Rising Tide That Lifts all Boats: How Europe, by Promoting Growth, Can Help Itself and Help the World," speech by the IMF Managing Director at the Austrian National Bank Seminar, Vienna, May 22, 2006 (www.imf.org/external/np/speeches/2006/052206.htm); Kofi A. Annan, "Millennium Development Goals Have Unprecedented Political Support, Secretary-General Says at London Event," address by UN Secretary-General to the St. Paul's Cathedral Event on the Millennium Development Goals, London, July 6, 2005 (www.un.org/News/Press/docs/2005/sgsm9984.doc.htm).

[97] Kemal Dervis, "Statement by the Administrator of the UNDP at the Executive Board of the UNDP/UNFPA," New York, January 24, 2006, p. 4 (http://content. undp.org/go/newsroom/june-2006/statement-dervis-exec-20060619.en).

[98] International Monetary Fund, "Common Ground and Differences of View Between the Bretton Woods Institutions (IMF and World Bank) and the World Council of Churches," Washington, DC, October 22, 2004, p. 1 (www.imf.org/ external/np/exr/docs/wcc102204.htm).

choice."[99] Above all, both sides disagreed over the proper role of states and markets. For the Bretton Woods institutions, most of the time "government intervention distorts and/or rigidifies markets and makes them function less well."[100] Kofi Annan, on the contrary, held that "there is no autopilot, no magic of the marketplace," and called for stronger public institutions, able to compensate the losers in globalization.[101]

Behind the new development consensus, the reform agenda proposed by the Bretton Woods institutions and by the UN continued to express the traditional clash of values between the left and the right. The financial institutions systematically emphasized the policy space already available to developing countries. They thus highlighted these countries' capacity for "self-help," as well as their leaders' need to pay more attention to good governance, corruption, fiscal adjustment, trade liberalization, and private-sector development. The World Bank, notably, drew a clear line between "good-policy" and "poor-policy" countries.[102] Global reforms considered by the Bretton Woods institutions remained limited in scope. The WTO largely focused on the opening of domestic markets. For its part, the IMF initiated a debate on a new international financial architecture, but discussions were essentially confined to issues such as greater policy transparency, stronger surveillance mechanisms, and improved interorganizational collaboration. The lack of representation of Southern countries in the Fund's governing bodies was recognized as a problem and small changes in voting procedures were implemented, but a genuine restructuring of the decision-making process did not materialize.

---

[99] Anne O. Krueger, "'Tis Not Too Late to Seek a Newer World: What Globalization Offers the Poor," address by the IMF First Deputy Managing Director to the Oxford Union, Oxford, May 9, 2005, p. 2 (www.imf.org/external/np/speeches/2005/050905.htm); Köhler, "Working for a Better Globalization," p. 2.

[100] Anne O. Krueger, "The Time is Always Ripe: Rushing Ahead with Economic Reform in Africa," lecture by the IMF First Deputy Managing Director to the Economic Society of South Africa, June 9, 2005, p. 3 (www.imf.org/external/np/speeches/2005/060905b.htm).

[101] Annan, "Millennium Development Goals Have Unprecedented Political Support."

[102] Ian Goldin, Halsey Rogers, and Nicholas Stern, *The Role and Effectiveness of Development Assistance: Lessons from World Bank Experience*, Washington, DC, World Bank, 2002, p. xix (http://wbln0018.worldbank.org/eurvp/web.nsf/Pages/ Paper+by+Ian+Goldin/$File/GOLDIN.PDF).

Hostile to the idea of integrating all multilateral bodies under the authority of the UN, the Bretton Woods institutions were resolved to maintain a separation between economic and social issues on the global agenda.

The UN ascribed much more weight to the systemic constraints on development, and pushed for governance reforms much more ambitious than those considered by the WTO or the IMF. Although the Monterrey agreement, for example, was welcomed as progress, it did not meet the UN's expectations. UNCTAD, in particular, strongly criticized the Monterrey accord for leaving economic development to "market forces."[103] The UN continued to call for a radical overhaul of multilateral trade rules, in order to provide "a level playing field" for all countries.[104] In addition to their emphasis on the need to democratize major economic forums and put the UN at the core of global governance, UN agencies proposed institutional innovations that included the launching of a Marshall Plan for the Third World, the introduction of global taxes, the creation of an Economic Security Council, the establishment of a bankruptcy court, and the creation of an international development fund.[105] These ideas were received guardedly at best by the Bretton Woods institutions.

Finally, the two sides maintained their own way of understanding the North–South division, each camp finding its inspiration in intellectual traditions associated with either the right or the left. The Bretton Woods institutions remained more comfortable with a framework categorizing countries as industrial, emerging, or low-income.[106] This

---

[103] UNCTAD, *Trade and Development Report 2006: Global Partnership and National Policies for Development*, New York and Geneva, United Nations, 2006, p. 57 (www.unctad.org/en/docs/tdr2006_en.pdf).

[104] Annan, *In Larger Freedom*, p. 22.

[105] United Nations, *Financing for Development: A Critical Global Collaboration*, Technical Note No. 4, New York, United Nations, 2002; UNRISD, *Visible Hands: Taking Responsibility for Social Development*, Geneva, UNRISD, 2000, pp. 25–32; UNCTAD, *Trade and Development Report, 2002: Developing Countries in World Trade*, Geneva, United Nations, 2002, p. i (www.unctad.org/en/docs/tdr2002_en.pdf); Juan Somavia, "Statement by Director-General of the ILO to the Sixty-fourth Meeting of the Development Committee," Ottawa, November 18, 2001 (www.ilo.org/public/english/bureau/dgo/speeches/somavia/2001/ottawa.htm).

[106] Anne O. Krueger, "From Despair to Hope: The Challenge of Promoting Poverty Reduction," lecture by the IMF First Deputy Managing Director at the

view of the world, inherited from the gradualist conception of history associated with the theory of modernization, suggested that under-development was not ineluctable, and that states who made the right decisions could achieve prosperity. UN agencies, for their part, were more inclined to stick to the old core–periphery vision. These terms, however, were given a different meaning from the one they had in the 1970s, when they were popularized by dependency theory. As UNDP head Kemal Dervis put it: "It is no longer a geographical center, but a sociological center, and the periphery is the people around it and they may include the suburbs of Paris or New Orleans."[107] Dervis' analysis, which reconceptualized the unequal and antagonistic nature of the global system, provided a forceful reminder that, in the field of development, the values and beliefs of the left remained altogether distinct from those of the right.

Conclusion

At the end of the twentieth century, a rapprochement took place between the left and the right. In national politics, this movement toward the center saw the right soften its stance on market competi-tion, individualism, and a leaner state, while the left was coming to terms with the legitimacy of the market, the virtues of competition, and the need for efficiency. On the left, the most articulate rendition of this ideological adjustment came from Third Way advocates such as Tony Blair, Gerhard Schröder, and Anthony Giddens, who proposed a modernized social-democracy, sensible to the challenges raised by globalization, neoliberalism, post-industrialism, and new social move-ments. In global politics, a similar process took shape around the idea of a new development consensus, able to combine the right's prefer-ence for markets and competition with the left's concern for social justice. For a time, this new compromise seemed sufficiently powerful

Annual Boehm-Bawek Lecture, Innsbruck, November 17, 2005, p. 2 (www.imf.org/external/np/speeches/2005/111705.htm).

[107] Kemal Dervis, "Globalization: Key Challenges for Governance and Multilateralism," keynote speech by the Administrator of the UNDP at the Conference on "The Challenge of Globalization: Reinventing Good Global Governance," November 4, 2005, p. 3 (http://gstudynet.org/governance/panels/keynote.php).

to bridge the long-standing gap between the views defended by the global financial institutions and those of the United Nations.

The rapprochement, however, soon showed its limits. In global politics, it never erased the enduring and numerous differences between the left and the right over globalization, growth, inequality, and the governance of development. The UN agencies continued to be critical of a world that remained profoundly and increasingly unequal, while the IMF, the World Bank, and the WTO remained confident that the international system was heading in the right direction and could become more equitable with good policies and modest reforms. In domestic politics, Third Way discourses gradually gave way to more classical assertions of social-democratic values, as the right came back to power in most of the Western world in the beginning of the 2000s, and as the left was reaffirming its strength in Latin America and in other countries of the South.

Systematic studies of party programs in Western democracies between the Second World War and the end of the twentieth century show the remarkable stability of the left–right division over time and across space. In English-speaking democracies, there was a rightward shift of all parties in the 1980s, but the gap between the left and the right moved along, so that the distance between the two sides remained about the same; in continental Europe, this general shift to the right did not even take place.[108] Interestingly, European Union politics itself was defined and paced by the politics of left and right, as both intergovernmental relations and European elections reflected the relative strength of conservatives and social-democrats in member states.[109] Everything else being equal, parties of the left always spent

---

[108] Ian Budge and Michael D. McDonald, "Election and Party System Effects on Policy Representation: Bringing Time into a Comparative Perspective," *Electoral Studies*, vol. 26, no. 1, March 2007, 168–79, p. 171; Torben Iversen, "Class Politics is Dead! Long Live Class Politics! A Political Economy Perspective on the New Partisan Politics," *APSA–CP Newsletter* (American Political Science Association Comparative Politics Newsletter), vol. 17, no. 2, Summer 2006, 1–6, pp. 2–3.

[109] Manow, Schäfer and Zorn, "European Social Policy and Europe's Party-Political Center of Gravity," p. 32–33; Liesbet Hooghe, Gary Marks, and Carole J. Wilson, "Does Left/Right Structure Party Positions on European Integration?," in Gary Marks and Marco R. Steenbergen (eds.), *European Integration and Political Conflict*, Cambridge University Press, 2004, p. 121; Daniele Caramani, "Is There a European Electorate and What Does It Look

more and redistributed more than parties of the right, they invested more in human capital formation, and they created more public employment and social services, leading women to become more leftist than men.[110] The left in power had more success, too, in reducing poverty at home, and it was also more generous in offering development assistance to promote justice abroad.[111] In global politics, actors and institutions on the left, NGOs and UN agencies in particular, continued to oppose purely market-oriented approaches to globalization, and favored more equality and more democratic governance structures. In sum, the debate between the left and the right had evolved, as the two sides adjusted to a new world context, but it continued to define the most enduring and fundamental divide of global politics.

Like? Evidence from Electoral Volatility Measures, 1976–2004," *West European Politics*, vol. 29, no. 1, January 2006, 1–27.

[110] David Bradley, Evelyn Huber, Stephanie Moller, François Nielsen, and John Stephens, "Distribution and Redistribution in Postindustrial Democracies," *World Politics*, vol. 55, no. 2, 2003, 193–228; Iversen, "Class Politics Is Dead!," pp. 4–6; Torben Iversen, "Electoral Institutions and the Politics of Coalitions: Why Some Democracies Redistribute More Than Others," *American Political Science Review*, vol. 100, no. 2, May 2006, 165–81, p. 165; Torben Iversen and Frances Rosenbluth, "The Political Economy of Gender: Explaining Cross-National Variation in the Gender Division of Labor and the Gender Voting Gap," *American Journal of Political Science*, vol. 50, no. 1, January 2006, 12–18.

[111] Lyle Scruggs and James P. Allan, "The Material Consequences of Welfare States: Benefit Generosity and Absolute Poverty in 16 OECD Countries," *Comparative Political Studies*, vol. 39, no. 7, September 2006, 880–904; Jean-Philippe Thérien and Alain Noël, "Political Parties and Foreign Aid," *American Political Science Review*, vol. 94, no. 1, March 2000, 151–62; Alain Noël and Jean-Philippe Thérien, "Public Opinion and Global Justice," *Comparative Political Studies*, vol. 35, no. 6, August 2002, 627–52.

8 | *The core currency of political exchange*

The left–right distinction, observe political scientists Michael McDonald, Silvia Mendes, and Myunghee Kim, is the "core currency of political exchange." Like price and quantity in economic exchange, these notions provide a simple and universal language that helps citizens, politicians, and experts make sense of politics. Without them, collective decisions and popular control over elected politicians would be very difficult, and indeed almost impossible.[1] Intercultural and international debates would also lose much coherence and become hard to comprehend. But is the left–right distinction powerful enough to extend beyond the politics of equality and distribution it usually captures, and help us understand other global issues? And what does this language mean for the study of global politics?

The first question concerns the heuristic value of the left–right dichotomy. Even among those who would agree that the cleavage between the left and the right is an enduring and encompassing one, many would contend that, in the end, it remains too simplistic to account for the complex universe of contemporary world politics. Many issues, they would argue, simply reflect other divisions, outside left–right dynamics. There is no denying that global politics does not begin and end with the left and the right. Religious differences, for instance, have been and remain a major source of conflict in the world. Still, as the core currency of political exchange, the left–right cleavage covers and shapes most questions. This chapter's first section considers three dominant issues of our time that have often been presented as beyond the left–right opposition – the politics of identity, the war on terrorism, and the global environmental debate – to illustrate the remarkable reach of this global symbolic currency.

[1] Michael D. McDonald, Silvia M. Mendes, and Myunghee Kim, "Cross-Temporal and Cross-National Comparisons of Party Left–Right Positions," *Electoral Studies*, vol. 26, no. 1, March 2007, 62–75, p. 63.

The second question addressed in this chapter concerns the study of politics, both domestic and international. Indeed, if the left–right divide is so fundamental, it may seem surprising that scholars interested in global affairs have paid so little attention to it. In the field of international relations, in particular, one hardly ever hears of the left and the right. In the last section of this chapter, we trace this peculiarity to the fact that political scientists themselves remain divided along a left–right axis, a reality they usually prefer not to see, to maintain their claim to scientific objectivity. Ideological divisions within political science are, however, unavoidable, and they are there to stay. Understanding them better is enlightening, and it could help build the study of global politics on more solid and integrated ground.

Emerging global issues

The politics of identity

The collapse of the Soviet bloc at the end of the 1980s brought to the fore a dimension of social life long hidden by an East–West confrontation focused on socialism and capitalism: the politics of identity. Against the optimistic predictions of those who had started celebrating the unmitigated triumph of liberalism, or even the end of history, the peoples of Eastern Europe reaffirmed their long-repressed claims to nationhood. Some did so pacifically and democratically, others in violent and exclusionary ways. The national flag sometimes served as an emblem of democracy, but it was also used to justify aggression and "ethnic cleansing," reminding the world of the dark side of nationalism.

In older democracies, the dominant neoliberal agenda also left a space open for a distinct politics of identity, promoted by social movements seeking new collective rights. Women, national minorities, indigenous peoples, ethnic communities, and various social and cultural groups took the political stage to demand recognition, respect, and equality. The conventional politics of income distribution and universal social rights that had been the hallmark of the left–right debate seemed fated, if not to vanish, at least to become less central in the life of established democracies.[2]

---

[2] Rogers M. Smith, *Stories of Peoplehood: The Politics and Morals of Political Membership*, Cambridge University Press, 2003, pp. 10–11; Samuel

This global politics of identity was often portrayed as antithetical to the left–right cleavage. The relatively ordered bipolar world of the Cold War, it was argued, was giving way to a chaotic universe of cultural conflicts, which were primordial and much more dangerous. On the right, in particular, commentators spoke of a rising "tribalism" that expressed "ancient hatreds," and they foresaw a "pandaemonium," a "coming anarchy," or a "clash of civilizations" whose manifestations would encompass harsh ethnic conflicts in post-communist countries, brutal civil wars in the South, and endless multicultural demands in affluent democracies.[3] Less pessimistic, many observers on the left nevertheless concurred in seeing this new politics of identity as contrary to the conventional politics of left and right, and as a development that risked distracting political actors from more important debates about equality, redistribution, and justice. While the left was "marching on the English Department," quipped Todd Gitlin, "the right took the White House."[4]

The politics of identity undeniably has a logic of its own. Rooted in strong cultural traits and in emotions that help define interpersonal trust and the worth of one's social group, collective identities run deeper than the relatively Cartesian politics of left and right.[5] Around the world and across the political spectrum, parties and social movements have regularly tried to bypass or dissolve divisions based on identity, but most of the time they ended up acknowledging and accommodating them. Likewise, in the nineteenth and twentieth centuries, authoritarian, liberal, and communist regimes made colossal efforts to build new nations out of distinct ethnic and national groups, but they rarely succeeded in displacing or entirely assimilating resilient

P. Huntington, *The Clash of Civilizations and the Remaking of World Order*, New York, Simon & Schuster, 1996, pp. 19–20.

[3] Daniel Patrick Moynihan, *Pandaemonium: Ethnicity in International Politics*, Oxford University Press, 1993, pp. 6–25; Robert D. Kaplan, "The Coming Anarchy: How Scarcity, Crime, Overpopulation, Tribalism, and Disease Are Rapidly Destroying the Social Fabric of Our Planet," *Atlantic Monthly*, vol. 273, no. 2, February 1994, 44–76; Huntington, *The Clash of Civilizations*, pp. 19–29.

[4] Todd Gitlin, quoted in Keith Banting and Will Kymlicka, "Introduction. Multiculturalism and the Welfate State: Setting the Context," in Keith Banting and Will Kymlicka (eds.), *Multiculturalism and the Welfate State: Recognition and Redistribution in Contemporary Democracies*, Oxford University Press, 2006, pp. 10–14.

[5] Smith, *Stories of Peoplehood*, pp. 56–59.

minority identities.[6] Still, in so far as they acquire a political expression, social identities almost always do so in the language of left and right. They rely, in other words, on the universal currency of political exchange.

Consider, first, large-scale national identities. In the 1930s and 1940s, just as Italian fascists and German Nazis articulated a right-wing and irredentist brand of nationalism to suit their purpose, the anti-fascist left built its resistance around an equally powerful "national and patriotic sentiment."[7] Nationalist discourses were thus constructed in the prevailing language of left and right politics. Likewise, in the 1950s and 1960s, decolonization was pursued by progressive nationalist movements, which proclaimed the intrinsic equality of all human beings. "National liberation," noted Eric Hobsbawm, then became "a slogan of the left."[8] In the post-Cold War years, nationalism proved just as malleable. In some countries, it was associated with authoritarianism, ethnic exactions, and violence, but in others, it inspired democratic movements. At first, these democratic movements used national identity to affirm the country's autonomy against a decaying Soviet empire; later, they evoked nationalism to consolidate popular sovereignty against autocrats presumably supported by foreign powers.[9] The popular revolutions of the early 2000s – rose revolution in Georgia (2003), orange in Ukraine (2004), tulip in Kyrgyzstan (2005), cedar in Lebanon (2005) – all involved protesters carrying the national flag to rally the population behind democracy, and prevent potential external interventions on behalf of contested rulers. In a similar fashion, the sub-state identities that sought recognition and autonomy in multinational countries were always tied either to the left or to the right, depending on the class and political alliances that defined them. In Belgium, for instance, "Walloon nationalism is on the left, Flemish nationalism is on the right."[10] Before the Second

[6] Walker Connor, *Ethnonationalism: The Quest for Understanding*, Princeton University Press, 1994, pp. 42–57.

[7] Eric J. Hobsbawm, *Nations and Nationalism since 1780: Programme, Myth, Reality*, second edition, Cambridge University Press, 1992, pp. 143–45.

[8] *Ibid.*, p. 150.

[9] Charles H. Fairbanks, Jr., "Revolution Reconsidered," *Journal of Democracy*, vol. 18, no. 1, January 2007, 42–57, p. 47.

[10] Jan Erk, "Sub-State Nationalism and the Left–Right Divide: Critical Junctures in the Formation of Nationalist Labour Movements in Belgium," *Nations and Nationalism*, vol. 11, no. 4, October 2005, 551–70, p. 566.

World War, Catalan and Québec nationalism were conservative ideologies; they are now social-democratic orientations.[11]

Scholars on the left are usually more attentive to these various and changing expressions of nationalism, and less likely than their conservative colleagues to paint all nationalisms as potentially malevolent. For one thing, they are less concerned by the need to maintain social order and more preoccupied by the possible injustice of any existing order. In line with their more optimistic view of human nature, they also tend to believe that conflicting identities "will work to check each other's excesses as they vie to win broad support in political contests."[12] These scholars, finally, are more sensitive to the distinct and legitimate character of demands from the underdogs, be they small nations or oppressed minorities.[13] Anthropologist Arjun Appadurai, for instance, contrasts "predatory" and "emancipatory" nationalisms, the former leading to the oppression and sometimes elimination of minority identities, the latter sustaining popular struggles against injustice.[14] Nationalism, in sum, varies in content, and it is normally of the right or of the left.

As for the domestic politics of identity linked to multiculturalism and new social movements, it is also very much a politics of the left and right. The opposition between progressives and conservatives on these questions is in fact so pronounced that many in the United States have spoken of culture wars. When they call for change, women, aboriginal peoples, blacks in the United States, ethnic and cultural minorities everywhere, and all kinds of disadvantaged groups undoubtedly do so as movements of the left, against conservative forces reluctant to modify the status quo.

The demands of identity groups are quintessential leftist demands because they concern recognition and respect, so as to achieve equality.

---

[11] Montserrat Guibernau, *Nations without States: Political Communities in a Global Age*, Cambridge, Polity Press, 1999, p. 95.

[12] Smith, *Stories of Peoplehood*, p. 159.

[13] Dominique Schnapper, *La communauté des citoyens*, Paris, Gallimard, 1994, pp. 30–31.

[14] Arjun Appadurai, "The Grounds of the Nation-State: Identity, Violence and Territory," in Kjell Goldmann, Ulf Hannerz, and Charles Westin (eds.), *Nationalism and Internationalism in the Post-Cold War Era*, London, Routledge, 2000, pp. 129–34; a similar distinction is made in Stanley Hoffman, "Nationalism and World Order," in Goldmann, Hannerz and Westin (eds.), *Nationalism and Internationalism*, pp. 204–6.

Some critics on the left have seen a contradiction between this focus on identity and the left's traditional politics of income redistribution, creating something like a "progressive's dilemma," whereby the pursuit of recognition would undermine the resolve and solidarity necessary to achieve greater equality. The empirical evidence, however, does not support this view. The adoption of multiculturalism policies does not lower public support for redistribution and does not affect a country's commitment to encompassing social programs.[15] Many factors may explain this. First, the claims of identity groups remain fundamentally compatible with the traditional demands of the left, because in the end they concern equality. To underline the intrinsic link between the quest for symbolic recognition of new social movements and their expectations about material rewards and redistribution, Matt James names the Canadian identity groups he studies "misrecognized materialists." Groups representing "visible" minorities, for instance, seek recognition precisely to combat racism, insecurity, and economic discrimination.[16] Second, no matter how important they are in public debates, multiculturalism policies remain marginal compared to the huge and slow-moving programs that constitute the welfare state, such as old age, health, or unemployment insurances. Third, given their nature, multiculturalism policies are more likely to be adopted and deployed in countries where the left is already strong, and thus able and committed to maintain generous welfare programs.

The case of indigenous peoples shows very well how identity and progressive politics can mesh. There are more than 370 million indigenous people in the world, spread over seventy countries, where they usually "occupy an encapsulated status as disempowered and dispersed subjects of a larger entity."[17] In the last decades, an indigenous international has emerged and has succeeded in having most states reject outright assimilation and accept elements of self-determination.

[15] Banting and Kymlicka, "Introduction," pp. 32–33.

[16] Matt James, *Misrecognized Materialists: Social Movements in Canadian Constitutional Politics*, Vancouver, UBC Press, 2006, pp. 79–80.

[17] Augie Fleras and Roger Maaka, quoted in Alan C. Cairns, "Citizenship and Indian Peoples: The Ambiguous Legacy of Internal Colonialism," in Engin F. Isin and Bryan S. Turner (eds.), *Handbook of Citizenship Studies*, London, Sage, 2002, p. 209; the data are from: United Nations Permanent Forum on Indigenous Issues, "About UNPFII/History," New York, UNPFII, 2006 (http://www.un.org/esa/socdev/unpfii/en/history.html).

In June 2006, this global movement also obtained a formal declaration on the rights of indigenous peoples, which was adopted by the United Nations Human Rights Council.[18] Combating internal colonialism, however, remains more complex than seeking conventional decolonization, because indigenous nations can rarely aspire to their own states.[19] They have to identify allies and seek compromises, and they always find such possibilities on the left. In Latin America, for instance, some progressives were worried that the pursuit of indigenous rights would be a distraction from the struggle against neoliberalism, but fruitful alliances were eventually forged. The strength indigenous peoples gained with the recognition of their rights allowed them, in fact, to play a key role in the revival of the "leftist–popular coalitions that opposed structural adjustment and trade liberalization."[20] Again, the politics of identity ended up being constructed as left–right politics.

The strongest opponents to the calls for recognition and equality associated with the politics of identity are indeed on the right. Conservatives often deride demands for respect as mere "political correctness," they claim that measures to help minorities are unfair to current generations that have not taken part in any injustice, they worry about the fate of national traditions and national culture, and consider that immigrants should be happy just to be accepted in the country they inhabit. In the end, writes Samuel Huntington, a truly

---

[18] Human Rights Council, *Report to the General Assembly on the First Session of the Human Rights Council*, New York, United Nations, June 30, 2006 (daccessdds.un.org/doc/ UNDOC/LTD/G06/128/65/PDF/G0612865.pdf? OpenElement). The Canadian government voted against this declaration, even though it contributed to its drafting, and even though bureaucrats in the Indian Affairs, Foreign Affairs, and Defence departments recommended approval. This was again a left–right question: the new Conservative government of Stephen Harper simply was not willing to go as far on aboriginal rights as the previous Liberal government of Paul Martin. Gloria Galloway, "Back UN on Native Rights, Ottawa Urged; Bureaucracy at Odds with PM's Position, Documents Show," *Globe and Mail*, June 8, 2007, p. A1 (www.theglobeandmail.com/servlet/story/LAC.20070608.INDIGENOUS08/TPStory).

[19] Cairns, "Citizenship and Indian Peoples," p. 209–12.

[20] Donna Lee Van Cott, "Multiculturalism versus Neoliberalism in Latin America," in Banting and Kymlicka (eds.), *Multiculturalism and the Welfare State*, pp. 272–94; Deborah J. Yashar, *Contesting Citizenship in Latin America: The Rise of Indigenous Movements and the Postliberal Challenge*, Cambridge University Press, 2005, pp. 281–308.

multicultural country would be doomed. It would simply lose its cultural core, and could "no longer endure as a coherent society." Knowing the opinion American conservatives have of the UN, Huntington formulates a dire warning: "a multicivilizational United States will not be the United States; it will be the United Nations."[21]

It is a fact, then, that the politics of identity has become more important than ever in world politics, and it is also true that it cannot be reduced entirely to an opposition between the left and the right. At the same time, national projects are always of the left or of the right, and identity claims consistently oppose progressives and conservatives. Indeed, neglecting the left–right underpinnings of identity politics would make it very difficult to understand this rising type of conflict.

The war on terrorism

Since the attacks of September 11, 2001, terrorism has become a prime concern in world affairs. Among elite groups as well as in the media, the debate on this question has developed largely along the fault line separating progressives and conservatives. In the United States, where, it is sometimes said, the left–right distinction has disappeared, the positions defended by the Republican Party and Fox News have unquestionably been different from those put forward by the Democratic Party or *The New York Times*. It is true, of course, that the debate on terrorism has included its share of ideological outliers. Various left-wing commentators have defended the invasion of Iraq on human rights grounds, while some pundits on the right condemned it in the name of realism and national interests. Yet in the United States, as elsewhere in the West, the fight against terrorism has generally mirrored the Cold War pattern: it opposed hawks, advocating a hard line, and doves, favoring compromise.

On the right, terrorism is understood as a security issue that jeopardizes the freedom and lifestyle of all civilized countries. Several politicians and analysts have depicted the phenomenon as one of the most telling manifestations of Huntington's "clash of civilizations."[22] A few days after 9/11, President Bush implicitly endorsed this interpretation when he stated: "What is at stake is not just America's

---

[21] Huntington, *The Clash of Civilizations*, p. 306.   [22] *Ibid.*

freedom. This is the world's fight. This is civilization's fight. This is the fight of all who believe in progress and pluralism, tolerance and freedom."[23] The successive strikes against Indonesia, Morocco, Spain, and Great Britain lent weight to the conservative thesis that terrorists strive for the destruction of democratic societies and liberal values. Rejecting any notion that the governments of the rich countries may be responsible – even indirectly – for the terrorist phenomenon, conservatives have ascribed it to individual fanatics or rogue states, ready to "strike at any place, at any time, and with virtually any weapon."[24] The magnitude of this perceived threat has justified making the fight against terrorism a political priority ranking above all others.

The hard line of the right has nowhere been expressed more clearly than in US foreign policy. Under the influence of a group of neo-conservative intellectuals for whom the elimination of the terrorist threat is essential for national security, the Bush administration has made the war on terrorism the cornerstone of its external relations. This general objective legitimized both the military intervention in Afghanistan in 2001 and the launching of the war in Iraq in 2003. In turn, the opening of these two battlefronts justified a spectacular expansion of the military budget. In the case of Iraq, where the debate became highly polarized, US policy-makers succeeded in imposing the necessity of a pre-emptive war, defined as "an act of anticipatory self-defense."[25] The argument was that the Iraqi government possessed weapons of mass destruction and thus represented "an imminent threat of unprovoked aggression."[26] For the American right, the fact that no terrorist attack had occurred in the United States since 2001 provided decisive proof that a tough foreign policy offered the best response to the scourge of international terrorism.

[23] George W. Bush, "Address to a Joint Session of Congress and the American People," Washington, DC, September 20, 2001 (www.whitehouse.gov/news/releases/2001/09/20010920-8.html).

[24] George W. Bush, *The Department of Homeland Security*, Washington, DC, 2002, p. 13 (www.whitehouse.gov/deptofhomeland/toc.html).

[25] Richard K. Betts, "Striking First: A History of Thankfully Lost Opportunities," New York, Carnegie Council for Ethics in International Affairs, March 2, 2003 (www.cceia.org/resources/journal/17_1/roundtable/866.html).

[26] Laura Neack, *Elusive Security: States First, People Last*, Lanham, Rowman & Littlefield, 2007, p. 122.

The American administration naturally presented the war on terrorism – and Operation Iraqi Freedom in particular – as one that rose above traditional political divisions. Among Western democracies, however, the US policy appeared much more legitimate to governments of the right. In Europe, notably, partisan differences were manifest.[27] At the end of 2003, among the fifteen countries that were then members of the European Union, six had agreed to participate in the coalition created by Washington and nine had refused. Of the six governments that dispatched troops to Iraq, five were led by parties of the center-right (Denmark, Italy, the Netherlands, Portugal, and Spain) and only one belonged to the center-left (United Kingdom). Among the nine opposed to the coalition, five were associated with the center-left (Belgium, Finland, Germany, Greece, and Sweden), and four with the center-right (Austria, France, Ireland, and Luxembourg). Left–right ideology did not predict policy orientations perfectly, but it clearly influenced the decisions of European governments with regard to the war in Iraq. The steadfast support of Great Britain and its New Labour government for the American strategy constituted a significant anomaly but, at the same time, one should acknowledge that Tony Blair's policy gave rise to sharp internal opposition, coming mainly from his own party and from groups identified with the left.[28]

In the domestic arena, conservatives have called for a hardening of internal security measures, as well as for substantial increases in the human, financial, and technical resources devoted to the fight against terrorism. New laws and regulations were adopted to give the police and the courts more latitude in the pursuit of terrorists.[29] Policies introduced in the aftermath of 9/11 granted exceptional powers of arrest to police officers, authorized the indefinite detention of foreigners, and reinforced immigration controls, particularly with regard to Middle Eastern populations. The anti-terrorist struggle also addressed fund-raising, money-laundering, weapon procurement, and

---

[27] Brian C. Rathbun, *Partisan Interventions: European Party Politics and Peace Enforcement in the Balkans*, Ithaca, Cornell University Press, 2004, p. 213. See also Jürgen Schuster and Herbert Maier, "The Rift: Explaining Europe's Divergent Iraq Policies in the Run-Up of the American-Led War on Iraq," *Foreign Policy Analysis*, vol. 2, no. 3, July 2006, 223–44.

[28] Rathbun, *Partisan Interventions*, p. 216.

[29] Doron Zimmermann and Andreas Wenger (eds.), *How States Fight Terrorism: Policy Dynamics in the West*, Boulder, Lynne Rienner, 2007.

diaspora mobilization.[30] In their campaign to reduce domestic vulnerability to the terrorist menace, conservatives often contended that the effectiveness of the means mattered more than their legitimacy. They maintained, accordingly, that the success of the fight against terrorism required a policy of strict confidentiality, and that, for security reasons, a good deal of information simply could not be made public.

The left, in contrast, tends to consider that the terrorist threat has been greatly exaggerated. John Mueller, for instance, argues that in most places the probability of someone becoming a victim of a terrorist attack remains "microscopic."[31] Except in 2001, he notes, in the United States, "fewer people have died from international terrorism [than] have drowned in bathtubs."[32] Progressives also insist that terrorism ought not to be reduced to a security problem whose solution can be achieved only through a military approach. Terrorists, explained UN Secretary-General Kofi Annan in 2003, "thrive on despair," and "there needs to be more on the horizon than simply winning a war against terrorism. There must be the promise of a better and fairer world, and a concrete plan to get there."[33] Convinced that peace and democracy cannot be imposed with bombs, liberals and socialists think that the use of force actually plays into the hands of extremists, and fuels hatred of the West. According to their analysis, the fight against terrorism must give greater consideration to its underlying economic and social causes, rely more heavily on diplomacy, and respect international human rights and norms.

Having given its mitigated support to the military intervention against the Taliban regime in Afghanistan, the left consistently disputed

---

[30] Peter Chalk and William Rosenau, *Confronting the "Enemy Within:" Security Intelligence, the Police, and Counterterrorism in Four Democracies*, Santa Monica, RAND Corporation, 2004, p. 25.

[31] John E. Mueller, "Terrorism, Overreaction, and Globalization," in Richard N. Rosecrance and Arthur A. Stein (eds.), *No More States: Globalization, National Self-Determination, and Terrorism*, Lanham, Rowman & Littlefield, 2006, p. 47.

[32] *Ibid.*, p. 48; John E. Mueller, "Is There Still a Terrorist Threat? The Myth of the Omnipresent Enemy," *Foreign Affairs*, vol. 85, no. 5, September/October 2006, 2–8.

[33] Kofi Annan, "Remarks at the Conference 'Fighting Terrorism for Humanity: A Conference on the Roots of Evil'," New York, September 22, 2003 (www.un.org/apps/sg/sgstats.asp?nid=511).

the involvement of Saddam Hussein's government in international terrorism. The fears associated with Saddam's weapons of mass destruction, observed Mueller, were "based more on selective perception, willful deception, and self-induced hysteria than on evidence."[34] From the very start, the invasion of Iraq, which was not approved by the Security Council, was denounced as a violation of the UN Charter. Contesting the doctrine of pre-emptive war, progressives presented this military operation as a maneuver to boost US control over the resources and populations of the Middle East. Far from enhancing democracy in Iraq, they contended, American policy plunged the country into a brutal civil war that could result in its disintegration. Finally, the left also denounced the war in Iraq as an immoral waste of resources and viewed as the ultimate irony the fact that the number of Americans killed in Iraq surpassed the number of victims of the 9/11 attacks.

In the domestic arena, human rights groups emphasized the need to bring the fight against terrorism back within the ambit of the rule of law and civil liberties.[35] To do otherwise could only set democratic regimes on the road to authoritarianism and serve the terrorists' ends. Hence, in the United States, the 2001 Patriot Act was repeatedly denounced for having been passed "with no discussion, debate or hearings."[36] Since the adoption of this controversial law, the opposition to anti-terrorist measures has only intensified, in large part because the FBI has been unable to identify a single sleeper cell of Al-Qaida in the country. In Great Britain, the country's highest court gave cause to critics when it ruled that parts of the Anti-Terrorism, Crime, and Security Act of 2001 violated European human rights legislation. One of the judges stated bluntly: "The real threat to the life of the nation, in the sense of a people living in accordance with its traditional laws and political values, comes not from terrorism but from laws such as these."[37] In a number of countries, the left has

---

[34] Mueller, "Terrorism, Overreaction, and Globalization," p. 67.

[35] S. Neil MacFarlane and Yuen Foong Khong, *Human Security: A Critical History*, Bloomington, Indiana University Press, 2006, p. 254.

[36] Neack, *Elusive Security*, p. 59.

[37] House of Lords, *Opinions of the Lords of Appeal for Judgment in the Cause "A (FC) and others (FC) (Appellants) v. Secretary of State for the Home Department (Respondent); X (FC) and another (FC) (Appellants) v. Secretary of State for the Home Department (Respondent)"*, London, UKHL 56, December 16, 2004, p. 53.

expressed concern about the lack of accountability of anti-terrorist agencies and the expanding role of the military in domestic politics. Taking note of the increasing number of cases of racial profiling involving Arabs and Muslims, progressives also deplored the fact that the fight against terrorism has engendered xenophobic sentiments contrary to democratic values.

Tony Blair, who struggled for years with his party's left over the war on terrorism, nicely summed up the left–right dimension of the debate – with his own Third Way twist – in an article he published in *The Economist* after he announced his departure: "Here is where I have always felt that the normal politics of left and right are a hindrance. The trouble is that the right is correct on the need to stand firm militarily and in support of freedom; and the left is correct on the need for justice."[38]

The global environmental debate

The recent multiplication of extreme weather events and ongoing debates about global warming have focused increasing attention on the environment as a global governance issue. It is sometimes argued that the environmental debate transcends traditional ideological divisions and that, in fact, a broad consensus has arisen in favor of sustainable development. This view, however, is far from convincing. Ever since the environment was put on the global agenda some four decades ago, the left has attributed more importance to this issue than the right. Robert Paehlke, one of those commentators who argue that environmentalism "can be blended with almost any left or right ideology," nevertheless concedes that, at the end of the day, the environmental movement "has most often been linked with the moderate left."[39]

The progressive character of environmentalism is the outcome of clear political choices. Most environmentalists consider the "lessening [of] socio-economic inequalities [as a] central and long-standing concern," and they have come to the conclusion that "egalitarian

---

[38] Tony Blair, "What I've Learned," *The Economist*, May 31, 2007, 26–28.
[39] Robert C. Paehlke, *Environmentalism and the Future of Progressive Politics*, New Haven, Yale University Press, 1989, pp. 190 and 309.

political mechanisms are to be preferred to centralized political ones."[40] Thus, for over twenty years, green parties have staked out a position as a new, more libertarian left, modifying the political landscape in a number of Western countries. At the cutting edge of this trend, the German greens have, for instance, defined themselves as part of a global community that includes "groups for the protection of life, nature and environment, citizens' initiatives, the workers' movement, Christian initiatives, peace, human rights, women's and Third World movements."[41]

The historical convergence of the environmental movement and the left should not obscure, of course, the ongoing tensions to which these two social forces are subject. Trade unions, for instance, often look upon the environmental cause with suspicion. Environmentalists themselves do not constitute a monolithic group. There are, in fact, "green conservatives," whose beliefs are based on religious, economic, or national security considerations.[42] Ultimately, however, the main cleavage places environmentalists on the left and their opponents on the right. Companies such as British Petroleum or General Electric may have jumped on to the environmental bandwagon, but overall business still tends to oppose environmental policies that threaten to reduce profits.[43] And although a few prominent American neo-conservatives have gone green and drive hybrid cars, "dominant conservative views" remain "indifferent or skeptical – if not polemically hostile – to environmental concerns."[44]

[40] Robert E. Goodin, *Green Political Theory*, Cambridge, Polity Press, 1992, p. 15; John Barry and Brian Doherty, "The Greens and Social Policy: Movements, Politics and Practice?," *Social Policy and Administration*, vol. 35, no. 5, December 2001, 587–607, p. 587.

[41] Die Grünen, *Programme of the German Green Party*, p. 6. Quoted in Douglas Torgerson, *The Promise of Green Politics: Environmentalism and the Public Sphere*, Durham, Duke University Press, 1999, p. 3.

[42] Nadivah Greenberg, "Shop Right: American Conservatisms, Consumption, and the Environment," *Global Environmental Politics*, vol. 6, no. 2, May 2006, 85–111.

[43] Pamela S. Chasek, David L. Downie, and Janet Welsh Brown, *Global Environmental Politics*, fourth edition, Boulder, Westview, 2006, p. 86. See also Paul G. Harris, "International Environmental Affairs and U.S. Foreign Policy," in Paul G. Harris (ed.), *The Environment, International Relations, and U.S. Foreign Policy*, Washington, DC, Georgetown University Press, 2001, p. 22.

[44] Greenberg, "Shop Right," p. 86.

In keeping with their more satisfied view of the world, conservatives tend to see the analyses of environmentalist movements as unduly alarmist. Many observers on the right, for instance, maintain that climate change remains an open question. In the absence of irrefutable scientific evidence, they contend, new studies are needed to determine whether global warming is really the result of human activity or simply a natural phenomenon, and to assess the extent to which rising temperatures have already affected the various regions of the world.[45] The same positive view leads these skeptics to put their trust in the potential of technology to solve the problems that may eventually stem from the deterioration of ecosystems and from resource depletion. In their view, "humans will not deplete any resources ... as long as technology is given free rein and prices are allowed to fluctuate enough to stimulate the search for substitutes."[46] At the same time, arguing that environmental protection should not open the door to unfair competition, the right demands that developing countries adopt stricter environmental policies.[47] After all, conservatives point out, countries like China and India are among the biggest polluters in the world, whereas the governments and enterprises of rich countries are the main contributors to the development of clean technologies.

In international as well as in national political debates, conservatives maintain that, even though it may be justified, the protection of the environment should not jeopardize economic growth. Just before the 1992 Earth Summit in Rio, former American president George H. Bush is reported to have said that "our life-style is not open to negotiation."[48] Some ten years later, his son George W. Bush surmised that the application of the Kyoto Protocol, a multilateral treaty aimed at reducing greenhouse gas emissions, would "wreck" the American

---

[45] "Scientists, Governments Clash as Report Reveals Dangers of Climate Change," *USA Today*, April 6, 2007 (www.usatoday.com/weather/climate/globalwarming/2007-04-06-global- warming-report_N.htm).

[46] Chasek, Downie, and Welsh Brown, *Global Environmental Politics*, p. 27.

[47] Aaron M. McCright and Riley E. Dunlap, "Defeating Kyoto: The Conservative Movement's Impact on U.S. Climate Change Policy," *Social Problems*, vol. 50, no. 3, August 2003, 348–73, p. 349.

[48] Quoted in Robert W. Cox (with Michael G. Schechter), *The Political Economy of a Plural World: Critical Reflections on Power, Morals and Civilization*, London, Routledge, 2002, p. 88.

economy.[49] In the end, the right considers the maintenance of a liberal economic order its absolute political priority. It thus favors a form of "liberal environmentalism," which would rely on "the market ... as the preferred means to solve environmental problems."[50]

Advocates of liberal environmentalism consistently lean toward voluntary rather than coercive measures to respond to environmental challenges. By nature more flexible, such measures are more in tune with the operation of markets than are binding regulations. Not surprisingly, the American government was at the outset among the most ardent proponents of the establishment of carbon markets to counter climate change.[51] Ironically, as the left's interest in carbon markets grew, the right began to distance itself from the idea, having realized that it could not be implemented without active public interventions. The resistance of conservatives toward binding regulations has been expressed in a variety of contexts. Most notably, opposition to the Kyoto Protocol was built to a large extent on a rejection of the treaty's requirement for firm governmental commitments.[52] Traditionally hostile to the intervention of international institutions in environmental matters, the right has also shown little enthusiasm for the creation of a World Environment Organization or an Environmental Security Council.

Making a different reading of the evidence available, the greens and the left regard the protection of the environment as crucial for the future of humanity. Taking the long-term view, their approach lays stress on the principle of "inter-generational equity," whereby today's generations have responsibilities toward future generations.[53] Environmentalists are also more critical of a development model centered on capitalist growth and expansion. Moderates like Nicholas Stern

---

[49] Associated Press, "Bush Defends Kyoto Opposition," *The Philadelphia Inquirer*, July 1, 2005.

[50] Steven Bernstein, *The Compromise of Liberal Environmentalism*, New York, Columbia University Press, 2001, p. 121.

[51] David G. Victor, *The Collapse of the Kyoto Protocol and the Struggle to Slow Global Warming*, Princeton University Press, 2001, p. 5.

[52] Charli E. Coon, "Why President Bush Is Right to Abandon the Kyoto Protocol," Backgrounder no. 1437, Washington, DC, The Heritage Foundation, May 11, 2001 (www.heritage.org/Research/Energyand Environment/BG1437.cfm).

[53] World Commission on Environment and Development, *Our Common Future*, Oxford University Press, 1987, p. 348.

propose a better integration of social costs in the price of goods, so as to more accurately reflect their ecological effects.[54] Radicals such as Susan George simply refuse to reduce the environment to a commodity, preferring to see "the biosphere as the total system and the economy as the subsystem."[55] Yet moderates and radicals agree that "conventional free-market economic policies systematically underprice or ignore natural resources."[56]

The left defends an overtly political conception of the environment. In the 1980s, the Brundtland Commission had already taken the position that "many problems of environmental stress arise from disparities in economic and political power,"[57] and environmentalists today repeatedly state that the deterioration of the environment has a direct bearing on the occurrence of poverty, conflict, migration, and famine. This holistic vision points in particular to the developed countries, who are the biggest per capita energy and resource consumers. For environmentalists, the available resources simply preclude the extension of the North's lifestyle to the entire world population. The governments of rich countries thus have a political, economic, and moral duty to help poor countries develop in an environmentally sustainable way.

The solutions promoted by people on the left proceed from the principle that a *laissez-faire* approach would entail the destruction of the planet. In their view, domestic and international norms and institutions must be strengthened. When it comes to compliance, environmental groups put more faith in financial incentives and in sanctions than in voluntary, "sunshine methods."[58] With respect to financial incentives, it is worth noting that while development assistance remains the most popular instrument, a growing faction within the left sees carbon markets as an innovative instrument for reducing

---

[54] Nicholas Stern, *The Economics of Climate Change: The Stern Review*, Cambridge University Press, 2007.

[55] Susan George, *Another World Is Possible If...*, London, Verso, 2004, p. 50.

[56] Chasek, Downie, and Welsh Brown, *Global Environmental Politics*, p. 31.

[57] World Commission on Environment and Development, *Our Common Future*, p. 46.

[58] Harold K. Jacobson and Edith Brown Weiss, "Assessing the Record and Designing Strategies to Engage Countries," in Edith Brown Weiss and Harold K. Jacobson (eds.), *Engaging Countries: Strengthening Compliance with International Environmental Accords*, Cambridge, MA, MIT Press, 2000, p. 550.

greenhouse gases. Another notion typically associated with the environmental left is the principle of precaution, which states that "where there are threats of serious or irreversible damage, lack of full scientific certainty shall not be used as a reason for postponing cost-effective measures to prevent environmental degradation."[59] Finally, environmentalists strongly believe that the current crisis cannot be resolved without a massive influx of public funds. They therefore call for new taxes that could be applied, for example, to the use of non-renewable energy sources such as petroleum. The right, which mistrusts state intervention, systematically opposes such approaches. Like the politics of identity and the politics of terrorism, the global environmental debate is, through and through, a conflict between the left and the right.

Left and right in the study of politics

Political science is, by all accounts, a divided discipline.[60] Political scientists disagree on the purpose of their endeavor, on the scope of their domain of inquiry, on their concepts and theories, and on their methods and scientific norms. Charles Lindblom put it bluntly when he concluded that political science is "a name given not to a field of conventional scientific inquiry but to a continuing debate [which] tends to be endless rather than declining (or terminating in a finding)."[61] In a similar way, James Farr and Raymond Seidelman argue that it is a series of "long-standing debates, not some agreement on fundamental principles, that give the discipline the identity it now has."[62] Yet it seems unclear what these endless debates are about. While they all

---

[59] United Nations Environment Programme, "Rio Declaration on Environment and Development," 1992 (www.unep.org/Documents.Multilingual/Default.asp?DocumentID=78&ArticleID=116).

[60] Gabriel A. Almond, *A Discipline Divided: Schools and Sects in Political Science*, Newbury Park, Sage, 1990, p. 14; Ira Katznelson and Helen V. Milner, "American Political Science: The Discipline's State and the State of the Discipline," in Ira Katznelson and Helen V. Milner (eds.), *Political Science: The State of the Discipline*, New York, W. W. Norton, 2002, p. 1.

[61] Charles Lindblom, quoted in Katznelson and Milner, "American Political Science," p. 2.

[62] James Farr and Raymond Seidelman, "General Introduction," in James Farr and Raymond Seidelman (eds.), *Discipline and History: Political Science in the United States*, Ann Arbor, University of Michigan Press, 1993, p. 7.

point to the various fractures that divide the discipline, recent surveys of political science also admit that the exact nature of these fractures remains difficult to "pin down."[63]

Many political scientists insist on the gap between those who privilege the "hard," quantitative methods associated with the natural sciences and those who prefer the "soft," qualitative approaches inspired by the humanities. This conflict can also be cast as an opposition between those who aim for universal, law-like generalizations, and those who favor rich, context-specific explanations. The former would advocate a "method-driven" political science, and the latter a "problem-driven" discipline. The overall division, however, is not only a question of methodology or epistemology. Political scientists hold different views about power and democracy, and they defend a number of more or less opposed theories, to explain just about every phenomenon. Some, for instance, understand power in terms of individual behavior and preferences, others in terms of social structures and dominating worldviews. Hence, in the Weberian tradition, power can be seen as "the ability of one actor to get another to do something the latter would not otherwise do," that is to say as the capability one has to influence another actor's individual choices. In a more Marxist vein, power can alternatively be understood as a more profound effect of inequality and privilege, whereby the public agenda, the different actors' preferences, and language itself are defined and circumscribed by a society's unequal structures of representation.[64] Accordingly, some theories of comparative politics stress individual rationality, others insist more on institutional structures and cultural factors.[65] In international relations, similar divergences differentiate realist, liberal, neoMarxist, and constructivist approaches.

---

[63] Ian Shapiro, Rogers M. Smith, and Tarek E. Masoud, "Introduction: Problems and Methods in the Study of Politics," in Ian Shapiro, Rogers M. Smith, and Tarek E. Masoud (eds.), *Problems and Methods in the Study of Politics*, Cambridge University Press, 2004, p. 1; Katznelson and Milner, "American Political Science," p. 2; Farr and Seidelman, "General Introduction," p. 7; J. Tobin Grant, "What Divides Us? The Image and Organization of Political Science," *PS: Political Science and Politics*, vol. 38, no. 3, July 2005, 379–86, p. 379.

[64] Katznelson and Milner, "American Political Science," p. 15.

[65] Mark Irving Lichbach and Alan S. Zuckerman, "Research Traditions and Theory in Comparative Politics: An Introduction," in Mark Irving Lichbach and Alan S. Zuckerman (eds.), *Comparative Politics: Rationality, Culture, and Structure*, Cambridge University Press, 1997, p. 5.

One could delve endlessly in such nuances and differences. If we did so, we would find many complications, intriguing oddities, and a great number of theoretical outliers. We would also see that many scholars resist classification and belong to an "eclectic majority" that happily convenes at what Gabriel Almond called the "cafeteria of the center."[66] The main cleavages, however, are well defined and profound, too profound in fact to be only about methods, concepts, or approaches. They oppose, on each side of the "cafeteria of the center," tables occupied by the left and by the right, who distinguish themselves in a consistent and meaningful manner.

Consider, for instance, conceptions of democracy. In his 1981 presidential address to the American Political Science Association, Charles Lindblom contrasted the discipline's mainstream view of democracy as a "mutual-benefit" arrangement that allowed individuals to resolve conflicts and attack "problems in common," with a dissenting synthesis, which understood democracy as the "institutionalized form" of the "struggle" between "advantaged and disadvantaged groups."[67] Lindblom did not exactly say so, but his presentation left no doubt that he was talking about the right and the left in political science. It left no doubt either that, in his mind, political scientists should make it a priority to address this fundamental cleavage, to learn from it, and enrich the dialog between conventional and critical accounts.

The views of power presented above – power as the exercise of influence and power as a structure of domination – are also obviously of the right and of the left, as their antecedents in Weber and Marx indicate. The same can be said of the distinctive understandings of choice that Ira Katznelson and Helen Milner outline in their discussion of the state of the art. Many political scientists, they explain, are inspired by the sociological tradition and see as paramount the goal of understanding the social structures that preside over political choices. Others, closer to the perspective of economics, place "these confining structures in the background and [emphasize] acts of choice."[68] In other words, those who stand closer to sociology largely see constraints,

---

[66] Almond, *A Discipline Divided*, p. 24.
[67] Charles Lindblom, "Another State of Mind," in Farr and Seidelman (eds.), *Discipline and History*, pp. 328–30.
[68] Katznelson and Milner, "American Political Science," pp. 16–17.

and those who find their inspiration in economics point to choices. James Duesenberry, an economist, nicely sums up the difference between these two traditions, which shape the contending outlooks that divide political science: "economics is all about how people make choices; sociology is all about how they don't have any choices to make."[69]

This connection to sociology and economics is, fundamentally, a left–right connection. *Homo sociologicus*, indeed, is basically the good-natured man of Jean-Jacques Rousseau and of the left, who belongs to a society, follows social and cultural norms, and means well. When he fails, it is because social forces compel him to act wrongly. *Homo economicus*, on the other hand, is the calculating individual of Thomas Hobbes and of the right, who relentlessly pursues his own interest, to the point of becoming what Amartya Sen has called a "social moron."[70] When he is set free, this individual succeeds; collective and democratic institutions, however, may well fail.[71] Applied to politics, the assumption of self-interest borrowed from economics has clear ideological implications. The market, notes Swedish sociologist Lars Udehn, becomes "the sole institution with the wonderful ability of turning private vice into public virtue," while political action "on the contrary [leads] to suboptimal waste and serfdom. *Ergo:* the best society is a free market society."[72]

This core cleavage explains the methodological and epistemological differences that separate political scientists. Economics is indeed a deductive discipline, which seeks universal generalizations and builds "clean models" from assumptions about individual interests. Sociology is primarily inductive, and favors the "thick" descriptions that can be developed only by scholars with "dirty hands."[73] Economists

---

[69] James S. Duesenberry, quoted in Peter A. Hall, "The Dilemmas of Contemporary Social Science," *Boundary 2*, vol. 34, no. 3, Fall 2007, 121–41.

[70] Amartya K. Sen, "Rational Fools: A Critique of the Behavioral Foundations of Economic Theory," *Philosophy and Public Affairs*, vol. 6, no. 4, Summer 1977, 317–44, pp. 335–36.

[71] Lars Udehn, *The Limits of Public Choice: A Sociological Critique of the Economic Theory of Politics*, London, Routledge, 1996, p. 6; Paul Hirsch, Stuart Michaels, and Ray Friedman, " 'Dirty Hands' versus 'Clean Models:' Is Sociology in Danger of Being Seduced by Economics?," *Theory and Society*, vol. 16, no. 3, May 1987, 317–36, p. 321.

[72] Udehn, *The Limits of Public Choice*, pp. 194–95.

[73] Hirsch, Michaels, and Friedman, " 'Dirty Hands' Versus 'Clean Models'," pp. 320–21.

will always be faulted for sacrificing relevance and empirical validity to theoretical elegance; sociologists for being disorderly and messy in their approaches.[74]

Now, consider methodological debates in political science. The most ardent defenders of the economic – or "rational choice" – approach to politics have no qualms about describing rival, more sociological approaches as pre-scientific. In the last fifty years, write, for instance, Kenneth Shepsle and Mark Bonchek, political science has evolved "from storytelling and anecdote swapping, first to thick description and history writing, then to systematic measurement, and more recently to explanation and analysis," and this transformation "constitutes significant movement along a scientific trajectory."[75] Those relying on more inductive approaches are simply behind on the road toward science. In return, critics of the rational choice approach always point to the shaky empirical foundations of models that often bear little correspondence to reality, and to the approach's general disregard for social and political relevance.[76] This is where the cleavage between a "method-driven" and a "problem-driven" polit-ical science comes from. In the abstract, the cleavage is just another appellation for the confrontation between economic and sociological perspectives in political science, itself an expression of the more fun-damental left–right divide.

The ramifications of this divide are numerous and extended. In comparative politics, for instance, a specific debate opposes scholars who identify themselves as "area specialists" and take pride in knowing not only the politics, but also the language, the history, and the culture of a region of the world, to those who claim to be "social scientists" first, entirely devoted to the search for "lawful regularities" that can contribute to the development of political science. Robert Bates, who uses rational choice models to account for African pol-itics and is a strong advocate of the "scientific" approach, leaves no doubt about the ideological underpinnings of this methodological

---

[74] *Ibid.*; Robert Aaron Gordon, "Rigor and Relevance in a Changing Institutional Setting," *American Economic Review*, vol. 66, no. 1, March 1976, 1–14, p. 1.

[75] Kenneth A. Shepsle and Mark S. Bonchek, *Analyzing Politics: Rationality, Behavior, and Institutions*, New York, W. W. Norton, 1997, 166–69, p. 7.

[76] Donald P. Green and Ian Shapiro, *Pathologies of Rational Choice Theory: A Critique of Applications in Political Science*, New Haven, Yale University Press, 1994, pp. 5–6.

confrontation, and suggests that his opponents have a leftist bias: "The debate over area studies is often exacerbated by debates over the merits of the market, the state, or the impact of the West, with those who endorse area studies viewing those who use rational choice theory as being pro-market, anti-state, and given to applying historically contingent categories in a universalistic manner."[77] The accusations of area studies specialists can indeed be explicitly political. They sometimes suggest that their opponents are inspired by the market model of the "Chicago Economics Department," and generally contend that rational choice work reflects "the particular parochialisms of American culture."[78] Theoretical work, they add, should be "a means to understanding real-world problems of significance, rather than an end in itself."[79]

Similar debates have developed about the study of gender and race. Scholars seeking to revisit political science from a feminist perspective or from a standpoint more sensitive to "racial ordering and its consequences" have regularly denounced the tendency to reduce gender and race to simple variables in otherwise unchanged mainstream accounts, and criticized an "excessive reliance on the discipline of economics as a source of methodological and theoretical inspiration."[80] In the study of American politics, the dominance of rational choice models and quantitative methods has similarly been associated with a lack of attention to the most important substantive issues, and in particular to a neglect of the "massive and growing economic and political inequalities" that plague the United States.[81]

---

[77] Robert H. Bates, "Area Studies and the Discipline: A Useful Controversy?," *PS: Political Science and Politics*, vol. 30, no. 2, June 1997, 166–69, p. 169.

[78] Chalmers Johnson, "Preconceptions vs. Observations, or the Contributions of Rational Choice Theory and Area Studies to Contemporary Political Science," *PS: Political Science and Politics*, vol. 30, no. 2, June 1997, 170–74.

[79] Atul Kohli, "State, Society, and Development," in Katznelson and Milner (eds.), *Political Science: The State of the Discipline*, p. 116.

[80] Michael C. Dawson and Cathy Cohen, "Problems in the Study of the Politics of Race," in Katznelson and Milner (eds.), *Political Science: The State of the Discipline*, pp. 488–89; Helene Silverberg, "Gender Studies and Political Science: The History of the 'Behavioralist Compromise'," in Farr and Seidelman (eds.), *Discipline and History*, pp. 372 and 378.

[81] Paul Pierson, "The Costs of Marginalization: Qualitative Methods in the Study of American Politics," *Comparative Political Studies*, vol. 40, no. 2, February 2007, 146–69, p. 166.

The same contrast has been made in comparative politics between rational choice institutionalists who merely "focus research agendas on puzzles internally generated by their overarching theory" and historical institutionalists who have the foresight and courage to address "big questions and real-world puzzles."[82] Rational choice scholars know this accusation very well and usually reply that "what most impedes the development of knowledge in comparative politics" is precisely "our selection of big, inadequately defined outcomes to explain."[83] They prefer "generating testable hypotheses from models that may have high predictive power."[84] "Given these fundamental disagreements," concludes Atul Kohli wisely, "the best one can hope for is an agreement to disagree."[85]

A left–right cleavage thus traverses political science, dividing the discipline in fairly predictable ways over topics, methods, and concepts. Rarely do political scientists admit explicitly that their differences are a question of left and right. Gabriel Almond evoked this possibility in his discussion of the "separate tables" used by political scientists at their gatherings, but he mainly emphasized the eclectic majority that preferred to unite in the vast "cafeteria of the center."[86] When he delivered his presidential address to the American Political Science Association in 1992, Theodore Lowi faulted his colleagues "of left, right, and center" precisely for "their failure to maintain a clear and critical consciousness of political consciousness," that is to say for refusing to confront and take into account their obvious ideological divisions.[87] For Lowi, "totally aside from whatever merits it may have as a method and however true its truth may be," the rational choice approach became hegemonic "for political reasons," and most of its "luminaries...came from, serve in, or are substantially associated

---

[82] Paul Pierson and Theda Skocpol, "Historical Institutionalism in Contemporary Political Science," in Katznelson and Milner (eds.), *Political Science: The State of the Discipline*, pp. 696 and 716.

[83] Barbara Geddes, quoted in Margaret Levi, "The State of the Study of the State," in Katznelson and Milner (eds.), *Political Science: The State of the Discipline*, p. 52.

[84] Levi, "The State of the Study of the State," p. 52.

[85] Kohli, "State, Society, and Development," p. 116.

[86] Almond, *A Discipline Divided*, pp. 13–24.

[87] Theodore Lowi, "The State in Political Science: How We Become What We Study," in Farr and Seidelman (eds.), *Discipline and History*, p. 394.

with the same 'freshwater' universities that kept burning the flame of laissez-faire ideology."[88]

What about political philosophy, a sub-field presumably immune to pleas for either clean models or dirty hands? While it would be presumptuous to treat such a rich domain of inquiry in a paragraph, one observation seems worth making. In his survey of the field, Canadian philosopher Will Kymlicka begins by stating that the conventional view is that political philosophers can essentially be classified according to their position on a left–right continuum, with those on the left stressing equality and advocating "some form of socialism," and those on the right emphasizing freedom and leaning toward "some form of free-market capitalism." This representation, suggests Kymlicka has become unsatisfactory because all contemporary philosophers now believe in equality, or in the idea that "each citizen is entitled to equal concern and respect." The argument no longer concerns "whether to accept equality, but how best to interpret it:" "while leftists believe that equality of income or wealth is a precondition for treating people as equals, those on the right believe that equal rights over one's labour and property are a precondition for treating people as equals."[89] The central division of political philosophy thus remains one between the left and the right, and it opposes, just as we suggested in Chapter 1, different understandings of equality.

Could international relations possibly be the only field of political science to stand on the sidelines of this ubiquitous ideological confrontation? After all, within the discipline, the study of "IR" constitutes something like a domain apart, with its own questions, approaches, and theories. Unanimously acknowledged, the theoretical and empirical complexity of international relations seems to challenge the relevance of a distinction as simple as the left–right cleavage. Yet the incongruity is only apparent. In fact, the left–right opposition provides an unequaled roadmap for finding one's way in the conceptual labyrinth of world politics. Although this opposition is generally ignored by scholars, it offers a powerful narrative, able to impart greater consistency to the theoretical discussions of the field. By linking such discussions to an ideological continuum coming from domestic and

---

[88] *Ibid.*, p. 390.
[89] Will Kymlicka, *Contemporary Political Philosophy: An Introduction*, Oxford University Press, 1990, pp. 1–5.

everyday politics, the notions of left and right help in comparing approaches as well as understanding the "great debates" that have marked the history of international relations.

"Normal science" as disseminated in academic textbooks is a good place to start to see how neglected the left–right terminology is in international relations theory.[90] One should first know in this regard that a widespread practice of contemporary "normal" international relations is to summarize the theoretical debates of the field into typologies that are structured around a few basic criteria.[91] Admittedly, the standard classifications diverge as to both the number of theories and their exact names. Experts disagree, for example, on whether realism and neorealism are distinct schools of thought, or whether liberalism and neoliberal institutionalism ought to be amalgamated. Yet beyond these academic disputes, normal science recognizes four major intellectual traditions in international politics: realism, which stresses the promotion of the national interest; liberalism, which centers on the process of cooperation; neoMarxism, which highlights the inherently conflictual nature of capitalism; and constructivism, which emphasizes the role of ideas. Each tradition is typically characterized by its distinct concepts, its specific units of analysis, and its own view on the motives of actors and on the international system.

Despite their undeniable usefulness, standard typologies of international relations theory are far from perfect. They tend, for instance, to marginalize alternative schools of thought such as postmodernism and feminism. More importantly, however, they present the different theories as if they were mutually incommensurable, and, furthermore, most classifications exclude any idea of measurement.

The incommensurability of the classifications of international relations theories can be illustrated in two major ways. First, the

[90] Thomas S. Kuhn, *The Structure of Scientific Revolutions*, University of Chicago Press, 1962, p. 10.
[91] See, for example, Paul R. Viotti and Mark. V. Kauppi, *International Relations Theory: Realism, Pluralism, Globalism*, second edition, New York, Macmillan, 1993, p. 10; Stephen M. Walt, "International Relations: One World, Many Theories," *Foreign Policy*, no. 110, 1998, 29–46, p. 30; Karen A. Mingst, *Essentials of International Relations*, second edition, New York, W. W. Norton, 2003, p. 79; Charles W. Kegley, Jr., and Eugene R. Wittkopf, *World Politics: Trends and Transformation*, tenth edition, Belmont, Thomson-Wadsworth, 2006, pp. 47–48.

typologies provided by normal science pay little attention to inter-sections among competing schools of thought. They skim over the fact that some liberals accept the assumptions of realism regarding power and self-interest, that some constructivists share the liberal idea of progress and cooperation, or that some neoMarxists and construct-ivists agree on the importance of distinguishing "problem-solving theory" from "critical theory." Second, the standard typologies do not account very well for the nuances that exist within each paradigm. And yet the defensive realists' conception of power and security is not identical to that of offensive realists, there are various views on democracy and markets among liberals, not all neoMarxists attribute equal importance to structures of production, and constructivists do not all share the same epistemological perspective. Most of these subtleties are simply glossed over in conventional accounts of world politics.

The different theories of international relations are seen as incom-mensurable because, in a normal science perspective, they each coin-cide with a discrete and monolithic worldview, without sharing any common denominator with the others. Hence, usual classifications seem incapable of locating theories on a continuum or a scale like the left–right spectrum. One could possibly infer that by describing the characteristics of realism, liberalism, neoMarxism, and constructivism in that order, certain taxonomies rate each theory on the basis of its relative popularity in the academic community. But aside from the fact that this method is rarely made explicit, its scientific validity is in any case doubtful. Approaches dominant in North America are not the same as those prevailing in the Third World.[92]

The "normal science" method of classifying international relations theories has recently been challenged in an innovative way by Alexander Wendt. Drawing on social theory, Wendt considers "four sociologies" of international politics based on two key debates: one between materialists and idealists, and the other between individualists and

---

[92] See Stephanie G. Neuman, "International Relations Theory and the Third World: An Oxymoron?," in Stephanie G. Neuman (ed.), *International Relations Theory and the Third World*, New York, St. Martin's Press, 1998, pp. 1–29; and Arlene Tickner, "Seeing IR Differently: Notes from the Third World," *Millennium: Journal of International Studies*, vol. 32, no. 2, 2003, 295–324.

holists.[93] He represents these two debates graphically, with the horizontal axis corresponding to the materialism–idealism debate, and the vertical axis to the individualism–holism debate. Wendt thus distinguishes four sets of international relations theories: materialist–individualist, materialist–holist, idealist–individualist, and idealist–holist. Among these four, he identifies two sets around which current thinking tends to polarize: materialist–individualist (or rationalist) theories and idealist–holist (or constructivist) theories. Wendt then bridges the gap between his own typology and the standard typologies of international relations theory by associating the rationalist camp with neorealism and neoliberalism, and the constructivist camp with the English school, postmodernism, and feminism. In addition to being parsimonious, Wendt's model has the advantage of directly addressing the problem of the incommensurability of traditional classifications. Following his explanation, all theories can be understood on the basis of continuous variables because each one is more or less materialist and more or less individualist.

While Wendt's contribution was an intellectual breakthrough, the concepts of left and right can enrich the theorizing of international relations in unique ways. The left–right framework does not, of course, answer all the challenges arising from any classification of conceptual approaches. Yet it does offer a convenient scale for comparing theories and theorists. Moreover, it makes it possible to openly introduce a political dimension into the discussion.

Consider, first, the "normal science" typologies of international relations theories. The classical approaches identified by these typologies – realism, liberalism, and neoMarxism – can be readily situated on the left–right continuum because each of them defends a distinctive notion of equality and international change. Realism leans toward the right, liberalism hovers near the center, and neoMarxism is, of course, on the left. In line with this interpretation, the neorealist Kenneth Waltz affirms that "inequality is what much of politics is about," and that "inequality is inherent in the state system."[94] Taking a more moderate position, the liberal Robert Keohane acknowledges

[93] Alexander Wendt, *Social Theory of International Politics*, Cambridge University Press, 1999, pp. 22–33.

[94] Kenneth N. Waltz, *Theory of International Politics*, New York, McGraw-Hill, 1979, pp. 132 and 142.

that "the principles on which present patterns of cooperation are based show insufficient sensitivity to the interests of disadvantaged people in the Third World," but at the same time he argues that "on consequentialist grounds,...contemporary international economic regimes may be superior to politically feasible alternatives."[95] Finally, the neoMarxist Robert Cox asserts, far more critically, that the "inter-civilizational world" he advocates should be based on "mutual support in promoting social equity," and "a consensual understanding of basic human rights."[96] In terms of left and right, the political positions of these authors and the schools they represent are plain to see.

Constructivism, a more recent theory, is harder to pin down along the left–right continuum, and, in principle, constructivists could position themselves anywhere. In reality, however, constructivism developed as an extension of liberalism that is open to critical theory. One would therefore be justified in placing this approach at the center-left of the political spectrum. Wendt, for one, certainly regards as desirable the transformation of the "Lockean" culture that now dominates the international scene into a "Kantian" culture founded on friendship, solidarity, and a common identity.[97] Wendt's "thin" constructivism, it must nonetheless be mentioned, is generally seen as more conservative than the "thick" version adopted by some of his constructivist colleagues.

Further nuances inherent in each of the main images of international politics could also be transposed on to a left–right scale. Like political parties, all schools have their conservative and progressive wings. This said, the left–right spectrum does more than just set in order the standard typologies of international relations theories. It can also serve to contextualize the opposition between rationalists and constructivists, which is at the core of Wendt's work, and which many now see as "the main axis of debate in the field of international relations."[98] It is worth noting in this connection that in proposing

---

[95] Robert O. Keohane, *After Hegemony: Cooperation and Discord in the World Political Economy*, second edition, Princeton University Press, 2005, p. 256.

[96] Robert W. Cox (with Michael G. Schechter), *The Political Economy of a Plural World: Critical Reflections on Power, Morals and Civilization*, London, Routledge, 2002, p. 185.

[97] Wendt, *Social Theory of International Politics*, pp. 305–11.

[98] James Fearon and Alexander Wendt, "Rationalism v. Constructivism: A Skeptical View," in Walter Carlsnaes, Thomas Risse, and Beth A. Simmons (eds.), *Handbook of International Relations*, London, Sage, 2002, p. 52.

a binary categorization, the left–right model is *a priori* no more reductive than the "rationalism v. constructivism" debate, or any of the great debates that have framed the history of the discipline. More substantively, it should be stressed that the right clearly has greater affinities with rationalists, while the left is more in harmony with constructivists.

Of course, not all rationalists are conservatives, nor is every constructivist a progressive. Nevertheless, as in comparative politics, the right is more comfortable with the methodological individualism, the references to economics, and the problem-solving approach typical of rationalism. The left, for its part, certainly feels more at home with the cultural structuralism, the references to sociology, and the critical approach of constructivism. It is often said that the knowledge produced by rationalists is oriented more toward the status quo, while that produced by constructivists "is more useful for changing the world."[99] This distinction parallels the opposition between tradition and emancipation that is intrinsic to many definitions of left and right.[100] The ontological and epistemological issues that divide international relations scholars today are obviously too complex to be reduced to an opposition between progressives and conservatives. Still, the debate between rationalists and constructivists does not exist in a political vacuum, and within this conceptual conversation the left and the right have their respective preferences.

The entwinement of methodological controversies and ideological cleavages is nothing new in international relations. At least two of the great debates that have characterized the evolution of the discipline – the "idealism v. realism" debate of the interwar period, and the "positivism v. postpositivism" debate of the 1980s – displayed a rather obvious left–right pattern. The right generally lined up with the realists and the positivists, whereas the left aligned itself with the idealists and the postpositivists. Admittedly, the "traditionalism v. scientism" debate of the 1950s and 1960s is more difficult to decode using a left–right framework, which only confirms the notion that methodological issues transcend politics. At the same time, however, it is important to consider that there is no unanimity on the status of

[99] Wendt, *Social Theory of International Politics*, p. 378.
[100] Norberto Bobbio, *Left and Right: The Significance of a Political Distinction*, Chicago University Press, 1996, p. 47.

the "traditionalism v. scientism" debate in the history of international relations. Indeed, some experts suggest that this controversy had no bearing on the "substantive aspects of the subject matter of international politics," and thus regard it as a "pseudo-debate."[101]

In the end, the left–right cleavage in international relations very much concerns the way scholars represent the social relations that define their own community. Typically, the right has a more consensual, and the left a more conflictual view of the situation. In his 1999 International Studies Association (ISA) presidential address, Michael Brecher, for instance, proposed a clearly non-politicial vision of the field, which he described as a "mature social science discipline." Skeptical toward pluralism, he maintained that "continuing fratricides among paradigms and methodologies" could lead to the implosion of international relations theory. According to Brecher, not only should "synthesis in every facet of the field" be a goal in itself, but "it would also enhance our contribution to society, especially to foreign policy and national security decision-makers."[102] When Steve Smith presented his own ISA presidential speech a few years later, the tone was markedly different. Adopting a normative stance open to a variety of theoretical positions, he claimed that "there is no view from nowhere," and that academic perspectives are always linked to social forces. In his critical analysis, Smith further argued that the discipline of international relations had "effectively served as a handmaiden to Western power and interests."[103] Brecher and Smith held the same prestigious post, but stood for quite distinct values. There is little doubt as to where each one can be located in the left–right spectrum.

The left–right opposition enlightens our understanding of international relations theory because it helps historicize the debates of the discipline and clarify their political meaning. Such added value is particularly welcome because it encourages dialog and bridge-building among international relations, comparative politics, political

[101] Brian C. Schmidt, "On the History and Historiography of International Relations," in Carlsnaes, Risse, and Simmons (eds.), *Handbook of International Relations*, p. 14.

[102] Michael Brecher, "International Studies in the Twentieth Century and Beyond: Flawed Dichotomies, Synthesis, Cumulation," *International Studies Quarterly*, vol. 43, no. 2, 1999, 213–64, pp. 214 and 252.

[103] Steve Smith, "Singing Our World into Existence: International Relations Theory and September 11," *International Studies Quarterly*, vol. 48, no. 3, 2004, 499–515, pp. 500 and 513.

philosophy, and other social sciences. From a more applied perspective, the left–right distinction also has the potential to open up a fertile research program within constructivism. This theoretical approach is indeed defined by the importance it ascribes to ideas in world politics. Yet constructivists have to date paid relatively little attention to the ideologies that actually shape international relations. Global in scope, the left–right framework undoubtedly offers a useful approach to closing this gap, as well as being a core instrument in the elaboration of a grammar of international discourse.

Conclusion

The left–right metaphor does not explain everything. The politics of identity, the war on terrorism, and the global environmental debate have cultural and sociological foundations that are certainly distinct from the opposition between progressive and conservative ideas or forces. Identity politics, for instance, is anchored in deep psychological perceptions about a person's sense of belonging. Both the war on terrorism and the global environmental debate have to do, as well, with the interests of states. Still, each of these debates is undeniably fashioned and constructed as an opposition between the left and the right. Without this distinction, it would in fact be very difficult to comprehend these contemporary conflicts. In that sense, the left–right metaphor is truly the core currency of political exchange.

Political science and international relations scholarships are also shaped and defined by this ubiquitous opposition. In his recent survey of the social sciences, Peter Hall makes this connection transparent by noting that his colleagues have experienced their "own version of the culture wars, sparked by the imperial ambitions of those who seem to hope that rational choice analysis will provide a new master social science."[104] In both political science and international relations, scholars are indeed divided over methodology, epistemology, and relevance, and these divisions fundamentally reflect in sophisticated ways the enduring opposition between conservatives and progressives. Obviously, these divisions – or the widespread agreement to disagree – are there to stay. Scholars would be well advised, however, to acquire a better understanding of their differences, and to gain, as Theodore

[104] Hall, "The Dilemmas of Contemporary Social Science."

Lowi suggested, "a clear and critical consciousness of political consciousness."

Charles Lindblom, who has devoted much of his work to understanding the role of knowledge in democratic politics, provides
encouraging considerations with respect both to the ubiquity of the
left–right opposition in political life, and to its prevalence in the social
sciences. In a democracy, Lindblom argues, people "cannot think
successfully about their volitions if they regard themselves as unique.
Instead, they look for clues in the situations, attitudes, and beliefs of
others whom they regard as like themselves." At the same time,
"governments cannot respond to millions of diverse volitions...-
problem solving requires that people move their volitions toward
clusters of agreement."[105] The left and right "clusters of agreement"
certainly do a good job in helping people think with others, and in
forcing governments to take notice. Most importantly, in our age of
global politics, this universal metaphor helps to link people across
time and space, and over a broad range of issues. In other words, the
left–right opposition makes global politics intelligible. As for social
scientists, they have to come to terms with the fact, which may not
be so disturbing after all, that they partake, too, in this global debate.
"The waters," Lindblom notes, "are less dangerous than they appear,
for social scientists have never sailed in any other waters and are still
afloat. They have always been partisan."[106]

---

[105] Charles Lindblom, *Inquiry and Change: The Troubled Attempt to Understand
and Shape Society*, New Haven, Yale University Press, 1990, p. 235.
[106] *Ibid.*, p. 260.

Conclusion

Politics involves distinct social mechanisms, which cannot be adequately captured by the sociological notions of structure and culture, or by the economic concepts of rational choice and equilibrium. Some political actions are driven by social norms, and others by utilitarian calculations, but political life always contains an additional dimension: communication. Political scientists sometimes convey this distinction by speaking of a logic of arguing that exists alongside a sociological logic of appropriateness (norms) and an economic logic of consequentialism (utility). When they argue, social actors can challenge prevailing norms and the dominant rationality, and transform society as they communicate and deliberate.[1] Economist Albert Hirschman once made a similar distinction by contrasting the market, where one exercised choice through "exit" – by not buying – and politics, where "voice" and protest were the prevailing modes of operation.[2] Likewise, Jon Elster distinguished the market, where private preferences were expressed through purchases, and the forum, where an open and public conversation brought people to determine together the common good and the meaning of social justice.[3]

This deliberative dimension of politics is perfectly captured by the left–right opposition. Whereas the core concepts of economics translate into an instrumental rationality that tends to "close off debate,"[4]

---

[1] Thomas Risse, "Constructivism and International Institutions: Toward Conversations across Paradigms," in Ira Katznelson and Helen V. Milner (eds.), *Political Science: The State of the Discipline*, New York, W. W. Norton, 2002 p. 602.

[2] Albert O. Hirschman, *Exit, Voice and Loyalty: Responses to Decline in Firms, Organizations, and States*, Cambridge, MA, Harvard University Press, 1970, p. 15.

[3] Jon Elster, "The Market and the Forum: Three Varieties of Political Theories," in Jon Elster and Aanund Hylland (eds.), *Foundations of Social Choice Theory*, Cambridge University Press, 1986, pp. 103 and 111.

[4] Theodore Lowi, "The State in Political Science: How We Become What We Study," in James Farr and Raymond Seidelman (eds.), *Discipline and*

the left–right division, understood as the core currency of political exchange, suggests instead that debates are unavoidable, inherent in political life, and foundational for democracy.

Adding to the usual constructivist accounts, a focus on the left–right distinction also helps to see that there is a definite order to political debates. As explained in the first chapter, this order, which entails distinct conceptions of equality, emerged with democratic politics and gradually gained currency, to spread all over the world and encompass a wide range of questions and issues. The second chapter documents this ubiquity of the left and the right, and shows that people almost everywhere understand the distinction, and can locate themselves on a left–right continuum, in a manner that is consistent with their views about equality, the role of the state, and a host of related social values and attitudes. Only in authoritarian or newly democratic countries are these perceptions of left and right less focused, but the situation may be changing rapidly, as is suggested by the politics of Latin America in the 2000s. In international discourse, as Chapter 3 indicates, the same dichotomy can be found, and it organizes clearly opposed views of globalization, each side choosing to highlight certain facts and figures. Rarely used to analyze international relations, the left–right distinction undoubtedly captures important differences that are at stake in the contemporary debates about world politics.

The next chapters follow the evolution of this global ideological rift from the American Revolution in 1776 to the International Declaration on the Rights of Indigenous Peoples in 2006. Our survey is necessarily sketchy, because the objective was not to write a history of the left–right debate, but rather to explore the main dimensions of this universal cleavage. Chapter 4 starts with the foundations, and explains how democracy, war and peace, capitalism and socialism, and the colonial enterprise were all interpreted and debated through the lens of left–right politics. Chapter 5 then takes a closer look at the postwar era of embedded liberalism. This era was indeed a good one for the left, which was largely able to impose its views of macro-economic management for full employment, of organized industrial relations, and of universal and generous welfare policies. Internationally, though,

History: Political Science in the United States, Ann Arbor, University of Michigan Press, 1993, p. 391; John S. Dryzek, *Discursive Democracy: Politics, Policy, and Political Science*, Cambridge University Press, 1990, pp. 4–7.

the postwar period was one of high ideological left–right tensions, with the global confrontation between capitalism and socialism threatening the very fate of the earth, while the rise of an assertive and critical global South challenged the world's core structures of power.

As explained in Chapters 6 and 7, in the 1980s this tensed but apparently unsurpassable world order collapsed, to give place to an era dominated by market democracy and defined by a hegemonic neoliberal ideology, which reinstated the right's priorities in both domestic and international politics. In the South as well as in the North, the left seemed in disarray, at best able to maintain the institutions and policies that it had fought to impose in the previous decades. Eventually, however, at the end of the 1990s, a new left emerged that accepted some of the tenets of neoliberalism and integrated them into a vision, which was in turn presented as a Third Way or as a new development consensus. The left remained the left, however, and the right was still the right.

The debate between the two sides continued, not only over equality and development but, as we point out in Chapter 8, also over issues having to do with identity, terrorism, and the environment. Whatever the question, the main political actors interpreted it in the well-established language of left and right. Surprisingly perhaps, given the power of this ideological cleavage, political scientists remained reluctant to use the distinction as an analytical tool and, even more so, to apply it to their own debates and divergences. A fear of losing objectivity may explain this reluctance. Yet the social sciences are always, by necessity, involved in political debates, and the best we can hope for is probably to be transparent about this social implication, which can in fact also be a source of pride.

The late Michael Harrington was a rare species in American life. A committed social-democrat in a nation where the term "liberal" – which in Europe refers to people on the center-right – was used to paint those on the left-of-center as extremists, he denounced poverty and injustice, and fought for a country more preoccupied by equality and human emancipation than by economic growth and consumerism. Working in this rather hostile political environment, Harrington became acutely aware of the wide gap between the ideological universes of the left and of the right. Yet, beyond the differences, he also saw a structured and reasoned conversation. "Every serious social idea in the contemporary world," he wrote in one of his last books, "leads a double life. This is not because some mysterious symmetry is at work, but because only a very limited number of changes have any significant chance of succeeding. So the Left and the Right necessarily explore a relatively narrow range of possible futures and, when they are serious, respond to the same reality in fundamentally different ways."[5]

Throughout this book, we have seen this structured conversation at work over a remarkable range of ideas, from the nineteenth-century workers' right to vote to the contemporary claims of ethnic minorities to be recognized and treated as equal, and from the fight for socialism to the recent idea of a Global Compact. In a world where democratic politics seems hard-pressed to follow the rapid and global expansion of market forces, the universal prevalence of this language should be seen as a hopeful sign. The lack of cohesive and encompassing ideologies that can articulate the divergent expectations of citizens is indeed one of the most pressing problems of emerging democracies. Without a common currency to articulate differences, political debates tend to remain inchoate, and centered on personalities, images, and patronage.[6] Arguing collectively becomes difficult, and democratic deliberation is impaired. This book suggests that global politics is already endowed with such a common currency. This is good news for democracy, and good news for the world as well.

Some readers will see our book as a political essay rather than a work of social science. Others will consider that in insisting so much on the left and the right, we condemn ourselves to a simplistic, ideological view of the world. This type of reaction – which is probably unavoidable – raises the question of objectivity and relevance in the social sciences. In a manner that would nowadays seem quaint, Max Weber argued for universal aims in the social sciences, and suggested accordingly that "a correct scientific proof... must be acknowledged as correct even by a Chinese." In spite of his politically incorrect language, Weber was right to think that the scientific enterprise required rigorous theoretical arguments and a respect for empirical evidence that could stand the test of critical inquiry. At the same time,

---

[5] Michael Harrington, *The Next Left: The History of a Future*, New York, Henry Holt, 1986, p. 15.
[6] Thomas Carothers, *Confronting the Weakest Link: Aiding Political Parties in New Democracies*, Washington, DC, Carnegie Endowment for International Peace, 2006, p. 11.

Weber recognized that, as social scientists, we always remain "*cultural beings*, endowed with the capacity and the will to take a deliberate attitude towards the world and to lend it *significance*."[7]

We have tried to be as clear and as systematic as possible in our theoretical and empirical arguments. This work, however, like any other work in the social sciences, is not value-free. It is anchored in our own perspective, as political scientists informed by constructivism and as citizens of a small French-speaking society of North America. In underlining the ubiquity of the left–right division, the book seeks to offer a better and more relevant interpretation of globalization, which connects the domestic and international politics of economic development and social justice. Its findings are not intended to be authoritative, purely neutral, or definitive. In the social sciences, argues Charles Lindblom in *Usable Knowledge*, the best we can hope for, and this is already much, is to enlighten, to improve our common understanding of the world.[8]

The book is unlikely to be received in the same way on the right and on the left. If the comments we have heard in formal and informal presentations of this material are representative, readers on the left will appreciate it more than people on the right. This is hardly surprising, because it is the right that usually claims that the left–right distinction is *passé*. Keen to stress the consensual rather than the conflictual dimensions of social life, and attached to a more "natural science" view of social inquiry, conservatives are likely to be ill-at-ease with a book that gives so much importance to the divisions that social actors and social scientists across the world have constructed around their divergent conceptions of equality. The left, on the contrary, usually sees the world as unequal, unable to achieve social justice, and mired in conflicts. Progressive readers will thus feel more at home with a book that stresses cleavages and debates. In the social sciences, explains Canadian political scientist Robert Cox, "theory is always *for* someone and *for* some purpose."[9] As authors, we do not escape our categories. In the end, this book is undoubtedly of and for the left.

---

[7] Max Weber, *The Methodology of the Social Sciences*, Glencoe, Free Press, 1949, pp. 58 and 81 (italics as original).

[8] Charles Lindblom, *Usable Knowledge: Social Science and Social Problem Solving*, New Haven, Yale University Press, 1979, pp. 72–74.

[9] Robert W. Cox, "Social Forces, States, and World Orders: Beyond International Relations Theory," in Robert W. Cox (with Timothy J. Sinclair), *Approaches to World Order*, Cambridge University Press, 1996, p. 87.

Index

Note: Page numbers in bold refer to Tables; those in italics refer to Figures.

absolutist monarchy, and inclination
    to war 90
Adams, John, US President 86
affirmative action, in USA 18–19
Afghanistan
    Taliban regime 208
    war in 206
Africa 48
    colonial rule in 101
    and decolonization 105
    economic development 63–4
    emigration of professionals 77
    Millennium Development Goals 75
    share of trade 72
African National Congress 190
age, and left–right self-placement 46
agriculture, subsidies 73
AIDS/HIV
    and life expectancy in Africa 76
    progress against 64
Albania, left–right self-placement 42
Algeria 48
    left–right self-placement 40, 42
alienation, and inequality 21
Allende, Salvador, Chilean President
    133
Almond, Gabriel 217, 221
American Economic Association 141
American Political Science Association
    217, 221
American Revolution 85–7, 232
    Federalist–Republican division 86–7
Amin, Samir 133
Amnesty International 80, 172
Annan, Kofi, UN Secretary-General
    161, 181, 185, 192
    on terrorism 208
anti-colonialism 123

Appadurai, Arjun 202
Argentina 189
arms trade 78, 79, 127, 134
Asia
    central 71
    colonialism in 101
    economic crisis (from 1997) 168, 186
    newly industrializing countries 129
    trade growth 72
Asia Pacific region 48
Asian Development Bank 158
Atatürk, Mustafa Kemal, Turkish
    President 105
Austria 207
    empire 91
    rise of far right 187
authoritarianism 24–6, 88
    and liberalism 25, 25
    reversion to 88, 89, 91
    of Southern governments 135, 153

Bachelet, Michelle, Chilean President
    189
balance of power, in Europe 91, 92
Bandung Conference (1955) 123
Bangladesh 48
    left–right self-placement 39
Bank Charter Act (1844) 97
Bank of England, and monetary
    regulation 97
Bates, Robert 219
Beárt, Emmanuelle 23
Belgium 207
    nationalisms in 201
Berlin Conference (1884–85) 103
Berlin Wall
    fall of (1989) 137
    symbolism of 122

Berlusconi, Silvio, Italian Prime
Minister 187
A Better World for All (2000) 183, 185
Beveridge, William 119
Bhattacharya, Buddhadeb 171
Bismarck, Prince Otto von 92, 119
Blair, Tony, British Prime Minister 11
Commission for Africa 31
New Labour 166
and Third Way 175, 178
and war in Iraq 207
and war on terrorism 210
Bleaney, Michael 142
Blinder, Alan 142
Bobbio, Norberto 16, 179
Bolivia 189
Bonaparte, Napoleon 91, 102
Bonchek, Mark 219
Bosnia and Herzegovina, left–right
self-placement 42
Brandt International Commission
(1980) 131, 153
second report (1983) 154
Brandt, Willy, German Chancellor
131, 154
Brazil 189
capital markets 63
and global trade 160
and technological revolution 59
Brecher, Michael 228
Bretton Woods conference (1944) 124
Bretton Woods institutions 128,
135, 181
and 1973 oil shock 144
consensus with UN agencies 183, 186
continuing divergence from UN
agencies 190–5
growing influence of 157
tolerance of inequalities 191
see also International Monetary
Fund; World Bank
British Empire 101, 102
British Petroleum 211
Brown, Michael 6
Brundtland, Gro Harlem, World
Commission on Environment and
Development 31, 214
Buchanan, James 142
Bulgaria, economy 63
Buonarroti, Filippo Michele 87

bureaucracy, and neoliberal business
model 148
Burke, Edmund, view of colonialism 102
Bush, George H. W., US President
167, 212
Bush, George W., US President 11,
205, 212

Callaghan, James, British Prime
Minister 146
Canada
identity politics 203, 204
Liberal party 166
suffrage qualifications 88
see also Québec
Cancún Summit (1981) 153
capital markets 63
international financial system 73–4
capitalism
and collapse of communism 138
expansion of 84
industrial 95–7
presumed decline of 125
and socialism 95–101
socialist opposition to 99
as superior to communism 124–5
carbon markets 213
Carr, E. H. 93
Carter, Jimmy, US President 146
Castro, Fidel, Cuban President 126, 133
center, self-placement at 34, 34, 42
Central Asia, poverty in 71
Central and Eastern Europe 48
democratization 53
left–right self-placement 38
see also Eastern Europe
Chamberlain, Joseph 103
Chávez, Hugo, Venezuelan President 189
child-rearing, left–right differences
20, 55
Chile 123, 189
left–right self-placement 40
US intervention 127
China
economic inequality in 71
life expectancy 64
pollution 212
and technological revolution 59
Tiananmen Square 137
and USSR 125

Chirac, Jacques, French President 187
cholera epidemic (1832) 98
Chrétien, Jean, Canadian Prime
    Minister 166
Churchill, Winston, British Prime
    Minister 11
cities, collective rule in 84
civil liberties 67, 209
civil service, and business model 148
civil society
    global organizations 173
    rise of 80, 172
civilizations
    clash of 29–30
    and left–right self-placement 47–54
Clausewitz, Carl von 92
climate change 212
Clinton, Bill, US President 20, 166
    and Third Way 175
Cobden, Richard, MP 93
Cold War
    and anti-Americanism of Western
        left 126–7
    arms race 123, 134
    and East-West divide 122–7
    ideological conflict 107
collective bargaining 110, 116, 117
Colombia, left–right self-placement 40
colonialism 84, 101–6
    and anti-colonialism 123
    justifications for 102–4
    as moral duty 103
    nuances of opposition to 101–2
    see also decolonization
colors, as political metaphors 14
Commission for Africa 31
Commonwealth of Independent States
    (CIS) 137
communications technology
    impact of 56, 58
    inequality of access to 70
communism 22
    authoritarianism of 25
    collapse of 62, 137, 152, 199
    economic model 110
    right-wing reaction to 100
    rise of 99–100
    as threat to "free world" 122, 123
    and Western toleration of right-wing
        dictatorships 123

Comparative Study of Electoral
    Systems 34n
conservatism 19
    see also right
Conservative Party (UK)
    and Beveridge project 120
    and monetarism 145
    see also Thatcher, Margaret
constructivism 8, 232
    in international relations theory 223,
        226, 226–7
consumption 170
    statistics 75
Corn Laws, repeal of (1846) 97
corporations
    and environmentalism 211
    and Global Compact 185
    multinational 161
    transnational 73
Correa, Rafael, Ecuadorean President
    189
corruption, in developing countries
    135, 153
Cox, Robert 226, 235
Croatia, left–right self-placement
    42
Cuba 126
    US intervention 127
cultural attitudes
    divisions between 54–5
    and political inclination 23–4,
        47–54
culture, and identity politics 200
Czech Republic
    economy 63
    left–right self-placement 40
Czechoslovakia
    and fall of Berlin Wall 137
    revolution (1968) 126

da Silva, Luiz Inácio "Lula", Brazilian
    President 189
D'Alema, Massimo, Italian Prime
    Minister, and Third Way 175
Danton, Georges 102
Darwin, Charles 104
debate
    as basis of global politics 3–4,
        233–5
    and problems of definition 6–8

debt reduction
  developing countries 60, 74, 162
  and geo-political interests 164
  IMF initiatives 183–4
  Jubilee 2000 172
decolonization 104–6, 133
  as communist–capitalist conflict 108
  and democracy 128
  and nationalism 201
  and North–South conflict 128
  see also colonialism; developing
    countries
definitions, problem of 7–8, 10–11
democracy
  advancement of 68, 17, 80
  and cultural differences over equality
    48–51
  and decolonization 128
  democratic deficit 78–80
  development of 83, 84–9
  and equality 17, 89
  and French socialism 16
  global 67
  and inclination to peace 90, 93
  and international relations 84
  parliamentary 100
  in political science 217
  see also equality; liberal democracy;
    market democracy
democratization
  and adoption of left–right cleavage
    51–4, 55
  and armed conflicts 66
  of global governance 174
  see also market democracy
Denmark 207
  development aid 74, 162
  move to right 187
dependency theory 133
Dervis, Kemal, UNDP 107, 109, 195
Dessalines, Jean-Jacques 102
detention, indefinite 207
developing countries
  authoritarianism and corruption in
    135, 153
  debt reduction 60, 74, 162
  demand for special treatment 134
  economic growth in 59, 134
  and fall of communism 138
  foreign direct investment 161–2

lack of representation at IMF 193
  left commitment to 131
  and market liberalization 63–5, 186
  mixed economy models for 114
  neoclassical view of 130
  self-affirmation of 133
  statist economic model in 128
  and technological innovation 59
  and trade 59, 160, 174
  variations in competence of 193–4
  see also North–South divisions
development
  and environmentalism 213–15
  global organizations 172
  new agenda 158–64
  new consensus on global poverty
    168, 181–7
  and structural adjustment policies
    159, 161, 165
  "structuralist" analysis of 132
  and trade liberalization 159–61
  Washington Consensus 157–8
  see also Bretton Woods institutions
development aid 75, 74, 129, 135,
    162–4
  aid agencies 163
  "aid fatigue" 163
  private finance 163
  securitization of 164
"development economics" 158
Dickens, Charles, *Tale of Two Cities*
    56
dictatorships, right-wing, Western
  tolerance of 123
Diderot, Denis, view of colonialism
    102
disease, and poverty 76
distributive justice 13, 189
Doha Round (2001), WTO
  negotiations 160, 184
Dominican Republic, left–right self-
  placement 40
Downs, Anthony 142
Dubos, René *see* Ward, Barbara
Duesenberry, James 218
Dulles, John Foster, US Secretary of
  State 124
Dunn, John 87
Dupont de Nemours, Pierre Samuel
    102

Earth Summit, Rio (1992) 212
East Germany, fall of Berlin Wall
    137
East–West division
    Cold War as 108, 122–7
    and end of Cold War 152
    and politics of identity 199
Eastern Europe
    collapse of communism 137
    influence of USSR·in 124, 125
    and market liberalization 63
    poverty in 71
economic growth
    and 1981–82 recession 147
    British historical 95
    in developing countries 59, 134
    from globalization 58
    and imperialism 103
    in modernization theory 130
    and new social movements 169
    slowed 70, 168–9
    and social change 136
    and trade 72–3
    and welfare spending 118
economic inequality, increased 70, 69,
    69–71
economic policy
    and individual behavior 139,
        142–3
    macro-economic management 114
    micro-economic theory 143
    postwar mixed economy 109–17
    and social equality 110
    state intervention in 110, 139
    see also Keynesian consensus;
        monetarism
economics
    Chicago school 220
    and political science 217–19
Ecuador 189
education
    improvements in 64
    and left–right self-placement 47
Eisenhower, Dwight D., US President
    115, 124
El Salvador, left–right self-placement
    40
electoral systems 68
    and left–right self-placement 40
Elster, Jon 231

"embedded liberalism" 108
Engels, Friedrich 21, 98
    Communist Manifesto 99
English Civil Wars 85
Enlightenment, the 8
environment
    and developing countries 77–8
    global debate on 210–15, 229
    global organizations 172
    global progress on 65
    and precautionary principle 215
    voluntary measures 213, 214
equality
    as basis of political cleavage 3, 4,
        10, 30
    cultural perceptions 47–8
    and democracy 89
    and democratic debate 17
    and development consensus 191–2
    differing standards of 21–3
    differing values 42–7
    and freedom 144
    and French republicanism
        16–17, 87
    and global redistribution 131
    growth of 136
    and multiculturalism 202
    and opposition to colonialism 104
    and resurgence of center-right 189
    and role of state 110
    Third Way view of 178–80
Estonia, economy 63
Europe
    balance of power in 91, 92
    social-democratic governments 166,
        188, 196
    and US-led coalition against Iraq
        207
European Exchange Rate Agreement
    145
European Union
    European Council's social-
        democratic policies 180
    expansion 63
Eysenck, Hans 25

family
    left–right differences 20
    well-being of 65
Farr, James 215

fascism
  authoritarianism of 25
  and command economy 112
  economic model 110
  as reaction to communism 100
feminist theory 223
Ferry, Jules 16, 19, 103
financial system, international 73–4
  liberalization 63, 148
Finland 207
  left–right self-placement 40
First International 100
First World War 93, 94
Forbes Magazine 69
Ford Motor Company 111
foreign direct investment 63, 161–2
Fortuyn, Pim 187
Fox, Vicente, Mexican President 167
France 207
  colonialism 103
  cultural-political categorizations 23
  Declaration of the Rights of Man
    and the Citizen (1789) 87
  and economic planning 113
  economic policies 147
  and First World War 94
  hierarchies in 17
  left–right self-placement 38, 40
  National Assembly (1789) 14, 87
  rejection of Third Way 178, 180
  republicanism 15, 16
  rise of far right 187
  and rise of socialism 15–16
  universal male suffrage 88
Freedom House 68, 67
French physiocrats 96
French Revolution 14, 87–8
  and view of colonialism 102
  and view of war 90
Friedman, Milton 139–41
  Capitalism and Freedom 143

G-8 (Group of 8), debt cancellation 60
G-77 (Group of 77) 129, 133
Galbraith, John Kenneth 24
Gandhi, Mahatma 105
Gates, Bill 185
Gauchet, Marcel 12
General Agreement on Tariffs and
  Trade (GATT) 63, 124, 128

  and Washington consensus 157–8
General Electric company 211
George, Susan 214
Georgia 201
Germany 207
  and *Die Neue Mitte* 175
  economic planning 111
  election of centrist party 167
  Green Party 211
  move toward monetarism 144
  nationalism and Nazism 94, 201
  reunification 137
  social insurance 119
Giddens, Anthony 9, 175, 177, 188
  on equality 179
Gitlin, Tony 200
Global Compact (2000) 185, 234
global governance, democratization of
  174
global politics
  complexity of 26–30
  debate as basis of 3–4, 233–5
  left and right in 8–19
  postwar emergence of 109
  relationship to national politics 28–9
  and rise of new actors 56
  see also world community
globalization 9, 30
  and alter-globalization 173
  criticism of by left 69–80
  and interaction 56
  nuanced approaches to 81–2
  satisfaction of right with 57–69
  social critiques of 172
  and traditional politics 9
Glyn, Andrew 178
governance
  concern for improved 193
  global 174
Great Depression (1930s) 100, 109,
  112
  and social welfare programmes 119
Greece 207
Greece, classical 13, 17
Green Parties, rise of 170, 211
Greenpeace 172
Growing Sustainable Business Initiative
  (UNDP) 186
Guatemala, US intervention 127
Gupta, Partha Sarathi 101

Hacking, Ian 7n
Haider, Joerg 187
Haiti, independence 102
Hall, Peter 113, 229
Hamilton, Alexander 86
Harrington, Michael 233
Hayek, Friedrich A. von 19
    The Road to Serfdom 143
health, international improvement in 64
health care, state provision 150
Heath, Joseph 22
Held, David 9
Hertz, Robert 13
Hibbs, Douglas A. 116
hierarchies
    and liberal democracies 17–18
    in political structures
Higgott, Richard 31
Hirschman, Albert 231
Hitler, Adolf 11
Hobbes, Thomas 21, 218
Hobsbawm, Eric 97, 101, 201
Hobson, J. A. 103
human nature, views of 22, 24
human rights
    disregard for 79–80
    global organizations 172, 174
    and internal security measures 209
    UN concern with 192
    universal declaration (1948) 109,
        118
    violating states 67
Hungary 48
    democratization 53
    economy 63
    and fall of Berlin Wall 137
    left–right self-placement 42
    uprising (1956) 126
Huntington, Samuel 29, 51, 204, 205
Hussein, Saddam, Iraqi President 209

identity, politics of 199–205
immigration controls 207
imperialism 79, 84, 101, 102, 103,
    104–5
income inequality 70, 69–71
    in countries of the North 71
    and welfare cuts 150
income level, and left–right self-
    placement 47

income security, male breadwinner
    model 118
India 48
    economic growth 160, 160
    Kerala state 190
    left–right self-placement 38, 39, 42
    pollution 212
    remittances to 62
    revival of political left 10
    and technological revolution 59
    West Bengal state 171
indigenous peoples
    declaration of rights of (2006) 232
    and identity politics 203
individual rights 17, 88
individualism
    and economic policy 139, 142–3
    and market democracy 165
Indonesia 48
    left–right self-placement 39, 40
industrial revolution 95
    and working conditions 97
industry, decline of 169
inflation 116, 139, 171
    1970s crisis 144
    and monetary theory 140
Inglehart, Ronald 10, 40, 54
    World Values Survey 33, 34
insecurity, social 22
institutions, international
    American power over 79
    intervention by 132, 134
    left view of 135
    see also Bretton Woods institutions;
        United Nations
International Astronomical Union
    (IAU) 6
International Commission for the Study
    of Communication Problems
    (MacBride Commission) 134
International Criminal Court (ICC)
    156
International Labour Office (ILO)
    182
international law 93
International Monetary Fund (IMF) 79,
    124, 128, 146
    debate on governance 193
    Highly Indebted Poor Countries
        Initiative 60, 183–4

Multilateral Debt Relief Initiative
(2005) 184
Poverty Reduction Strategy Papers
(PRSPs) 184, 186
and structural adjustment policies
159, 161
and Washington consensus 157–8
international relations theory 222–9
and democracy 84
idealism v. realism debate 227
incommensurability of typologies
223–4
positivism v. postpositivism 227
traditionalism v. scientism 227
Wendt's "four sociologies"
224–5
International Studies Association (ISA)
228
International Workingmen's
Association (First International)
100
internet, global use of 59
Iran
and democratization 54
left–right self-placement 40
Iraq, debt forgiveness 164
Iraq, war against (2003) 78, 206
left–right split on 10, 209
Ireland 48, 207
famine (1845–50) 98
Islamic world
cultural divergence from West 54
left–right self-placement 38, 39
Israel 51
left–right self-placement 41, 42
issue-based politics 170
Italy 207
city-states 85
far right in 187
income inequality 71
nationalism and fascism 201

Jaélic, Jean 23
James, Matt 203
Japan 48
economic planning 113
welfare spending 118
Jaurès, Jean 94
Jefferson, Thomas, US President 86
Jordan, left–right self-placement 39

Jospin, Lionel, French Prime Minister
178, 180, 187
Jubilee 2000 movement 172
justice
global organizations 172
see also social justice

Kalecki, Michal 115
Kanbur, Ravi 1–3
Kant, Immanuel
Project for a Perpetual Peace 90
view of colonialism 102
Katznelson, Ira 217
Kazakstan 48
Keohane, Robert 225
Keynes, John Maynard 114
demand management 113
and Hayek 143
Keynesian consensus 108, 139–40
criticisms of 139
end of 144–5
monetarist argument against
139–42
political attack on 143–4
rationalist attack on 142–3
Khrushchev, Nikita, Russian Premier
127
Kim, Myunghee 198
Kirchner, Néstor, Argentinian
President 189
Kirkpatrick, Jeane 123
Köhler, Horst, IMF 184
Kohli, Atul 221
Kok, Wim, Dutch Prime Minister, and
Third Way 175
Korea, Republic of, left–right self-
placement 40
Kymlicka, Will 222
Kyoto Protocol 156, 212, 213
Kyrgyzstan 201

labor, North–South divide 76–7
labor market 97
socialist view of 99
structural unemployment 116
Labour Party (UK) 146
and Beveridge project 120
nationalization policies 113
and New Labour project 166, 180
see also Blair, Tony

Lafontaine, Oskar 177
Laïdi, Zaki 9, 10
laissez-faire 96
  effect of Great Depression on
    109, 112
Lakoff, George 20, 44
Lamy, Pascal, WTO 184
Laski, Harold 107
Latin America 48, 51, 232
  American domination of 101
  anti-Americanism in 190
  democratization in 51–3, 137
  economic crisis 168
  and indigenous rights 204
  left–right self-placement 40, 55
  poverty in 71
  revival of political left 10, 189
  trade growth 72
Latvia
  economy 63
  left–right self-placement 42
Le Pen, Jean-Marie 187
League of Nations 67, 93, 104
Lebanon 201
left
  anti-Americanism of 126–7
  and environmentalism 210–11
  and French republicanism 15, 16
  new objectives for 9
  and North–South interdependence
    131–5
  opposition to armies and militarism
    93
  political revival 10, 166–9
  renewal of (1990s) 169–75
  self-placement at *34*, 34
  and socialism 15–17
  and Third Way 175
  and threat of terrorism 208–10
  values of 44
  view of globalization 57, 69–80
  view of human nature 22, 44, 57
  view of imperialism 104–5
  view of war 90
  see also communism; socialism
left and right 8–19
  approaches to poverty 2–3
  and authoritarianism 24–6
  as contrasting worldviews 10, 19–26
  and cultural difference 29–30

  and debate on globalization 81–2
  as enduring global dichotomy 3, 27,
    187–95, 196–7, 198–9
  in French National Assembly 14
  ideological debate 233–5
  incorporation of new issues within
    27–8
  in international relations theory
    222–9
  moral nature of debate 20–1
  and multiculturalism 202–3
  and nationalisms 201–2
  origins of 12–14, 83, 106
  and problem of definition 10–11
  reality and persistence of 11–12,
    231–3
  and state economic intervention
    112, 115
  as too simplistic 26–7
  as unfashionable 2
  values 55
  and war and peace 84, 89–95
  and welfare state 120, 151–2
  see also left; right
Leibfried, Stephan 108
Leijonhufvud, Alex 142
Lenin, V. I. 11
  economic planning 111
  on imperialism 103
Leroy-Beaulieu, Paul 104
Levellers 85
liberal democracy
  and right 17–18
  triumph of 137
liberalism
  and authoritarianism 25, *25*
  and capitalism 124
  and equality 144
  in international relations theory
    223, 225
  postwar consensus 108–9
  rise of 83
  see also neo-liberalism
life expectancy 64
Lindblom, Charles 215, 217, 230
  Usable Knowledge 235
Lithuania, economy 63
Locke, John 21, 96
Louverture, Toussaint 102
Lowi, Theodore 221, 229

Lucas, Robert 142
Luxembourg 207
    development aid 74

McCarthy, Senator Joseph 127
McDonald, Michael 198
McGrew, Anthony 9
McLuhan, Marshall 58
McManus, Chris 12, 35
Macpherson, C.B. 85
Madison, James 85
Maier, Charles 113
Major, John, British Prime Minister 167
male–female distinctions 13, 46
Malloch Brown, Mark, UNDP 168
Malthus, Reverend Thomas Robert 96
Mandela, Nelson 11
Mao Zedong, Chairman of People's
    Republic of China 133
Marcos, Ferdinand, Philippine
    President 123
market democracy, shift to 137–65, 138
market liberalization 62–3
Marshall Plan 129
Marx, Karl 21, 98
    Capital 99
    on colonialism 104
    Communist Manifesto 99
    on planning 111
Marxism
    and Cold War 108
    and power 216
Mehmet, Ozay 114
men, left–right self-placement 46
Mendes, Silvia 198
Metternich, Prince 91
Mexico 167
    capital markets 63
    left–right self-placement 40
Middle East 48
military, expanding role in domestic
    politics 210
Millennium Development Goals
    (MDGs) 74–6, 182, 191
Mills, C. Wright 127
Milner, Helen 217
Mitterrand, François, French President
    147
mixed economy, postwar 109–17
modernity 19

modernization theory, economic 130
Moellendorf, Wichard von 111
monetarism 139–47, 165
    modification of 147
    quantity theory of money 139
monetary regulation 97
Montenegro, left–right self-placement
    39
Monterrey Summit on Development
    Financing (2002) 60, 154, 162,
    182, 194
Montesquieu, Charles de Secondat,
    Baron de 90
Montreal Protocol, on ozone-depleting
    substances 65
Morales, Evo, Bolivian President 189
Morocco, left–right self-placement 39
Mueller, John 208
Mulroney, Brian, Canadian Prime
    Minister 148
multiculturalism 200, 202–3
    and equality 202
multinational corporations 161
Myrdal, Gunnar 111

Nasser, Gamel Abdel, Egyptian
    President 133
nationalism 199
    and minority identities 200
    in social-democratic movements
    201–2
nationalization, economic 112, 113,
    117
neoclassical economics 130, 142
neoliberalism 19, 147–52, 165
    acceptance of 152
    and adjustment of social-democratic
    policies 170
    and Third Way 177
neoMarxism, in international relations
    theory 223, 225
Netherlands 207
    development aid 74, 162
    far right in 187
    left–right self-placement *41*, 40
new international economic order
    (NIEO) 129, 133
New Labour Party (UK) 166, 180
New Partnership for Africa's
    Development (NEPAD) 63

New Zealand, welfare reforms 150
Nicaragua 189
Nigeria, left–right self-placement 42
Nixon, Richard, US President 139
Non-Aligned Movement (1961) 123, 133
non-governmental organizations (NGOs)
  and democratization of global governance 174
  international 172
  and rise of civil society 80, 172
norms (appropriateness) 231
Norris, Pippa 40, 54, 181
North Atlantic Treaty Organisation (NATO) 123
North Korea 137
North–South divisions 128−35
  asymmetrical relationship in 132, 194
  and Cancún Summit (1981) 153
  conservative view of 128−31
  and environmentalism 214
  left view of 131−5
  marginalization of debate 152−8
  and move to market capitalism 138
  new agenda 158−64
  see also developing countries
Norway
  development aid 74, 162
  move to right 187
nuclear weapons
  deterrence 123
  and disarmament 127
Nutella 24
Nyerere, Julius, Tanzanian President 106

oil crisis (1973) 133, 144
Olson, Mancur 142
Organization of Petroleum Exporting Countries (OPEC) 133, 144
Ortega, Daniel, Nicaraguan President 189
Orwell, George 58
Ougaard, Morten 31
Owen, Robert 98

pacifism
  and socialism 95
  in world view 93

Paehlke, Robert 210
Pakistan, left–right self-placement 39, 42
Paul VI, Pope 131
Pauly, Louis 183
peace
  as absence of war 92
  development as 131
  see also war
peace movements 172
  international 93
pensions, public 150
Phelps, Edmund S. 141
Philippines 48, 123
  left–right self-placement 40
Phillips, Alban 141
Pierson, Paul 149
Pinochet, Augusto, Chilean President 11, 123
planet, definition of 6
planning, economic
  application of 112−14
  state role in 110, 111−12
Pluto, debate over status as planet 6
Poland, economy 63
Polanyi, Michael 27
"political correctness", and identity politics 204
political philosophy 222
political science
  inductive approach 219−22
  international relations theory 222−9
  left and right in 221
  methodological debates 219
  objectives of 215−16
  rational choice theory 219, 219−20, 220−2, 226−7
  and sociology 217−19
politics
  global nature of 3
  social factors in 231
  study of 199, 215−29
politics of identity 199−205, 229
Poor Law Amendment Act (1834) 97
Portugal 48, 207
postmodernism 223
poverty
  contending approaches to 1−2
  extreme hardship 76
  global reduction in *61*, 60−2, *61*

and labor market 97
in nations of the North 71
new global consensus on 168, 181–7
and redistributive tax measures 180
regional increases in 71
under communism 127
see also debt reduction;
    development aid
power
  and imperialism 102
  in political science 216, 217
pre-emptive war, doctrine of 206, 209
Prebisch, Raúl, UNCTAD 132
production, global system of 58
property 96
  private 143
  and suffrage qualifications 88
protectionism 72–3
Proudhon, Pierre 98
public opinion
  and inclination toward peace 93
  and self-placement on left–right scale
    10, 32, 33, 33–42
public sphere, expansion of 8
Puerto Rico, left–right self-placement
    40

Québec, nationalism 7, 202

racial profiling, in anti-terror measures
    210
Raphael, D.D. 13, 17
Rathbun, Brian 29
Rathenau, Walther 111
rational choice theory 219, 219–20,
    220–2, 226–7
  of economics 142–3, 231
rational expectations theory 142
Reagan, Ronald, US President 123,
    138, 146
  and Cancún Summit (1981) 154
  and welfare policies 149
  world view 152
realism, in international relations
    theory 28, 223, 225
reason and rationality, and inclination
    to peace 93
religion
  effect on politics 198
  and left–right dichotomy 13

Rémond, René 11, 26
republicanism
  and democracy 85
  France 15, 16
  and inclination towards peace 90
responsibility, to balance rights 176
revolution, as communist strategy 100
Rhodes, Cecil 103
Ricardo, David 97
Rieger, Elmar 108
right
  and conservatism 19
  and democracy 18
  development policies for Third
    World 128–31
  and environmentalism 212–13
  and liberalism 17–18
  move toward center 167, 188
  and pragmatic view of war 92
  rise of far right 187
  self-placement at 34, 34
  values of 44
  view of globalization 56, 57–69
  view of human nature 22, 45, 56
  view of imperialism 104
Righter, Rosemary 129
rights
  indigenous 204, 232
  individual 17, 88
  and responsibilities 176
  see also human rights
Roe v. *Wade* (1973) 6
Romania 63
Roosevelt, Franklin Delano, US
    President 11
Rostow, Walt W., *The Stages of
    Economic Growth* 130
Rousseau, Jean-Jacques 21, 218
  Project Towards a Perpetual Peace 90
  view of colonialism 102
Royal Dutch Shell 73
Ruggie, John Gerard 108
Russian Federation
  economic crisis 168
  left–right self-placement 40
  see also Soviet Union
Russian Revolution (1917) 100

Sachs, Jeffrey 81, 165
Saint-Simon, Henri de 98

Sarkozy, Nicolas, Franch President 189
Say, Jean-Baptiste 97, 120
Scandinavia, universalist welfare
    programmes 121
Schröder, Gerhard, German Chancellor
    167
    and Third Way (Die Neue Mitte) 175
Schumpeter, Joseph 108
Schwartz, Anna 140
Seattle, WTO meeting (1999)
    173, 184
Second International (1889) 100
Second World War 94
security
    domestic policies on 207–10
    and global terrorism 68
Seidelman, Raymond 215
self-placement 232
    at center *34*, 34
    on left *34*, 34
    on left–right scale *34*, 10, 32, 33,
        33–42
    non-responses **36**, 35–9
    on right *34*, 34
    socio-economic correlates **46, 49**,
        46–7, 48
Sen, Amartya 218
September 11, 2001 attacks 68,
    164, 205
service sector, expansion of 169
Shepsle, Kenneth 219
Sieyès, Emmanuel Joseph, on Third
    Estate 87
slavery, abolition by revolutionary
    France 102
Slovakia, economy 63
Slovenia 48
    economy 63
    left–right self-placement 40, 42
Smith, Adam
    The Wealth of Nations 96
    view of colonialism 102
Smith, Steve 228
social insurance, early 118
social justice
    ancient political debates 13
    distributive 13, 189
social movements
    global 171
    new 169–70

socialism
    and capitalism 95–101
    and left in France 15–17
    origins of 98–100
    and parliamentary democracy
        100
    rise of 15–16
    and war and peace 94
sociology 217–19
South Africa 190
South Commission (1990) 154
South Korea 190
    capital markets 63
Soviet Union
    and Cold War 122
    and decline of development aid
        163
    disintegration of 137, 199
    economic planning 111
    founding of 100
    influence of 126
    and popular democracy 126
    rise of 107
    "socialism in one country" 94
    space age 127
    as superpower 125
    see also Russian Federation
space technology 127
Spain 207
    Catalan nationalism 202
    left–right self-placement 39
Stalin, Joseph 94
state
    development of modern 83
    and planning 110, 111–12
    role of 22, 148, 176
    see also welfare state
Stein, Herbert 140, 146
Stern, Alan 6
Stern, Nicholas 213
Stone, Deborah 7
structural unemployment 116
Sub-Saharan Africa 71
    poverty 76
suffrage
    qualifications 88
    universal male 17, 88
    for women 89
Summers, Lawrence H., US Treasury
    Secretary 1

Sweden 207
  development aid 74, 162
  income inequality 71
  trade unions 116
  welfare spending 118
Switzerland, women's suffrage 89

Taiwan 62, 190
  left–right self-placement 40
Tanzania, left–right self-placement
    39, 42
taxation
  redistributive 180
  and welfare spending 151
Taylor, Charles 8
Taylor, Frederick W., scientific
    management 111
technology
  and climate change debate 212
  innovation in developing countries
    59
  see also communications technology
terrorism
  causes of 208
  as global threat 68, 206
  international 78
  "war" on 164, 205–10
Thatcher, Margaret, British Prime
    Minister 19, 23, 138
  monetarist policies 145
  and welfare state 149
  world view 152
Third International (1919) 100
Third Way 3, 9, 167–9, 175–81, 195
  redundancy of 188
  view of equality 178–80
Thorez, Maurice 25
Tocqueville, Alexis de 87
Toye, John 158
trade
  and development 59, 134
  and economic growth 72–3
  generalized system of preferences
    135
  growth in international 58
  and inclination to peace 93
  liberalization 62–3, 159–61
  in modernization theory 130
  protectionism 110
  tariffs and subsidies 72–3

trade unionism 116–17
  origins of 98–9, 100
trade unions, and environmentalism
    211
transnational corporations 73
transnational social movements
    organizations (TSMOs) 172
tribal societies, left–right distinctions
    13
Truman, Harry, US President 107
Tullock, Gordon 142
Turkey 48, 105
  left–right self-placement 39
Turner, Ted 185

Udehn, Lars 218
Uganda, left–right self-placement 42
Ukraine 201
unemployment
  1970s rise in 144
  acceptance of higher levels of 171
  and monetary theory 140
  non-accelerating inflation rate of
    (NAIRU) 141
  structural 116
  welfare benefits 151
United Kingdom
  1997 election 166
  Anti-Terrorism, Crime and Security
    Act (2001) 209
  economic planning 113
  imperialism 101
  industrial capitalism 95–7
  left–right self-placement 41, 38,
    40, 42
  move toward monetarism 145
  suffrage qualifications 88
  and war in Iraq 207
  welfare state 119–20, 150
  see also Conservative Party; Labour
    Party
United Nations 67, 79, 191
  and American funding 156
  and colonies 105
  consensus with Bretton Woods
    institutions 183, 186
  continuing divergence from Bretton
    Woods institutions 190–5
  and development 128, 156, 161,
    185–6, 194–5

United Nations (*cont.*)
economic development policies 114,
155, 181
Economic Security Council
(proposed) 194
Environmental Security Council
(proposed) 213
International Declaration on Rights
of Indigenous Peoples (2006)
232
and invasion of Iraq 209
loss of influence 155–6
membership 129
Millennium Declaration (2000)
182, 191
Millennium Project 81
principle of equal sovereignty 132
resolution on development aid 135
Security Council 79, 209
World Summit (2005) 182
United Nations Capital Development
Fund 186
United Nations Conference on Trade
and Development (UNCTAD)
128, 132, 161, 194
United Nations Development
Programme (UNDP) 128, 185, 195
United Nations Educational, Scientific
and Cultural Organization
(UNESCO) 155
United Nations Environment
Programme (UNEP) 77
United Nations Human Rights Council
204
United Nations Industrial Development
Organization (UNIDO) 128
United States of America 66, 79,
107, 127
1992 Presidential election 166
affirmative action 18–19
and Cold War 122
criticism of United Nations 155
economic growth 118
economic policies 112–13, 115, 136
income inequality 71
left–right polarization 189
move towards monetarism 146–7
multiculturalism in 202, 205
New Deal 112
Patriot Act (2001) 209

power over international institutions
79
revival of Republicanism 188
September 11, 2001 attacks 68, 164,
205
suffrage qualifications 88, 89
Taft-Hartley Act (1947) 112
Taylorism in 111
and Third World development 154
and toleration of dictatorships 123
trade unionism 117
and war against Iraq (2003) 78
and war on terrorism 205–7
welfare policies 121
Universal Declaration of Human
Rights (1948) 109, 118
Uruguay 51, 52, 189
Uruguay Round (1986–94), WTO
negotiations 160, 184
and intellectual property rights 161
utility (consequentialism) 231

Vagts, Alfred 94
Vaillant, Édouard 8, 11
values 43, 42–4
equality 42–7
left–right divide 55
socio-economic correlates 46, 49,
46–7
to encourage in children 45, 44
view of human nature 45, 45
Vasquéz, Tabaré, Uruguayan President
189
Venezuela 189
left–right self-placement 40
Vietnam 48
left–right self-placement 39, 42
USA and 127
World Values Survey 34
Vietnam War 127, 133
Volcker, Paul, chairman of US Federal
Reserve 146

Wal Mart 73
Waltz, Kenneth 225
war
decline in number of 66
and democratic deficit 78
and development of left and right 84,
89–95

and interests of ruling classes 90
see also peace
"war on terrorism" 164, 205–10,
    229
  and internal security policies
      207–10
Ward, Barbara, and René Dubos, *We
    Have Only One Earth* 31
Washington consensus 157–8
Washington, George 86
water, access to 78
Weber, Max 57, 216, 234
welfare state 117–22
  benefit cuts 149
  debate on reform 168
  limitations of 121–2, 148
  neo-liberal modifications 148–52
  and universalism 120–1
Wendt, Alexander 224, 226
Wickham-Jones, Mark 177
William I, German Emperor 119
Williamson, John 158
Wolcott, Jesse W., US congressman
    112
Wolf, Martin 58, 81
Wolfensohn, James, head of World
    Bank 1, 183
Wolfowitz, Paul 183
women
  economic discrimination against 71
  left–right self-placement 46
  promotion of equality 65
women's rights organizations 172
Woods, Ngaire 158
workers
  mobility 62
  remittances by 62
  see also trade unionism

"workfare" 151
working classes, and rise of socialism
    99
working conditions 97
World Bank 79, 124
  on development aid 163
  and poverty reduction 61, 60, 183
  and structural adjustment policies
      159, 161
  view of inequality 192
  and Washington consensus 157–8
  World Development Report (2000/
      2001) 1
World Commission on Environment
    and Development 31
world community
  complexity of 56
  concept of 31
  democratic deficit in 79, 174
  and postwar international solidarity
      129
World Economic Forum, Davos (1999)
    173
World Environment Organization
    (proposed) 213
World Health Organization 132
World Social Forum 80
World Trade Organization (WTO) 63,
    79, 160
  and foreign direct investment 161
  pro-development policies 184
  Seattle meeting (1999) 173, 184
  and trade liberalization 160
  and Washington consensus 157–8
World Values Survey (WVS) 33–5, 44

Zimbabwe, left–right self placement
    39